Introduction to the Eurasian Economic Union

Evgeny Vinokurov

Introduction to the Eurasian Economic Union

palgrave
macmillan

Evgeny Vinokurov
Eurasian Development Bank
St Petersburg, Russia

ISBN 978-3-319-92824-1 ISBN 978-3-319-92825-8 (eBook)
https://doi.org/10.1007/978-3-319-92825-8

Library of Congress Control Number: 2018947386

Cover credit: Aleksei Naumov / Alamy Stock Vector

This Palgrave Macmillan imprint is published by the registered company Springer Nature Switzerland AG
The registered company address is: Gewerbestrasse 11, 6330 Cham, Switzerland

"Introduction to the Eurasian Economic Union by Evgeny Vinokurov is a must read for all experts and practitioners specializing in the Eurasian space. Introduction to the Eurasian Economic Union by Evgeny Vinokurov includes all what you need to know about its evolution, structure, policies and practices. Balanced, reliable and clearly written, this book is an essential companion to students and all interested in the region. Easy to follow but complex in content, this is an ultimate introduction to the Eurasian Economic Union showing its development, successes and failures. Perfect for students and general public."

—Piotr Dutkiewicz, *Professor of Political Science Carleton University, Ottawa*

"The Eurasian Economic Union has become an important instrument in Russia's regional and global strategies. Its history and mechanisms are here described very thoroughly and readably. A valuable handbook for scholars and diplomats. Evgeny Vinokurov is for sure the best person as an insider to explain it all to the outsider. Any future prospects for EU-Russian relations have to take this new regional integration organisation into account".

—Michael Emerson, *Centre for European Policy Studies, Brussels*

"Introduction to the Eurasian Economic Union closes an important gap in the research on post-Soviet regionalism and in comparative regionalism studies in general. It is a comprehensive survey of various aspects of the functioning of the EAEU – from the institutional aspects and the external economic relations to the history of the organization and its place among other regional alliances. The study manages to combine a deep and detailed analysis with being clear and open to a wide audience. Being based on a sober and non-ideological approach to the EAEU, it is a real encyclopaedia of the current state of the post-Soviet regionalism – a must read for the students of post-Soviet economy and politics!"

—Alexander Libman, *University of Munich*

Contents

List of Abbreviations

ACF	Anti-Crisis Fund of the Eurasian Economic Community
APEC	Asia-Pacific Economic Cooperation
ASEAN	Association of South-East Asia Nations
BRI	Belt and Road Initiative
BRICS	a group of five countries: Brazil, Russia, India, China, and South Africa
CAEC	Central Asian Economic Community
CCT	Common Customs Tariff
CEFIR	Centre for Economic and Financial Research
CFE	Treaty on Conventional Armed Forces in Europe
CIS	Commonwealth of Independent States
CJSC	closed joint-stock company
CSTO	Collective Security Treaty Organization
CU	Customs Union
EAEU	Eurasian Economic Union
EAPC	Euro-Atlantic Partnership Council
EAU	Eurasian Union (a term used in 1990s–2000s)
EBRD	European Bank for Reconstruction and Development
EDB	Eurasian Development Bank
EEC	Eurasian Economic Commission
EFSD	Eurasian Fund for Stabilization and Development
EU	European Union
EurAsEC	Eurasian Economic Community

FDI	foreign direct investment
FTA	free trade area
GCC	Cooperation Council for the Arab States of the Gulf
GDP	gross domestic product
GUAM	a regional organization consisting of four countries: Georgia, Ukraine, Azerbaijan, and Moldova
HS Code	Harmonized System Code
IMEMO	Primakov National Research Institute of World Economy and International Relations (Russian Academy of Sciences)
IMF	International Monetary Fund
IT	information technologies
MERCOSUR	Southern Common Market
NAFTA	North American Free Trade Agreement
NATO	North Atlantic Treaty Organization
NTB	non-tariff barrier
OJSC	open joint-stock company
PJSC	public joint-stock company
PPP	purchasing power parity
PRC	People's Republic of China
RO	regional organization
SACU	Southern African Customs Union
SCO	Shanghai Cooperation Organization
SEEC	Supreme Eurasian Economic Council (Supreme Council)
SES	Single Economic Space
TNC	transnational company
UESCA	United Energy System of Central Asia
UN	United Nations
UNCTAD	United Nations Conference on Trade and Development
USA	United States of America
USRB	Union State of Russia and Belarus
USSR	Union of Soviet Socialist Republics
VAT	value-added tax
WIIW	Vienna Institute for International Economic Studies
WTO	World Trade Organization

List of Figures

List of Tables

List of Boxes

Introduction

25 Years: Integration Requires Patience

This book is on the Eurasian Economic Union (EAEU)—its content; evolution; organization; economic integration issues; operation of common markets for goods, services, capital, and labour; and foreign economic relations. I strive to provide a balanced analysis using a variety of approaches. Not only do I provide rich data about the economics, politics, institutions, common markets, and foreign economic relations of the Union, but I also try to explain why Eurasian integration processes have developed the way they have and not otherwise. In the last chapter of the book, I indicate the potential objectives and likely problems of the next years.

The EAEU is a young regional organization. It began functioning as a customs union in 2011. It began operating as an aspiring economic union in 2015. Member states established the EAEU based on a certain understanding of their long-term political and economic objectives. In this context, its main purpose is to help member states realize the potential of regional economic ties, modernize national economies, and create the conditions necessary to enter global markets. Establishing a single market for goods, services, capital, and labour is the main aim of Eurasian integration. Additional infrastructure supporting Eurasian integration—Court of the EAEU, Eurasian Development Bank, Eurasian Fund for

Stabilization and Development—is already functioning within the EAEU. Initiatives to form political institutions (e.g., a parliament) are not on the agenda.

The EAEU represents a serious achievement for its members after several "integration false starts" in the 1990s–2000s. Member states must overcome a multitude of obstacles in the future, but the Union is already a reality today. This assertion engenders no particular objections if critics do not hold the EAEU to inflated standards, for example, do not compare it with the European Union—the "model" of regional integration. If readers place the EAEU beside other regional integration projects of varying depth and success—such as NAFTA, MERCOSUR, ASEAN, and the GCC—it is easier to analyse the evolution of the Eurasian integration.

The EAEU has significant successes, but there are also limitations on its further growth. In 2015, the phase of rapid initial progress came to an end (I will show this in the analysis below). In 2016, the integration bloc hit its first wave of conflict and difficulty. Will it be able to advance further? Will it retrogress? The purpose of this book is to discuss the EAEU in terms of facts and hard data.

Ideologically, President of Kazakhstan Nursultan Nazarbayev's speech in March 1994 at Moscow State University may be called the starting point for the implementation of this large-scale interstate project (see Sect. 1.1; officially, the starting point is 2007—see Sect. 1.2). He proposed an integration paradigm that was fundamentally new at the time: more towards a Eurasian Union based on economics and common defence.

The mechanisms of the Commonwealth of Independent States (CIS) worked throughout the entire decade of the 1990s, actively suppressing various destructive disintegration processes. Industrial councils for transportation and electrical energy, which largely helped maintain the technological integrity of railway systems and power grids, played a special role. Yet the CIS failed to solve the problem of a "civilized divorce".

In 1995, Belarus, Kazakhstan, and Russia signed the Customs Union Treaty. However, the Customs Union did not actually start working. This was the first false start.

In 2000, five states—Belarus, Kazakhstan, Kyrgyzstan, Russia, and Tajikistan—established the Eurasian Economic Community (EurAsEC). Leaders have signed more than 100 agreements through the framework of the EurAsEC. Moreover, the EurAsEC served as the institutional springboard for the initiatives of 2006–2010. For example, the commission to create the Customs Union technically worked within the EurAsEC. The EurAsEC was officially abolished on 1 January 2015 in parallel with the establishment of the EAEU. In 2003, Belarus, Kazakhstan, Russia, and Ukraine signed a treaty to form the Single Economic Space. This initiative also failed to take off due to the Orange Revolution. This was the second false start.

In October 2007, Russia, Belarus, and Kazakhstan signed an agreement to create a common customs territory and form the Customs Union (CU). They expected the action plan adopted at that time, with respect to the creation of the CU, to take two years. There were understandable doubts about the prospects of the latest attempt. However, on 19 December 2009, the heads of these three states signed the Joint Declaration of the Formation of the Customs Union, and on 1 January 2010, the Common Customs Tariff took effect. As early as 2011, the CU of Belarus, Russia, and Kazakhstan began its normal operation, and on 1 January 2012, 17 agreements forming the basis of the Single Economic Space (SES) took effect. These agreements governed a number of key topics in the economic convergence of the "Eurasian troika"—from coordinating macroeconomic policy to labour migration.

Finally, on 1 January 2015, the Treaty on the Eurasian Economic Union took effect. The treaty codified and expanded all prior agreements regarding both the work of the Customs Union and the development of additional areas of integration. It enshrined the EAEU's institutional structure (see Chap. 3) and detailed a road map for the elimination of exemptions from the common market (Chap. 4). The EurAsEC formally terminated at the same time. New institutions entirely swallowed up its mandate and jurisdiction. Armenia joined the integration union on 2 January 2015, and Kyrgyzstan joined on 8 May 2015 (the decision was ratified and enacted in August 2015).[1]

Structure of the Book

The book has six chapters.

Chapter 1 is a brief excursion into the history of post-Soviet integration since the 1990s, including the disintegration processes of the 1990s and part of the 2000s. Everything started with the "civilized divorce" of the former Soviet republics and the responsible politicians' and technocrats' persistent attempts to save critical elements of trade, economic, and infrastructural relationships between countries. Several "integration false starts"—unsuccessful attempts to inaugurate economic integration—followed. In the end, this last attempt proved successful: the book outlines the path from the Customs Union Commission and enactment of the Common Customs Tariff to the signing of the agreements on the Single Economic Space and, finally, to the enactment of the Treaty on the Eurasian Economic Union.

Chapter 2 begins with a brief description of member states' economies and their dependence on the largest economy of the region. Russia's enormous influence in the Union, both in terms of economy and population, presents certain challenges to the integration project (but it also creates several opportunities that promote stability). Importantly, the raw material dependence of the Union's economy, whether direct or indirect, has huge significance for common trade policy and the building of common markets. Next, I briefly characterize the high density of economic ties to justify the need for integration, separately considering indicators of economic convergence and trends in public opinion regarding questions of economic integration.

Chapter 3 presents a detailed description of EAEU institutions—mainly the Supreme and Intergovernmental Councils, Eurasian Economic Commission, as well as the EAEU Court, Eurasian Development Bank, and the Eurasian Fund for Stabilization and Development. The underlying document—the EAEU Treaty—is examined in detail.

Chapter 4 examines the common markets for goods, services, labour, and capital. The common market is the "heart" of the integration project. The book examines trends in mutual trade and mutual investments. It evaluates the progress of eliminating exemption from the common markets (EAEU Treaty road map). Then, it considers the complex but singularly important question of unifying and minimizing trade barriers. I describe how the single labour market is set up, how it functions, and what its constituent parts are (a question that affects the lives of millions of migrant workers and their families every day). Finally, the text sets forth approaches for coordinating the currency, budgetary, and monetary policies of EAEU member states.

Chapter 5 addresses the EAEU's foreign economic relationships: its expansion, the forming network of free trade zones, and relationships with the European Union, United States, and China.

Chapter 6, the concluding chapter of the book, provides an understanding of the theory and ideology of Eurasian integration, its objectives in the coming years, a set of international comparisons, and a brief discussion on the difficult challenges that the EAEU is likely to encounter.

I would also like to draw the reader's attention to the Appendix. It is a chronology of Eurasian integration for 1991–2017 (with approximately one page per year), in which I highlight the most significant economic and political events.

In writing this book, I strived to be as concise as possible. The objective was to provide the market with a book for a wider audience—economists, political scientists, experts on international affairs, sociologists, students, and general audience with the interest in the EAEU and the diverse processes in and around it. Nevertheless, I warn you up front that certain parts of the book may still be… well, boring. This mainly applies to the sections in Chap. 3 on the EAEU institutions—the Commission, Court, and the Intergovernmental and Supreme Councils. Furthermore, reading a description of the EAEU Treaty may also be boring. You have been forewarned and thus forearmed: you can leaf through these sections when reading and then use them later as a reference. But I felt I could not exclude this information from the comprehensive treatment of the Eurasian Union.

The virtual absence of a published book that serves as a *full-fledged introduction to the EAEU*—a book that students and specialists from various fields (economists, political scientists, experts on international affairs, and social scientists) could use to acquaint themselves with the EAEU—motivated me to prepare and publish this work. This can be explained not only by the EAEU's young age but also by the widespread scepticism towards Eurasian integration. I hope my monograph will help dispel some of this scepticism: the EAEU is an entirely "normal" and active regional organization with its own successes and failures.

Without claiming to make a complete survey of the literature, I will mention four substantial monographs—Dragneva and Wolczuk (2013), Vymyatnina and Antonova (2014), Dutkiewicz and Sakwa (2015), and Lane (2017). The first of these books mainly addresses legal and institutional matters. The second is an economic analysis with a horizon through 2012; the third analyses the economic, political, social, and security developments in the region with the particular focus on the country level with a horizon through 2013; the last one is about the EAEU's potential role in the global community and its foreign policy. Furthermore, a chapter by Hancock and Libman (2016) in *The Oxford Handbook of Comparative Regionalism* deserves special mention. It is excellent in its content and balanced in its opinions.

Acknowledgements

This book is a child of research pursued by the Centre for Integration Studies, an in-house think-tank of the Eurasian Development Bank. I am thus in debt of all colleagues at the Centre. I am also grateful to numerous colleagues around the world whose comments strengthened the arguments and logic of this monograph. I would like to express deep gratitude to Anna Isakova for meticulous technical assistance.

Note

1. Systematic surveys of the evolution of Eurasian integration are presented in Hancock and Libman (2016) and Libman and Vinokurov (2012).

References

Dragneva, R. and Wolczuk, K. (eds.) (2013). Eurasian Economic Integration: Law, Policy and Politics. Cheltenham: Edwar Elgar.

Vymyatnina, Y. and Antonova, D. (2014). Creating a Eurasian Union: Economic Integration of the Former Soviet Republics. Basingstoke: Palgrave Macmillan.

Dutkiewicz, P. and Sakwa, R. (eds.) (2015). Eurasian Integration: The View from Within. Abingdon: Routledge.

Lane, D. (ed.) (2017). The Eurasian Project in Global Perspective. London: Routledge.

Hancock, K. J. and Libman, A. (2016). Eurasia. In: Börzel, T. A. and Risse, T. (eds.) The Oxford Handbook of Comparative Regionalism. Oxford: Oxford University Press, pp. 202–224.

Libman, A. and Vinokurov, E. (2012). Holding-Together Regionalism: Twenty Years of Post-Soviet Integration. Basingstoke: Palgrave Macmillan.

1

The History of Eurasian Integration: 1991–2016

1.1 "Civilized Divorce" and False Starts of the 1990s and 2000s

Comprehensive and far-reaching international projects often have difficulty getting off the ground. The establishment of the Eurasian Economic Union (EAEU) is a serious achievement for its members after the collapse of the USSR and the disruption of production chains formed over centuries even in the days of the Russian Empire. *At the beginning of the 1990s, Soviet republics prioritized minimizing losses above all else.* The bodies and industry councils of the Commonwealth of Independent States (CIS) pursued this critically important objective. The uninterrupted operation of the railways and power grids depended on its successful achievement. At that time, politicians and experts simultaneously tried to create a working plan for economic integration under the new conditions of independence and the transition to a market economy.

The starting point for discussing questions of post-Soviet regional integration was the need to come to an agreement regarding the future fate of the USSR in 1991. Amid the precipitous collapse, the state idea of creating a "weak" confederation—the Union of Sovereign States—did not find support among the Soviet republics. In December 1991, three heads

E. Vinokurov, *Introduction to the Eurasian Economic Union*,
https://doi.org/10.1007/978-3-319-92825-8_1

of state, representing Russia, Ukraine, and Belarus, signed an agreement to terminate the existence of the Soviet Union and to simultaneously set up the CIS. Soon afterwards, Central Asian states joined the CIS.

From the very beginning, the CIS did not harbour any ambitions to become a federated state one day. The organization's membership formed quickly: 12 of 15 Soviet republics (all except the Baltic States) joined the CIS by 1993. However, the list of agreements that had to be signed by all CIS member states was modest at that time and did not even include the CIS Charter. Legislatively, the CIS distinguishes between a Commonwealth "member" and "associate" depending on whether the state has ratified the CIS Charter. Member states had the right to refuse virtually every agreement, which they in fact did systematically; many countries signed certain agreements with specific provisions and limitations. However, in 1992–1993, post-Soviet integration was explicitly linked to the CIS; most of the agreements signed in this period related directly to this organization. However, this was also the most contradictory period in the integration process. In these years, more than integration, the countries of the former USSR worried about finding a peaceful resolution to potential differences and conflicts associated with disintegration through a process frequently referred to in the literature as a "civilized divorce".

The idea of a Eurasian Union (EAU) first appeared at a high level in a speech by Nursultan Nazarbayev at Moscow State University on 29 March 1994. The previous week, while speaking at the Chatham House in London, the president of Kazakhstan noted that two trends defined the development of the post-Soviet space: on the one hand, the nation-building and—on the other hand—the need for integration, so it was "reasonable to create a real working union of states on the basis of a 'nucleus of countries'".[1] In his Moscow speech, Nazarbayev directly mentioned two components of a future Eurasian Union: deep economic integration (precisely what EAEU institutions are working on) and a defence union (implemented as the Collective Security Treaty Organization [CSTO]).

> The time has come to take our countries' relationships to a qualitatively new level through new interstate associations and based on the principles of voluntary action and equality. This association could have been the

> Eurasian Union (EAU), which was to be built on principles other than those of the CIS, since the new association's foundation was to be built by supranational bodies called on to handle two critical tasks: form the Single Economic Space and support a policy of joint defence. However, it is important to emphasize that all other matters pertaining to sovereignty, domestic state and political structure, and each member's foreign policy activities, remain inviolable and assumes non-interference in each other's internal affairs.[2]

In 1995, the "troika" (Belarus, Kazakhstan, and Russia), which today remain the *core* of Eurasian integration,[3] signed the *Customs Union Treaty*. The document called for the elimination of barriers to free economic interaction between the parties' commercial entities and support for free exchange of goods and honest competition. However, the agreements were not actually implemented: the centrifugal forces of the 1990s were too powerful. In 1995, the Customs Union (CU) became the first integration false start.

2 April 1997 saw the birth of another integration association that stands alone in the history of Eurasian integration—the *Union State of Russia and Belarus (USRB)*. On 26 January 2000, these countries enacted the Union State Treaty, which had been separately signed in 1999. We will not go into detail about the USRB: its activities are tangential to the main track of Eurasian integration following the CIS-EurAsEC-CU/SES-EAEU line, chiefly due to the bilateral nature of the association. Still, we will briefly enumerate a few of the achievements of the Union State. The most important of them is the abolishment of border control. Travellers were the first to notice: trains cross the Russo-Belarusian border "unheeded", just like the borders of countries in the Schengen area. This does not happen anywhere else in the post-Soviet space, even between Russia and Kazakhstan. There are also several less substantial results—in terms of the labour market and close interaction between parliaments in the Parliamentary Assembly.

On 26 February 1999 in Moscow, the presidents of Belarus, Kazakhstan, Kyrgyzstan, Russia, and Tajikistan signed the Treaty on the Customs Union and the Single Economic Space (SES).

On 23 May 2000 in Minsk at a meeting of the Intergovernmental Council, the Council decided to create, before September 2000, a draft of a treaty to form an interstate integration association consisting of Belarus, Kazakhstan, Kyrgyzstan, the Russian Federation, and Tajikistan. On 10 October 2000 in Astana, the five states established the *Eurasian Economic Community (EurAsEC)*. The primary difference between the EurAsEC and the CIS was the abandonment of the ability to selectively participate in agreements. Another difference is voting by a weighted majority of votes (in the CIS, decisions are adopted only through consensus; however, in practice the EurAsEC also made decisions through consensus).[4]

Overall, the EurAsEC has not been able to meet the expectations placed upon it in 2000. Integration deepened slightly in spite of the large flow of agreements and other documents. However, it would also be entirely wrong to regard this organization as a failure. A mass of bilateral agreements between separate states—Russia and Kazakhstan, Russia and Belarus, and so on—achieved an increase in the overall level of actual integration.[5] Moreover, the EurAsEC blazed the trail for the EAEU—more on this below.

In 2003, the presidents of Belarus, Kazakhstan, Russia, and Ukraine signed an agreement to create the SES. The Orange Revolution of 2004 destroyed hopes for the success of this endeavour, which is a source of regret to this day. After all, member states took Ukraine's involvement in the Eurasian integration processes seriously and considered it to be economically expedient. This was the second false start.

Overall, integration progressed slowly at the institutional level in the first half of the 2000s, chiefly due to the integration bloc's misfortune involving Ukraine, on which the member states pinned big hopes. The situation began to change in the second half of the 2000s. Thanks to the sharp rise in oil prices, Russia and Kazakhstan received resources for economic development. Mutual trade, mutual investments, and labour migration—the elements of so-called bottom-up integration—began to grow explosively. The growing wealth had a positive effect on the economies of neighbouring states through several transmission channels—trade, investment, credit, and remittances.

These strengthening economic ties require institutional support. The Eurasian Development Bank (EDB), the new wave's first integration tool, which was founded by Kazakhstan and Russia in 2006 with $1.5 billion capital, is an example of an institution providing this support. At least 50% of the Bank's credit facilities pertain to integration. They aim at projects that create growth in mutual investments and trade. Symbolically, the Bank's headquarters is in Almaty (see Sect. 3.4).

The real breakthrough in building Eurasian integration institutions occurred only at the end of the 2000s amid the response to the global economic crisis. At the end of 2009, member states signed documents on the CU. In this same year, they also signed documents to create the EurAsEC Anti-Crisis Fund (ACF) (see Sect. 3.5).

1.2 The CU, SES, and Eurasian Economic Union (2007–2015)

The global financial crisis of 2007–2009 had a huge impact on all Eurasian economies. The negative effects came through diverse channels—prices (export prices for raw materials), remittances, investment flows, and many others. The greatest decline in GDP took place in 2009. The crisis simultaneously devalued national currency, and major government interventions took place. These actions only slightly softened the blow of the crisis. The theoretical literature traditionally notes that economic crises have a negative effect on integration: countries are inclined to close up and raise customs protections for domestic markets. However, in the "integration core" of the post-Soviet space, the crisis incentivized them to find new solutions! In Sect. 6.2, we discuss in detail the concept of holding-together integration, which explains why this happened. In practice, at least two major decisions followed in 2009–2010: first, the decision to create the CU (discussed below), and second, the decision to form the EurAsEC Anti-Crisis Fund with roughly $8.5 billion in on-call capital (see Sect. 3.5).

A little bit of history. In October 2007, Russia, Belarus, and Kazakhstan made the decision to move towards the CU. The stated goals of the action plan were to ensure the free movement of goods under mutual trade, create favourable conditions for trade with third parties, and advance economic integration.

Few believed this new attempt would succeed given the disappointment of the previous endeavours. However, precisely after the two planned years of preparation, on 19 December 2009 in the city of Almaty, Presidents A.G. Lukashenko, D.A. Medvedev, and N.A. Nazarbayev signed the Joint Declaration of the Formation of the CU. Then on 1 January 2010, the Common Customs Tariff (CCT) took effect. The economic crisis triggered this success, which pushed the countries towards unification.[6] We also believe that specific people made an important contribution: the activities of the CU Commission received organization support from the entire EurAsEC secretariat. Of course, the will and constant attention of the political leaders of the three states played a huge role. Without them, the national bureaucrats would have probably watered down the CU.

The CU of Russia, Kazakhstan, and Belarus was the breakthrough from which followed the Single Economic Space Agreement of 2012, the EAEU Treaty of 2015, and the long-awaited Customs Code. In 2010, the CCT took effect. It seriously influenced the trade policy of the Union's member states. Several countries made major adjustments to their customs tariffs. Moreover, Russia left 82% of customs tariffs unchanged, reducing only 14% of tariffs while increasing 4% of tariffs; Kazakhstan retained 45% of tariffs, reducing 10% of them and increasing 45% of them. Furthermore, it was far from clear at that point whether the CU would come to life: Belarus was highly critical of this integration project, mainly due to issues associated with the oil trade. Ultimately, all three countries signed the agreement and the CCT took effect.

The CU is the first post-Soviet initiative that is a full-fledged, active, and truly supranational institution. From the outset, the CU actively utilized a decision-making process that impacted trade. Before 2010, the region's states managed to maintain a certain level of cooperation only in specific areas: railway shipments, aviation safety standards, and power grids.

After the creation of the CU, the EAEU put in place the next layer of economic integration: it enacted 17 agreements (Box 1.1) after 1 January 2012; they formed the basis of the SES and defined the Eurasian project's content and progress for several years—right up to the enactment of the EAEU Treaty. These agreements governed a number of key topics in the economic convergence of the "trio"—from coordinating macroeconomic policy to labour migration. The SES agreements augmented the CU's regulations. Member states subsequently expanded and codified these agreements in the EAEU Treaty and its appendices.

Box 1.1 List of Single Economic Space Agreements Enacted Since 1 January 2012

1. Agreement on Common Principles and Rules of Competition
2. Agreement on Common Rules of State Support for Agriculture
3. Agreement on Common Rules for Providing Industrial Subsidies
4. Agreement on Regulation of Access to Railway Transportation Services, Including the Fundamentals of Tariff Policy
5. Agreement on Trading in Services and Investments in Member States of the Single Economic Space
6. Agreement on Common Principles of Regulation in the Defence and Protection of Intellectual Property
7. Agreement on Common Principles and Rules of Technical Regulation
8. Agreement on State (Municipal) Procurement
9. Agreement on the Legal Status of Migrant Workers and Their Family Members
10. Agreement on Cooperation to Combat Illegal Labour Migration from Third States
11. Agreement on Coordinated Macroeconomic Policy
12. Agreement on Coordinated Principles of Currency Policy
13. Agreement on the Creation of Financial Market Conditions to Ensure Free Movement of Capital
14. Agreement on Common Principles and Rules of Regulation of the Activities of Natural Monopolies
15. Agreement to Ensure Access to Services of Natural Monopolies in the Power Industry, Including the Fundamentals of Price-Setting and Tariff Policy
16. Agreement on Rules of Access to Services of Natural Monopolies in Gas Supply Using Gas Supply Systems, Including the Fundamentals of Price-Setting and Tariff Policy
17. Agreement on the Procedure for the Organization, Management, Operation, and Development of Common Markets for Oil and Oil Products

On 29 May 2014, at a meeting of the Supreme Eurasian Economic Council (SEEC), the presidents of the member states of the CU and the SES signed the Eurasian Economic Union Treaty, which signified the Eurasian economic project's transition to a new, deeper level of integration.

On 1 January 2015, the Eurasian Economic Union Treaty took effect. On 2 January, Armenia joined the integration union, and in May Kyrgyzstan signed an agreement to join (the document took effect in August 2015).

In February 2016, the first four-year term of the Eurasian Economic Commission (EEC) ended. This required a change in the top leaders (chairman and members of the EEC Board). Tigran Sargsyan, former prime minister of Armenia, became head of the college for the next four-year term (until 2020). This can be viewed as a positive signal. First, the mechanism for an interstate rotation through the post of chairman of the board worked (a representative of Belarus is to become the next head of the EEC in 2020). Second, a top-level politician with work experience directly related to integration building headed the Commission. In Chap. 3, we consider in detail how the Commission and other bodies of the Eurasian Union operate.

The signing and enactment of the EAEU Treaty are not the final words in the integration process. On the contrary, the Treaty outlines a plan to move towards the common markets that had not been created as of the beginning of 2015. They include a common market for drugs and medical products (enacted in May 2017); common market for electrical energy (planned for 2019); common financial markets (2022–2025); and a common market for oil, gas, and oil products (2024–2025). These are discussed in Chap. 4.

In the next chapter, we discuss in greater detail the economic features of EAEU member states and how they influence the regional organization (RO's) institutional design. Although we specifically focus on the economy (which is only natural since the EAEU pursues economic integration), we must mention at least one underlying political characteristic. The EAEU is a union of primarily autocratic states. The literature frequently makes the argument that autocracies are fundamentally incapable of implementing economic regional integration associations. This argument is easily overthrown by the empirical evidence—simply look at the regional integration in the Gulf, the EAEU, or the South African Custom Union before the 1990s (many ASEAN countries are also no beacons of democracy).

In fact, under certain conditions, regional integration agreements are implemented between autocratic states. Libman and Vinokurov (2018) showed that an economic regional integration agreement is implemented under either of the following two circumstances: (a) if there is an intermediate level of dependence (in this case the implementation is not merely a response to pressure from a large state and could happen proactively) and (b) if there is a high level of vulnerability dependence with a large country pushing for implementation. At the same time, autocratic integration has some inherent restraints. The EAEU corroborates these findings.

We will now move to the chapter entitled "Economic and Social Ties". An important caveat: in our analysis we place particular emphasis on (1) macroeconomic characteristics, (2) trade flows, (3) investment flows, and (4) labour migration. We do not explicitly discuss welfare effects on the EAEU. Various organizations including World Bank, EBRD, EDB, WIIW, the Gaidar Institute, and CEFIR made such assessments; however, they are forward-looking and vary widely. At present, it may be too early to assess the Eurasian Union's actual impact on the economies of its member states, though surely this will soon be possible.

Notes

1. Cited in: Nurymbetova and Kudaibergenov (2010). P. 15.
2. Nazarbayev (2012).
3. The idea of an "integration core" for Eurasian integration is quantitatively based on the first issue of the "System of Indicators of Eurasian Integration" (Vinokurov et al. 2009).
4. For more information about the institutional structure of the CIS and EurAsEC, see (Kaveshnikov 2011; Libman 2014).
5. Gleason (2004).

6. There is a widely accepted theoretical argument that crises hinder integration because the level of protectionism rises in a crisis. We will provide evidence for the opposite hypothesis: economic crises can be a catalyst for integration processes if there are close ties between the countries and a lack of real political and economic alternatives (Vinokurov and Libman 2014).

References

Gleason, G. (2004). The Reintegration of Eurasia: Functional Theory and Inter-state Policy Coordination. In: Khudoley, K. (ed.) Post-Communist Countries in the Globalizing World. Saint Petersburg: Saint Petersburg State University Press.

Kaveshnikov, N. (2011). Development of the Institutional Structure of the Eurasian Economic Community. Eurasian Economic Integration, 2 (11), pp. 19–35. Available at: https://eabr.org/upload/iblock/366/n2_2011_3.pdf.

Libman, A. (2014). Commonwealth of Independent States (CIS) and Eurasian Economic Community (EurAsEC). In: Levi, L., Finizio, G. and Vallinoto, N. (eds.) The Democratization of International Institutions. First International Democracy Report. London: Routledge.

Libman, A. and Vinokurov, E. (2018, forthcoming). Autocracies and Regional Integration: The Eurasian Case. Post-Communist Economies.

Nazarbayev, N. (2012). "Our peoples have lived together for centuries, and the strengthening of neighbourly relations is consistent with the vital interests of millions of people". Speech by the President of the Republic of Kazakhstan at Moscow State University. Moscow, 29 March 1994. In: N. Nazarbayev. When a Thought Becomes Reality. Moscow: Khudozhestvennaya Literatura, pp. 28–33.

Nurymbetova, G. and Kudaibergenov, R. (2010). Foreign Policy Initiatives of the President of Kazakhstan N.A. Nazarbayev. Historical and Documentary Research. Almaty: Kazakh Encyclopaedia.

Vinokurov, E. and Libman, A. (2014). Do Economic Crises Impede or Advance Regional Economic Integration in the Post-Soviet Space? Post-Communist Economies, 3 (26), pp. 341–358.

Vinokurov, E., Libman, A., De Lombaerde, Ph., Maqsimchook, N., Moldabekov, Ye. (2009). The System of Indicators of Eurasian Integration 2009. Almaty: Eurasian Development Bank. Available at: https://eabr.org/en/analytics/integration-research/cii-reports/edb-system-of-indicators-of-eurasian-integration/.

2

Economic and Social Ties

2.1 Economies of EAEU Countries

As an economic community, the EAEU has several structural characteristics that are largely dictated by its past and define its present and, probably, future:

1. Russia's dominant influence in the Union's economy (in terms of GDP, population size, and trade and investment flows). Roughly 86% of total GDP is generated in Russia, approximately 10% in Kazakhstan, and the remaining 4% in Belarus, Armenia, and Kyrgyzstan (see Fig. 2.1). As for population size, Russia represents 146.8 million people or 80% of the total population of the EAEU. Kazakhstan takes second place with 17.9 million people (10%) (see Fig. 2.2). The remaining member states collectively account for roughly 10% of the Union's population.[1] These numbers are simply some of the basic facts that justify integration building. Accordingly, readers should not give positive or negative estimates and forecasts on the basis of these numbers alone. We would especially like to warn against a one-sided

E. Vinokurov, *Introduction to the Eurasian Economic Union*,
https://doi.org/10.1007/978-3-319-92825-8_2

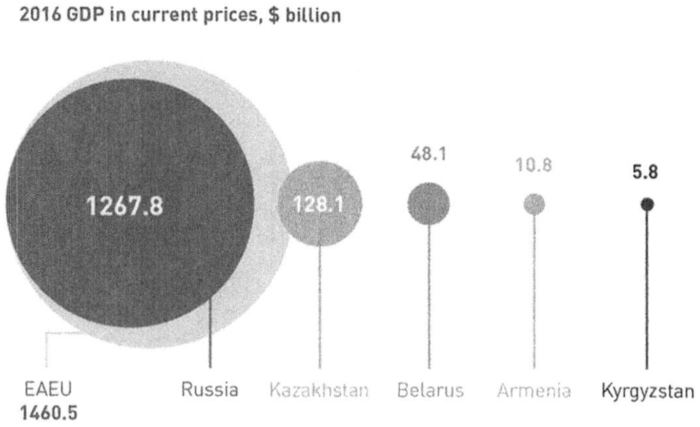

Fig. 2.1 Distribution of GDP in the EAEU in 2016. (Source: EDB Centre for Integration Studies 2017)

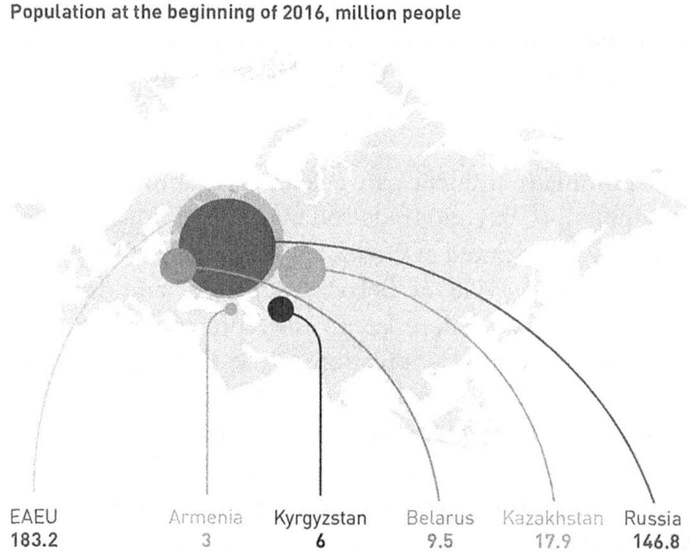

Fig. 2.2 Distribution of population in the EAEU in 2016. (Source: EDB Centre for Integration Studies 2017)

negative perception and remind the reader that a dominant partner is a reality for many regional integration entities, including the world's oldest Southern African Customs Union as well as NAFTA, GCC, and MERCOSUR.

2. Dependence on raw material exports. Both Russia and Kazakhstan are heavily oriented towards exports of oil, gas, and ferrous and non-ferrous metals, while the other EAEU countries are indirectly dependent on raw material exports through close economic ties with Russia and Kazakhstan.
3. The shared economic past (USSR and Russian Empire), which has left a legacy of several thousands of production chains, a common infrastructure (oil and gas pipelines, railways, and electric power network), very similar technical regulations, a common language, and close familial and social ties between people.
4. Huge distances and the high costs of transportation are serious obstacles to mutual trade. Considering the vast size of Russia, the distances between certain member states (e.g., Belarus and Kazakhstan) are very large. Mutual trade is also limited by the fact that Armenia is an exclave relative to other member states: trade flows reach Armenia almost exclusively through the territory of Georgia.
5. Small trade volumes in the Union (excluding Russia). In practice, EAEU members trade mainly with Russia, but not with one another. The Kazakhstan-Kyrgyzstan pair forms an exception, with substantial mutual trade.

After the economic collapse of the 1990s, all five EAEU member states have seen their per-capita GDP rise since the beginning of the 2000s (see Table 2.1). However, there have always been substantial differences in production and production growth levels. There is an approximately sevenfold average difference between the wealthiest countries (Kazakhstan and Russia) and the poorest country (Kyrgyzstan).

The post-Soviet history of the region's economic development may be divided into four main stages whose characteristics can be seen in GDP trends (see Fig. 2.3):

Table 2.1 Indicators of socioeconomic development of EAEU member states, 2016

Indicator name		Armenia	Belarus	Kazakhstan	Kyrgyzstan	Russia
GDP	Nominal, $ billion	10.8	48.1	128.1	5.8	1267.8
	PPP, $ billion	26.6	165.4	460.7	21.0	3745.1
	Nominal, per capita, $	3595.9	5092.0	7138.1	956.3	8838.2
	Real yearly growth for 2010–2016, %	3.5	1.6	4.6	3.8	1.4
Population, million people		3.0	9.5	17.9	6.1	146.8
Foreign trade turnover $ billion		4.0	35.6	52.3	3.9	456.5

Sources: IMF, World Bank, national statistics agencies, authors' calculations

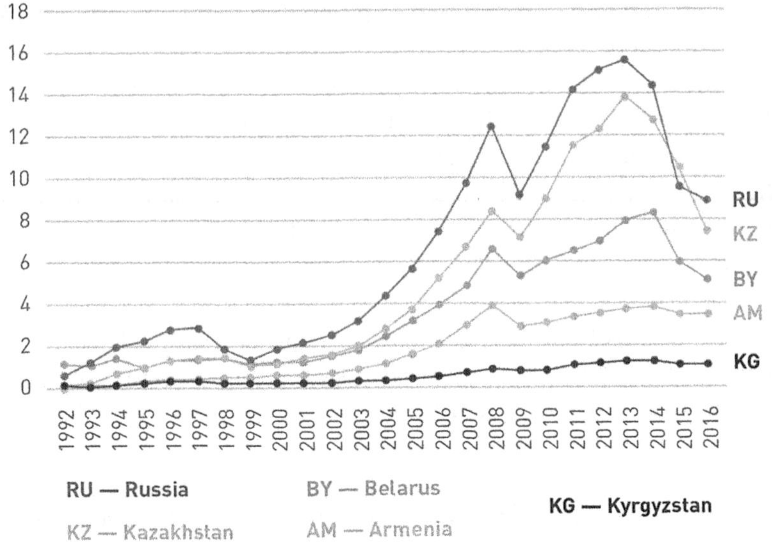

Fig. 2.3 Per-capita GDP of EAEU member states, $ thousands. (Source: IMF)

1. Abrupt collapse of the 1990s. During this time, the countries of the post-Soviet space tried to find their place in the world economy and restore the production capacity that had been disrupted by the collapse of the USSR.
2. The rapid growth of the 2000s, which can in part be explained by the general boom in developing economies and in part was caused by the exponential growth of the economies of Russia and Kazakhstan thanks

to the surge in prices for energy resources. This stage came to an end in 2008 when the global financial and economic crisis popped the first bubble in the energy resource market.

3. Economic recovery of the region following the crisis of 2008. This period is distinguished by less rapid growth rates and Russia's deceleration starting in 2011. Russia still remained the region's engine, but with substantially reduced influence. The growth rates of migrants' money transfers (mainly to Armenia and Kyrgyzstan) also contracted. Another sharp drop in oil prices caused the final stage in the Russian economic crisis that began at the end of 2014.
4. Beginning in 2015, the economies adapted to the new reality of lower prices for energy resources and some other exports. In this context, various effects of the drop in energy resource prices influence the economies of Belarus, Armenia, and Kyrgyzstan, which do not export oil directly. On the one hand, domestic production benefits from the less expensive energy resources. On the other hand, the economies become subject to abrupt changes in Russia and Kazakhstan. The defining characteristics of this period include falling consumption and, as a result, declining trade, frozen investments, a smaller volume of preferential lending, and fewer transfers by migrant workers.

Not only is the absolute level of economic growth important but also the comparative growth rates of member states relative to one another, that is, economic convergence (in principle, this indicator is paramount for economic integration). Three of the four countries are steadily converging with Russia and shrinking the development gap by roughly 0.7–1.4% per year. The only country where this trend is absent is Kyrgyzstan (see Sect. 4.7).

2.1.1 Russia

Russia's nominal GDP for 2016 was $1267 billion, and the country ranks 12th globally for this metric. When GDP is recalculated using purchasing power parity (PPP), the Russian economy rises to 6th place (according to data from the IMF and World Bank); however Russia's GDP (PPP) per capita for 2016 ranks 48th. Mining and extraction operations, especially for oil and gas, are still the economy's primary driver. However, in recent years the percentage of GDP from oil and gas has decreased.

Before the 2008 crisis began, the average annual growth rate of real GDP was 7.5%, the ruble exchange rate had strengthened against the dollar, and inflation had fallen below 10% by 2007. However, the global financial crisis dealt a powerful blow to Russia. The high share of foreign financing in the domestic banking sector intensified the shock. With the credit situation in the economy and the sharp reduction in external demand, GDP plummeted in 2009. After a modest upsurge in 2010 and 2011, growth of Russia's real GDP slowed in 2013 to approximately 1.5% year on year. This was the result of the deceleration in real consumption and the slump in investment activities.

The main reason for the economic slowdown in the post-crisis period is the lower growth potential. The Russian economy faces serious structural limitations. As of the end of 2016, Russian GDP was at about the same level as precrisis 2008 (according to the latest estimate from *Rosstat*, in 2016 GDP was only 2.8% higher than in 2008). In this sense, we can say that the Russian economy lost a decade.

2.1.2 Kazakhstan

Kazakhstan is the largest economy in Central Asia and the second-largest economy after Russia in the post-Soviet space. It would have been difficult 20 years ago to imagine that Kazakhstan's GDP would ever be greater than Ukraine's.

Kazakhstan exports raw materials produced by the mining, fuel, metallurgical, and chemical industry. As with Russia, oil and oil products dominate Kazakh exports, accounting for 35%. Ferrous and non-ferrous metals account for roughly 30%. The structural similarity of the Kazakh and Russian economies reduces the likelihood of asymmetric external shocks in these two countries and thus increases the stability of integration processes.

Kazakhstan's main trading partner is Russia, but the PRC's role grew rapidly in the 2000s. These statistics demonstrate China's growing influence in the Kazakh economy (the PRC's share of foreign trade in 2016 was approximately 16%). The PRC's investment policy (investments in oil production, oil and gas pipelines) is promoting growth in trade.

The global financial crisis seriously slowed the growth of the Kazakh economy. From its average annual precrisis level of 10%, GDP growth contracted to 7.5% in 2010 and 2011 and then further to roughly 4.5% in 2014. However, Kazakhstan's economy never contracted in any year. This is a major achievement. We believe this was possible due to the confluence of several factors: a relatively low social burden on the budget, fiscal stimulus, effective state policy, and low government debt.

State finances are stable. Large-scale raw material exports before the crisis made it possible to reduce the government debt, which was already small, to less than 6% of GDP (according to IMF data for 2007). Following the crisis, countercyclical fiscal policy led to a budget deficit, and the debt level rose again, but it remains low by international standards (13% of GDP).

Kazakh economic growth has recently slowed notably due to falling oil prices and weak external demand. In an attempt to maintain the country's competitiveness, the authorities weakened the *tenge* by nearly 50% and moved to a floating exchange rate in 2015. Despite the fact that this step temporarily bolstered internal demand, inflation grew, partially neutralizing the increased competitiveness of industry and agriculture. Inflation in Kazakhstan has historically fluctuated between 5% and 10%, except for the year 2008 when it briefly jumped to almost 20% due to high global prices for food products. By the beginning of 2016, inflation had again accelerated to double digits (roughly 17%), largely as a result of the tenge's devaluation in 2015. By the end of 2016, inflation had returned to single digits.

2.1.3 Belarus

In terms of EAEU integration processes, the following basic features are characteristic of the Belarusian economy:

1. A transit point for Russian goods on the way to Europe.
2. Strong dependence on Russia; Russia is the main sales market for Belarusian goods, as well as the main source of FDI for the Belarusian economy; Russia makes parts for the Belarusian mechanical engineering industry.

3. Small trade volumes with EAEU members other than Russia.
4. Large share of state in the GDP (ca. 75%) hindering foreign investments.

The country consistently suffers from rather high inflation (generally the highest among the economies of EAEU member states). Moreover, at the beginning of the 2010s, Belarus experienced rapid growth in foreign national debt.

The sudden growth of the Belarusian economy in 2003–2008 can be explained by steady external demand, high rates of construction using budgetary funds, as well as the terms of oil contracts with Russia. However, the period of nearly 10% economic growth also ended in the other countries of the region with the start of the financial crisis. The economy of Belarus demonstrated weak growth (1%) in 2009. Negative trends created a crisis in the balance of payments and a steep devaluation of the Belarusian ruble in the second half of 2011. Several factors contributed to the subsequent recession: households' need to restore their savings and the tight monetary policy introduced to promote stability coincided with weak external demand. These factors far outweighed the effects of increased competitiveness from the devaluation of the currency.

In 2016, the economy of Belarus continued to experience negative growth. GDP shrank by 2.6% (in 2015—by 3.9%). Output continued to fall given weak internal and external demand amid conservative monetary and fiscal policy. The reduction of crude oil supplies from Russia, which has affected industrial production volumes, was another factor holding back the economic recovery in the second half of 2016. Output declined in nearly every major sector of the economy except for agriculture.

2.1.4 Armenia

Analysing the Armenian economy from the perspective of integration processes reveals its distinguishing features:

1. The exclave nature of its geographic position relative to the rest of the Union and an actual economic blockade by Turkey and Azerbaijan.

2. Strong dependence on Russia; Russia is the primary sales market for Armenian goods, as well as the main source of FDI for the Armenian economy (more than 40% according to EDB).
3. Small trade volumes with EAEU members other than Russia.
4. Significant share of transfers by migrant workers and diaspora (19% of GDP in 2014 according to the World Bank).

Three important periods can be identified in the Armenian economy's development since the start of the 2000s.

First, there was a period through 2007 in which remittances grew and the real value of the currency rose rapidly. At that time, the Armenian economy's growth rates were measured in the double digits. The economic boom in Russia increased the volume of money transfers from the Armenian diaspora, helping to reduce poverty and increasing personal consumption and housing construction. At the same time, a huge influx of capital (including FDI) and money transfers put significant pressure on the dram, which helped curb inflation despite the powerful growth. Armenian exports became less competitive as the real value of the currency climbed and the trade deficit increased from approximately 12% of GDP in 2005 to nearly 19% in 2007. Moreover, as a percentage of GDP, exports steadily fell from about 20% to slightly over 10%.

The second stage is the global economic crisis of 2008–2009. The crisis walloped the Armenian economy. An abrupt decrease in money transfers, lower external demand, and reduced FDI resulted in the nearly 14% economic collapse of 2009, despite the fact that the Armenian financial sector was relatively isolated from global markets and its banking system remained stable. The crisis hit hardest the main drivers of the precrisis economy—the construction and mining industries.

The third stage is a gradual economic recovery after 2009. Since the beginning of 2010, the Armenian economy has begun to grow once again, though not as strongly as before. The main factors contributing to the recovery of private sector demand were low real interest rates and the money transfers that have gradually resumed. Government demand also played its role in the economy's recovery, because the authorities continued to pursue a countercyclical policy with the help of international organizations. However, the economic boost was relatively modest: GDP growth fluctuated around 4%, considerably lower than its precrisis level.

In 2016, Armenia's economy grew slightly. Internal demand remained weak, despite the reduction in the refinancing rate, stimulating tax and budgetary policy, and some support at the end of the year from money transfers from Russia. Exports retained their key position among drivers of economic growth in Armenia. This was facilitated both by government's policy to stimulate exports and by positive integration effects within the EAEU. Indeed, growth in Armenian exports (chiefly food products) is largely linked to the effects of joining the EAEU. Overall, in 2016, Armenian GDP growth slowed to 0.2% after growth of 3% the previous year.

2.1.5 Kyrgyzstan

Kyrgyzstan's economy features the following traits, which are structurally important within the context of its EAEU membership:

1. Unlike Belarus and Armenia, Kyrgyzstan depends not only on Russia but also on Kazakhstan in terms of trade and investments. Both countries are primary sales markets for Kyrgyz goods and the main sources of FDI.
2. A long history of political instability. Russia and the EAEU currently act as stabilizing anchors.
3. A significant percentage of the country's GDP comes from remittances (30.3% of GDP for 2014 according to the World Bank). This circumstance seriously influenced the republic's decision to apply to enter the Eurasian Union.

Like many other developing countries in the region before 2008, Kyrgyzstan experienced an economic boom caused by a considerable inflow of capital and remittances. However, the most negative effect on the country's economic growth came from political instability culminating in two revolutions—one in 2004 and another in 2010. In these conditions, investment activity remains very low, and the risks of conducting business are exceptionally high.

The situation has been normalizing since the beginning of the 2010s. Businesses can now plan investments for years into the future rather than weeks. Economic growth indicators and inflation figures reflect this. Thus, the *country's entry into the EAEU in 2015 serves as a kind of anchor for political and economic stability*. Institutional ties with Russia and Kazakhstan investments should be understood in this light and not only in the narrow context of trade and investments.

The growth of food prices in 2010–2011 had a particularly strong impact on the economy of Kyrgyzstan. In this period, the global economy experienced a shock to food prices (similar to what happened in 2007–2008). In 2010 and 2011, global prices for food products grew 17% and 23%, respectively. In 2012–2013, changes in the price and production of gold also affected economic development. The fact is that gold mining at the Kumtor deposit is systemically important for the country's economy, representing 7% of GDP and up to 40% of exports.

2.2 The Practice of Integration: Close Economic Ties in the Post-Soviet Space

Eurasian economic integration has its origins in the Soviet Union and Russian Empire. This is a positive, not a normative judgement. Countries in the post-Soviet space are interdependent in terms of railway transport (1520 mm standard), oil and gas pipelines, and power grids. The member countries find it nearly impossible to separate themselves from each other infrastructurally, and if they do so, they pay dearly.

Member states have accumulated numerous industrial relationships. For example, the Russian textile industry is adapted to using Uzbek cotton. Similarly, at least in the past century, Uzbek cotton production has been set up specifically to accommodate the needs of the Russian textile industry and vice versa. This interdependence is gradually diminishing due to the modernization of equipment and diversification of sales markets (the process is often painful and very costly). However, in practice, thousands of unique industrial and production relationships continue to function.

The space using 1520 mm gauge railways is particularly important. It includes without exception each of the republics of the former Soviet Union, as well as Finland. Historically, railways have been tremendously important for the vast land mass of northern and central Eurasia due to the lack of alternatives (the ability to use maritime transport is limited, and rivers only flow meridionally)—far more important than in other areas and countries of the world. Sixty per cent of the world's railways use 1435 mm gauge track. On the Eurasian continent, this percentage is significantly lower (a total of eight types of track are used in its vast expanses). Furthermore, member states are currently building the Belt and Road strategy based on the railway system: investments in railway transport, increased containerization, progress in multimodal transport, realization of the potential for a China-EU route through countries of the EAEU, and construction of high-speed highways.

Member states also maintain close industrial relationships in the energy industry. Even during the breakup of the 1990s and 2000s, considerable energy trading volumes existed, largely due to the layout of the preserved Soviet generating facilities. For example, the historically inexpensive coal-fired power plants of the Ekibastuz Basin in northern Kazakhstan partially operate in adjoining regions of Russia. Similarly, power plants on the Volga export energy to the energy-deficient territory of western Kazakhstan. Capital investments in generation and distribution systems are so large that complete autonomy would be difficult to achieve even if desired. Moreover, true energy security, especially for medium-sized power systems, lies in industrial and economic integration with neighbouring states. This helps balance the national power system and serves as an "insurance policy" against emergencies and peak loads.

The common power system of the USSR collapsed rather quickly in the 1990s. But one of its significant elements—the common power system of Central Asia with a shared dispatch centre in Tashkent—lasted until 2009. Member states are currently preparing the regulatory framework for the EAEU's future common electricity market, which is to come into existence by 2019 according to the Treaty. Its advantages are considerable both in terms of economic efficiency and increased stability in power systems.

This "new" form of EAEU integration stands on new foundations—the recognition of member states' sovereignty and market conditions (rather than administrative orders). The main challenge for the Eurasian Union is to create the broadest and most flexible common market built on these principles.

In doing so, what is the shared level of economic integration in the region? Are disintegration processes still at work, or have they been successfully halted and even reversed? Answering these questions requires data series for a long period of time, because economic processes have a lot of inertia. The analysis in the EDB System of Indicators of Eurasian Integration[2] covers 2000–2012 and allows us to make the following conclusions.

First, (dis)integration in the post-Soviet space is taking place non-uniformly in various areas of interaction between the countries.

Second, as early as 2004–2005, a gradual transition from disintegration to convergence can be seen in those countries we have called the *integration core*: Belarus, Kazakhstan, and Russia. Indicators of cooperation between these countries have either stabilized or are beginning to improve. The emergence of the CU in the form of the "trio" is no coincidence: it reflects the economic processes that took shape a few years before the formation of the Customs Union.

Third, when it comes to each country's overall level of integration with all of the countries in the post-Soviet space, Kyrgyzstan and Armenia have been among the top three since 2008. In this context, it is not at all surprising that they joined the EAEU in 2015.

2.3 Public Opinion on Eurasian Integration

Regular monitoring of public opinion on regional integration is a standard instrument. The European Commission is responsible for the Eurobarometer project in the European Union. In Latin America, a major international non-profit organization is in charge of the Latinobarómetro. In the EAEU, the Eurasian Development Bank assumed this task so far. Each year since 2012, it has conducted large-scale public opinion polls.

Box 2.1 Integration Barometer: A Note on the Methodology

EDB Integration Barometer is a project to perform annual monitoring of the foreign political, foreign economic, and sociocultural preferences of citizens of EAEU member states and CIS countries. In 2017, the research was conducted in seven countries: Armenia, Belarus, Kazakhstan, Kyrgyzstan, Moldova, Russia, and Tajikistan, with a total of 8250 people surveyed (at least 1000 in each country). The sample provides a wealth of information when broken down by "city versus village", "women versus men", age (several age groups), education, and income (several income groups).

The main objective of the EDB Integration Barometer is to study the attitudes of citizens in member states towards the creation of the EAEU, as well as the opinions of citizens of other countries regarding the possibility of them joining the Union. In 2012–2014, it measured the attitudes towards the Customs Union and the Single Economic Space, and since 2015, it has measured attitudes towards the EAEU.

Over the past five years, public opinion towards the Eurasian integration project in the current five member states was mostly positive—even very positive in international comparison. However, there is considerable variation from country to country and from year to year.

The Eurasian association enjoys the most consistent support in its three founding members—Kazakhstan, Russia, and Belarus, which comprise the Union's "integration nucleus". In each of these years, at least 60% of the population of these countries viewed their integration positively (see Fig. 2.4).

Public support for Eurasian integration in the "integration core" peaked in 2014, when the heads of the three states signed the EAEU Treaty—an event widely covered in the media and online. That same year, the national leaders' decision to create the EAEU received approval from 84% of the residents of Kazakhstan, 79% of residents of Russia, and 68% of residents of Belarus. However, attitudes towards the EAEU subsequently became more reserved.

The year 2016 saw the highest level of public support for the EAEU in Kazakhstan, where approval reached 74%. With an indicator of 69%, Russia is second place in terms of approval of integration. However, compared with 2015, this figure has decreased by 9%. In 2013, both countries saw the very lowest level of approval of integration in the five years of monitoring.

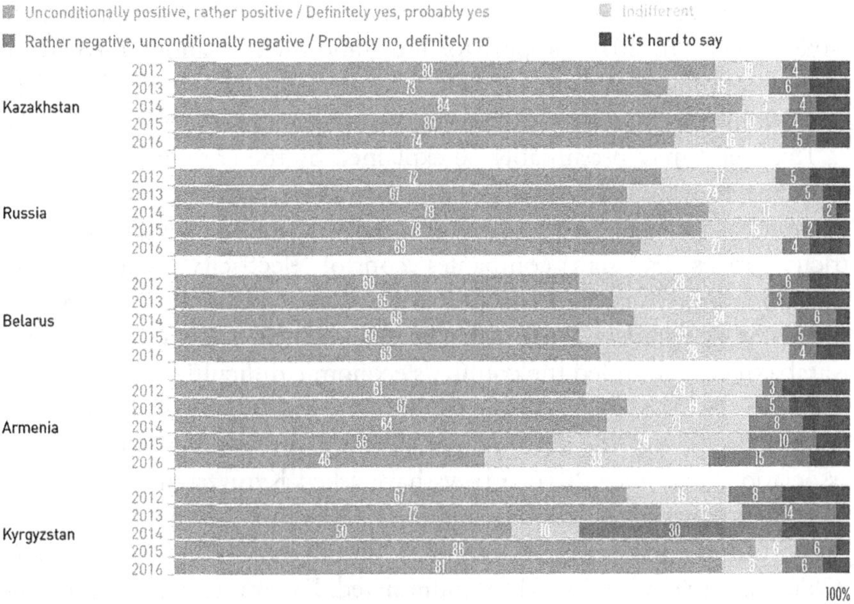

Fig. 2.4 Public opinion of the EAEU in member states in 2012–2016 (% of different answers). (Note: survey participants were asked the following question: "Armenia, Belarus, Kazakhstan, Kyrgyzstan, and Russia joined the EAEU (essentially a single market for the five countries). What is your opinion of this decision?". Source: EDB Integration Barometer 2016)

Among the Union's three founding members, public opinion towards Eurasian integration remained most reserved in 2012–2016 in Belarus, though the approval level did not fall below 60%. In 2016, we observed a level of 63%.

Because Armenia and Kyrgyzstan joined the EAEU only in 2015, their populations had previously been studied with respect to their desire to join the CU and the EAEU. Public perception of Eurasian integration in both countries has been characterized by significant fluctuations.

In Armenia, survey results recorded the highest level of support for potentially joining the association in 2013, when 67% of the population expressed a positive opinion. However, since 2014 this indicator has slowly decreased, and the level of negative attitudes towards integration has increased. As early as Armenia's first year of membership in the EAEU, public support for the country's involvement in the Union dropped from 64% to 56%. In 2016 support for integration fell by another 10–46%. Moreover, 15% of Armenians held a negative opinion of the EAEU in 2016, while this figure was 10% a year earlier and in 2012 it was only 3%.

This trend may presumably be explained by the crisis in the Russian economy, to which the Armenian economy is closely tied, since this connection has impacted Armenians' prosperity. In addition, increased electricity prices (Russian companies control electricity generation in Armenia) as well as dissatisfaction with Russia's position regarding the Armenian-Azerbaijani conflict that escalated in 2015–2016 in Nagorno-Karabakh compounded the country's economic difficulties.

Before 2015, surveys conducted in Kyrgyzstan only studied public opinion on the expediency of potentially joining the Eurasian integration association, but since 2016 surveys have asked Kyrgyzstanis about their attitude towards the decision to join the EAEU. In 2012 and 2013, public support for the prospect of the country joining the CU stood at 67% and 72%, respectively, but in 2014 it plummeted. For example, the percentage of citizens who supported Kyrgyzstan's joining the Union decreased from 72% to 50%, while opponents grew from 14% to 30%. By all appearances, this change in sentiment was a response to the devaluation of the Russian currency, which resulted in lower wages for migrant workers and a weaker national currency for Kyrgyzstan. Tightened control over Kyrgyzstan's re-exports of Chinese products, which had vast significance for the national economy, may have also influenced public opinion.

However, as early as 2015, when Kyrgyzstan signed the EAEU Treaty and was on the path to full membership in the Union, the public support for Eurasian integration in the republic grew sharply from 50% to 86%, while negative attitudes towards the association also decreased abruptly from 30% to 6%. Favourable media coverage regarding Kyrgyzstan's entry into the EAEU, which assumed the republic's workers would have free access to Union's common labour market, creation of a Kyrgyzstani-Russian Development Fund for adapting the national economy to EAEU conditions, and so on was instrumental. In 2016, 81% of the population of Kyrgyzstan expressed support for Kyrgyzstan's entry into the EAEU, which was this indicator's highest level for the year throughout the Union.

It is worth mentioning that in nearly every indicated instance, the decrease in support for Eurasian integration occurred due to growth in the percentage of citizens who were indifferent to the Union, and in Armenia it was also due to a rise in the number of negative opinions (by five percentage points) (see Fig. 2.4).

In general, it makes sense to expect a gradual decline in citizens' interest in and approval of the Eurasian Union. Scepticism and increased indifference towards Eurasian integration represent a distinctive phase in the evolution of an integration association. The long-observed Euroscepticism in EU countries is a vivid example. We can assume that a new phenomenon, *Eurasianscepticism*, is gradually emerging in Eurasia. As with Euroscepticism, it is manifest both in the collective consciousness and changes in the opinions of business and government elites, representatives of small- and medium-sized businesses, and the expert community.

There is nothing new in the critical attitudes towards post-Soviet reintegration; similar attitudes have been present during every attempt at (re)integration for the last 25 years. Both internal and external critics have called into question the goals and methods of these processes. Today's scepticism is qualitatively different in that it is an organic part of an integration project acknowledged as established by supporters and opponents alike. As the EAEU's companion, Eurasianscepticism is still in its infancy. However, it is highly probably that critical attitudes towards the CU, SES, and nascent EAEU may rise in the coming years.

The period of euphoria from the successful launch of the Customs Union and Single Economic Space is over. Amid this background, the level of public approval for Eurasian integration is also falling. With increasing frequency, the public is asking itself this question: "What exactly has the Union given me?" Attitudes towards Eurasian integration are becoming more utilitarian. The dissatisfaction of small- and medium-sized national businesses may be related to foreign manufacturers' strengthened positions (e.g., Russian manufacturers' positions in Kazakhstan). And at the level of governments and large companies, the abundance of non-tariff barriers (NTBs) protecting domestic markets is a source of special discontent.[3]

Accordingly, it is helpful to consider various income groups' opinions regarding membership in the EAEU (see Table 2.2). For example, in 2016 well-to-do segments of the population expressed positive attitudes towards the EAEU more often than the poor. In Kazakhstan and Belarus, support from high-income groups was 76% and 74%, respectively, while support from low-income groups was 65% and 57%, respectively. In Russia and Kyrgyzstan, representatives of various income groups demonstrated relative unity in their support for EAEU membership (in Russia, at least 64% in both income groups; in Kyrgyzstan, at least 79%). Moreover, respondents with low income were more likely to express indifference or a negative attitude towards the EAEU.

The difference in the opinions of various age cohorts is interesting (see Fig. 2.5). For example, in 2015 in Armenia and Kazakhstan, youth (18–34 years old) expressed support for their countries' membership in the EAEU more often (by 6–7% on average) than the adult population (35 years and older). Conversely, in Russia and Belarus, youth supported the EAEU less often than the adult population (in Belarus—by 19% on average). In 2015, Kyrgyzstan saw approximately equal support for the prospect of joining the EAEU from all age groups (youth supported the EAEU only 4% less than adults).[4]

Among states that are not part of the EAEU, the populations of Tajikistan and Uzbekistan expressed the greatest interest in potentially joining the Union in 2012–2016 (Fig. 2.6). The Barometer's data also make it possible to analyse how attitudes towards the Eurasian project are changing in Azerbaijan, Georgia, Ukraine, and Moldova (see Fig. 2.6).

An important precondition for two countries to draw closer together is mutual trust, which may manifest itself at the level of national elites and ordinary citizens. As part of the EDB Integration Barometer, the surveys ask citizens of CIS countries which countries they believe are friendly and capable of rendering support to their country in a time of need. This question actually reveals which countries are trusted by the population of various other countries. In all five years of observations, at least 53% of the population of all 12 CIS countries included in the study gave preference to their regional neighbours, most often Russia. Citizens of Kyrgyzstan, Kazakhstan, and Tajikistan have demonstrated the highest level of trust of their neighbours in the CIS region over the entire period of the study (in

Table 2.2 Public opinion in EAEU member states regarding membership in the Union (by population segments with different levels of income) (% of different answers)

	Armenia		Belarus		Kazakhstan		Kyrgyzstan		Russia	
	Groups based on economic position (wealthy/poor)									
	Wealthy	Poor	Wealthy	Poor	Wealthy	Poor	Wealthy	Poor	Wealthy	Poor
Positive	49	36	74	57	76	65	80	79	69	64
Indifferent	34	38	15	33	14	20	13	3	25	21
Negative	16	19	4	6	6	12	5	12	4	6

Source: EDB Integration Barometer (2016)

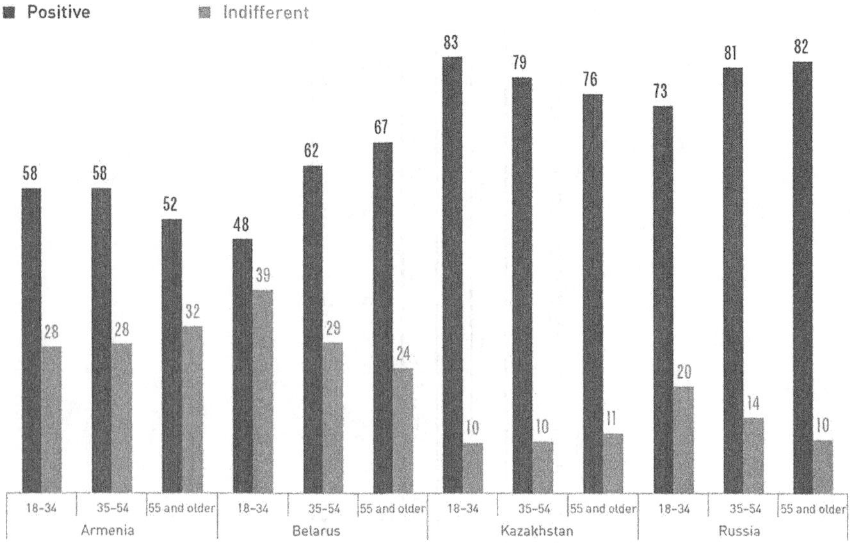

Fig. 2.5 Public opinion regarding support for a country's membership in the EAEU, grouped by age (% of different answers). (Source: EDB Integration Barometer 2015)

2016, 94%, 91%, 90% of the population, respectively). Looking at the distribution of answers for specific countries, we see that in Kazakhstan and Kazakhstan 89% and 81% of the population, respectively, give preference to Russia.[5] In Belarus, for five years, at least 83% of the population has considered neighbouring countries of the CIS region to be the friendliest. Furthermore, in 2016, 82% of citizens preferred Russia, 48% Kazakhstan (in 2015—54%), and 33% Armenia. As for Russia, its population is mostly inclined to trust neighbouring countries in the CIS region. In 2016, such preferences represented 77% of the population. Russians' preferences for specific allies in 2016 looked like this: 65% preferred Belarus, 51% Kazakhstan, 41% China, and 35% Armenia.

These data let us conclude that EAEU member states and Tajikistan (the most realistic candidate for joining the Union) are characterized by the highest level of mutual trust among their populations. This is a precondition of no small importance for the stability of the Eurasian integration project, including in the event that Tajikistan joins. Uzbekistan, Moldova, and Turkmenistan are in varying degrees also part

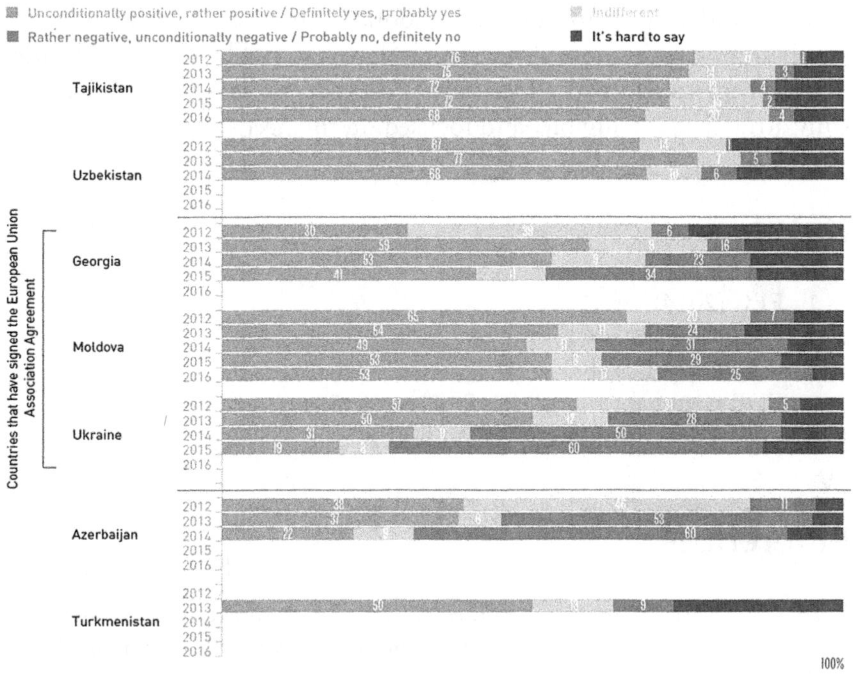

Fig. 2.6 Public opinion of the EAEU in non-member states in 2012–2016 (% of different answers). (Note: The surveys asked the following question in countries that are not EAEU members: "Armenia, Belarus, Kazakhstan, Kyrgyzstan, and Russia joined the Eurasian Economic Union (essentially a single market for five countries). Do you think it would be desirable for our country to join this Union?". Source: EDB Integration Barometer 2016)

of the circle of Eurasian mutual trust. The current preferences of the populations of Azerbaijan, Ukraine, and Georgia are incompatible with involvement in Eurasian integration.

A unique feature of the post-Soviet space is extremely close family ties and friendships between citizens of different countries. There is nowhere in the world where this occurs more. On average, 60% of survey respondents indicated they have relatives, close friends, and colleagues with whom they maintain regular contact in neighbouring countries.

Let us summarize. Most citizens of the Union's member states, including the younger generation, really do support the idea of Eurasian integration. This positive attitude is its own kind of public support for national leaders' pursuit of the corresponding policies. Additionally, it is highly important to consider warning signals in public opinion in order to have time to adjust the Eurasian integration project's path, making it truly attractive, intelligible, and focused on the needs of society.

Notes

1. EEC (2014).
2. Vinokurov (2014a).
3. Vinokurov (2014b).
4. EDB Centre for Integration Studies (2015).
5. EDB Centre for Integration Studies (2016).

References

EDB Centre for Integration Studies (2015). EDB Integration Barometer – 2015. Report No. 33. Saint Petersburg: Eurasian Development Bank. Available at: https://eabr.org/en/analytics/integration-research/cii-reports/integratsionnyy-barometr-eabr-2014/.

EDB Centre for Integration Studies (2016). EDB Integration Barometer – 2016 (Fifth Wave of the Survey). Report No. 40. Saint Petersburg: Eurasian Development Bank. Available at: https://eabr.org/en/analytics/integration-research/cii-reports/integratsionnyy-barometr-eabr-2016/.

EDB Centre for Integration Studies (2017). Eurasian Economic Integration – 2017. Report No. 43. Saint Petersburg: Eurasian Development Bank. Available at: https://eabr.org/en/analytics/integration-research/cii-reports/eurasian-economic-integration-2017/.

Eurasian Economic Commission (EEC) (2014). Eurasian Economic Union. Questions and Answers. Figures and Facts. Moscow: EEC. Available at: http://www.eurasiancommission.org/ru/Documents/eaes_voprosy_otvety.pdf.

Vinokurov, E. (ed.) (2014a). System of Indicators of Eurasian Integration II. Report No. 22. Saint Petersburg: Eurasian Development Bank. Available at: https://eabr.org/en/analytics/integration-research/cii-reports/edb-system-of-indicators-of-eurasian-integration/

Vinokurov, E. (2014b). The Birth of Eurasiaskepticism: Are There Reasons for Panic? Russia in Global Affairs, 1, March 21. Available at: http://eng.globalaffairs.ru/number/The-Birth-of-Eurasiaskepticism-16498.

3

EAEU Institutions

3.1 Features of the EAEU Treaty

The EAEU's main legal document is the Treaty on the Eurasian Economic Union (hereinafter referred to as the "EAEU Treaty" or the "Treaty"). It consists of 680 pages, of which 100 are the Treaty itself and the rest are its 33 appendices.[1] Recall that the presidents of Belarus, Kazakhstan, and Russia signed the Treaty on 29 May 2014. It took effect on 1 January 2015. On 2 January, Armenia acceded to the Treaty, and in May of that same year, Kyrgyzstan also acceded.

Studying this document is helpful to understanding the essence of Eurasian economic integration. One feature of the Treaty is that some of its important details are expressed in appendices to its main text.

On the next pages, we present a succinct analysis of the Treaty's most important provisions. It is indispensable to understanding the legal foundations of the Union. If the reader finds these legal materials too dry, he or she may simply look at Fig. 3.1, which depicts all major areas of regulation.

The Treaty consists of four parts.

Part one is the introduction and includes four sections. Section I contains general provisions about the establishment of the EAEU and its

E. Vinokurov, *Introduction to the Eurasian Economic Union*,
https://doi.org/10.1007/978-3-319-92825-8_3

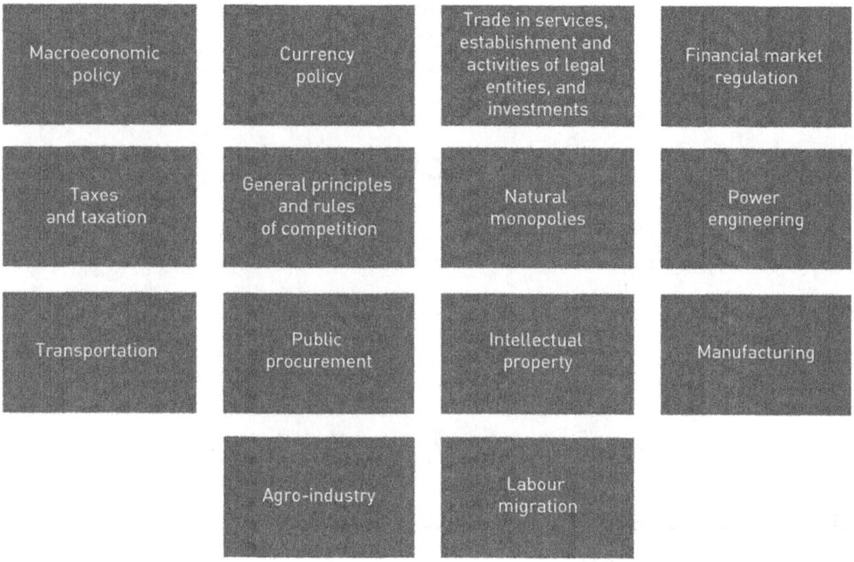

Fig. 3.1 Sections of the EAEU Treaty regulating the Single Economic Space. (Source: EDB Centre for Integration Studies)

status as a legal person. "The Union shall be an international organisation of regional economic integration and shall have international legal personality." The EAEU "…[ensures] free movement of goods, services, capital, and labour, [pursuit of a] coordinated, agreed, or common policy in the economic sectors determined under this Treaty and international treaties within the Union" (Article 1).

Section II sets forth the main operational principles, objectives, and jurisdiction of the Union. The EAEU Treaty identifies the following objectives: "to create proper conditions for sustainable economic development of the Member States in order to improve the living standards of their population; to seek the creation of a single market for goods, services, capital, and labour within the Union; to ensure comprehensive modernisation, cooperation, and competitiveness of national economies within the global economy" (Article 4).

This same section of the Treaty regulates the EAEU's legal framework and its international activities. In particular, there is an explanation of which documents and supranational bodies govern legal relations within the EAEU, and the Union's relations with third parties and the Union's supranational power are specified.

The Law of the Union consists of the EAEU Treaty, as well as "international treaties within the Union; international treaties of the Union with a third party; decisions and directives of the Supreme Eurasian Economic Council, the Eurasian Intergovernmental Council, and the Eurasian Economic Commission adopted within the powers provided for by this Treaty and international treaties within the Union" (Article 6).

Section III defines the procedure and powers of EAEU bodies, which are the Supreme Eurasian Economic Council (SEEC), the Eurasian Intergovernmental Council, Eurasian Economic Commission (EEC), and the Court of the EAEU. The bodies of the Union are examined in greater detail in Sects. 3.2 and 3.3. Specific matters—status, jurisdiction, powers, and operating procedures of the EEC and the Court of the EAEU—are governed by Appendices No. 1 and 2 to the EAEU Treaty.

Part one of the Treaty concludes with Section IV, which defines the procedure for creating the Union's budget, funding the activities of EAEU bodies, performing an independent audit and inspection (oversight) of the financial and commercial activities of the bodies of the Union. For example, budget matters are handled by the SEEC, while oversight is performed by groups of representatives of member states' corresponding state financial oversight bodies.

Part two of the EAEU Treaty (Sections V–XII) is dedicated to matters regarding the operation of the Customs Union within the EAEU.

Section V regulates the exchange of information in all areas, including use of the Union's integrated information system and creation of the EAEU's official statistical information. We note that all of the Union's official statistics (foreign and mutual trade statistics, financial and socio-economic statistics, etc.) are published in a special section of EEC website, entitled "EAEU Statistics".[2]

Section VI is dedicated to the operation of the Customs Union. The Treaty establishes the following common principles for the regulation of trade within the common customs territory of the EAEU:

Within the Customs Union of the Member States:

1. an internal market for goods shall be in place;
2. the Common Customs Tariff of the Eurasian Economic Union and other common measures regulating foreign trade with third parties shall be applied;
3. a common trade regime shall be applied to relations with third parties;
4. Common customs regulations shall be applied;
5. free movement of goods between the territories of the Member States shall be ensured without the use of customs declarations and state control (transport, sanitary, veterinary-sanitary, phytosanitary quarantine), except as provided for by this Treaty (Article 25).

The Treaty establishes rules for the operation of the internal market, according to which "the Member States shall not apply import and export customs duties (other duties, taxes and fees having equivalent effect), non-tariff regulatory measures, safeguards, anti-dumping and countervailing measures in mutual trade, except as provided for by this Treaty" (Article 28). Moreover, the Treaty stipulates EAEU member states' right to apply exemptions and restrictions in mutual trade, if necessary, but on a non-discriminatory basis. As before, there are a large number of obstacles to mutual trade between the Union's member states that cannot be removed quickly, especially in sensitive segments of national economies. The Treaty provides for transition periods for the elimination of these obstacles and preparation for the operation of single or common internal markets in various segments.[3]

Section VII of the Treaty regulates the formation of common markets for drugs and medical products, which assume uniformity in requirements, rules, and methods concerning the circulation of these goods within the common customs territory of the EAEU (read more about the difficult fate of these common markets in Sect. 4.1 of the monograph).

Section VIII provides for common customs regulations pursuant to the EAEU Customs Code, as well as other international treaties and acts taken into consideration in the EAEU Customs Code. The Customs Code is a regulatory act that defines the rules for customs relations between bodies within the Customs Union. The EAEU Customs Code simplifies and accelerates customs declaration procedures and product shipments within the Union.

Section IX of the Treaty is one of its foundational sections. It is entirely devoted to EAEU foreign trade policy. This is the section that specifically regulates the Union's conclusion of free trade agreements and participation in international organizations, as well as the foreign trade policy measures and mechanisms that member states may employ autonomously.

A single system of tariff preferences applies within the Union with respect to the goods supplied from the developing and least developed countries. This system serves to promote the economic development of these countries. It ensures that import customs duties amounting to between 75% and 0% of the EAEU's Common Customs Tariff (CCT) are applied to a specific list of goods imported by the Union. The Union's common rules for determining the origin of goods imported into the EAEU customs territory are determined by the EEC or a corresponding free trade agreement between the EAEU and a third party.

Importantly, the Union lacks supranational jurisdiction in the coordination of trading in services and making investments under agreements with third parties. For now, these matters remain part of the foreign policy competence of EAEU member states.

Articles 39 and 40 of the Treaty regulate the elimination of restrictive measures from third parties in trade with the EAEU and application of the Union's response measures. Both of these instances are within the jurisdiction of the EEC. However, member states have the right to apply response measures unilaterally on the basis of international treaties they concluded with a third party before the EAEU Treaty took effect.

Moreover, pursuant to Articles 46–48, the Union may apply non-tariff regulatory measures, safeguards, and anti-dumping, countervailing, and other measures to protect the internal market. For example, stipulated non-tariff regulatory measures include bans, quantitative restrictions and an approval process for importing/exporting goods, automatic licensing (supervision), or an exclusive right to export/import goods—with observation of the principles of openness and non-discrimination.

Article 42 of the Treaty regulates application of the EAEU's common Harmonized System (HS) Code and the EAEU's CCT. Specifically, the CCT employs the following types of common import customs duties: ad valorem rates (established as a percentage of the customs value of goods), specific rates (established depending on the physical characteristics of goods), combined rates, and seasonal rates (with a term of no more than six months per year). The ability to change import customs duties on sensitive goods is within the competence of the Council of the Commission. The list of such goods is confirmed by the SEEC. The EEC has authority in all other matters of customs and tariff regulation, including the granting of tariff preferences, tariff discounts, and quotas.

Section X of the Treaty is dedicated to technical regulation. Technical regulation is carried out on the basis of technical regulations that apply directly throughout the entire territory of the EAEU and contain mandatory requirements on the Union's single list of products and its life cycle. Products that comply with the EAEU's technical regulations must have the label which stands for *Eurasian Compliance*. Nearly all goods sold within the Union's common customs territory bear this label on their packaging.

Moreover, in order to protect the life and health of humans, animals, and plants, the Union pursues an agreed policy in the application of sanitary, veterinary-sanitary, and phytosanitary quarantine measures on the basis of scientifically valid principles. These measures apply chiefly to the products included on the single list and are regulated by Section XI.

Finally, within the common customs territory, the EAEU pursues an agreed consumer protection policy that guarantees that consumer rights will be observed with respect to all persons residing within the EAEU territory (Section XII).

Part three of the EAEU Treaty regulates the operation of the Single Economic Space within the Union and encompasses the broadest range of agreed member-state policies (Fig. 3.1).

Section XIII regulates agreed macroeconomic policy within the Union whose objective is to achieve balanced economic growth for the member states. It focuses mainly on realizing the EAEU's integration potential and each member state's specific advantages and creating conditions to improve the internal stability of their economies and their immunity to external influence. Moreover, according to Article 63 of the Treaty, the following values of quantitative macroeconomic indicators are the benchmarks for sustainable economic growth:

1. The annual consolidated state budget deficit shall not exceed 3% of GDP.
2. The public sector shall not exceed 50% of GDP.
3. Annual inflation shall not exceed the lowest inflation level among member states by more than five percentage points.

The agreed currency policy stipulated in Section XIV is implemented in the EAEU to promote member states' cooperation in currency and budgetary matters, increase international confidence in their national currencies, and strengthen national currencies in foreign trade and investment flows. Measures designed to carrying out the agreed currency policy include coordination of national currency exchange rate policies, creation of an integrated forex market for the Union, member states' provision of mutual access to their own money markets to the banks of neighbouring countries in the Union, and so on (we will postpone an in-depth discussion of the coordination of monetary and currency policy until Sect. 4.7 of the monograph).

Section XV focuses on guaranteeing freedom (including through the phased simplification of excessive internal regulation) of trade in services, business activities, establishment of legal entities, and investment activities within the territory of the Union. In all of these matters, member states give each other national treatment or "most favoured nation" status. This section stipulates that EAEU countries strive to create a single market for services in as many sectors as possible without exemptions or restrictions. According to the EEC, 43 sectors operate as part of a single market,[4] and the SEEC approved plans for the liberalization of an additional 18 sectors on 26 December 2016. However, each country in the Union has the right to apply individual restrictions. The Treaty's Appendix No. 16 contains an imposing list of "horizontal" restrictions retained by EAEU countries. The SEEC approves additional national lists of exemptions, restrictions, requirements, and conditions. For example, Kazakhstan retains a transition period for a number of service sectors until 2025.

This same appendix stipulates the right of the Union's member states to conclude international agreements on economic integration with third parties on the condition that said states give no less favourable treatment to EAEU countries than they give to the third party. Thus, EAEU states are autonomous when it comes to determining their foreign trade policy concerning trade in services, business activities, and investments with third parties.

Agreed financial market regulation, according to Section XVI of the Treaty, involves, among other things, giving national treatment and most favoured nation status to financial service providers within the Union, "enabling mutual recognition of licenses in the banking and insurance sectors, as well as in the service sector in the securities market" (Article 70). Member states retain restrictions recorded in the corresponding list in Appendix No. 17 to the Treaty regarding legal entities' and individuals' activities in financial services. When harmonization of EAEU countries' laws on financial markets is complete (which should happen by 2025), a supranational body will be formed to regulate the Union's financial market; the Treaty already specifies its future location—the city of Almaty.

The EAEU applies common principles regarding tax interactions. These principles imply, among other things, that taxes, duties, and payments will be collected on goods imported from neighbouring member states on conditions no less favourable than for similar goods from local manufacturers (Section XVII). For example, applying discriminatory VAT conditions to products shipped from neighbouring states is prohibited.

Section XVIII regulates the common principles and rules of competition in the cross-border goods markets of EAEU member states. In particular, member states must offer equal conditions when applying the competition (anti-monopoly) policy to entities in the Union's internal market. EAEU member states pursue an agreed competition (anti-monopoly) policy with respect to third parties. Additionally, this section assigns to the EEC the right to suppress violations of the common rules on competition in the cross-border markets of EAEU countries.

Section XIX of the EAEU Treaty regulates the activities of natural monopolies. EAEU member states are to strive to reduce areas of natural monopoly, by stimulating competition in these areas by making regulation more effective and lowering barriers to enter internal markets. Appendix No. 20 to the Treaty lists areas of natural monopolies in EAEU countries.

Section XX regulates the implementation of a coordinated energy policy and formation of common markets for the energy resources of member states. EAEU states must conclude corresponding international treaties to form such markets. For example, creation of a common electricity market is planned for no later than 1 July 2019 and implies the adoption of common rules on energy trading, access to the services of natural monopolies, and so on. Common gas market and common markets for oil and oil products are to be created no later than 1 January 2025 and will have common rules on unhindered access to gas, oil, and oil product supply systems, respectively. Common markets for energy resources specifically assume a transition to common principles for market-based price-setting and tariff policy, promotion of good-faith competition, and development of the transport infrastructure. Appendices Nos. 21–23 to the Treaty regulate all of the technical aspects of these measures, including the method used to perform interstate transfer of electrical energy between EAEU member states, rules on accessing the services of the relevant natural monopolies, and the procedure for managing the common markets.

Section XXI of the Treaty regulates the coordinated or agreed transportation policy and serves to create a single transport space within the EAEU. In fact, it assumes the formation of a common market for transportation services with common regulatory principles, which will make it possible to realize the EAEU's transportation potential and will facilitate the growth of transportation and logistical infrastructure at Union-wide scales. On 28 December 2016, the SEEC adopted a comprehensive document entitled "Main Areas of Agreed Transportation Policy of the Eurasian Economic Union". This road map for the phased creation of a single market for transportation services covers all types of transportation: maritime, railway, motor vehicle, and air. Appendix No. 24 clarifies every detail of the implementation of the agreed transportation policy; common approaches, rules, and the procedure for performing transport (motor vehicle) control at the Union's external border; access to railway transportation services and railway infrastructure.

Section XXII of the Treaty and Appendix No. 25 to the Treaty define the objectives, principles, and procedure for regulation of state (municipal) procurement within the Union. Within the Union, member states give each other national treatment with respect to procurement and ensure that potential suppliers from member states are unhindered in their ability to participate in procurement operations, which must be conducted electronically. National (central) banks form an exception. Regulations on public procurement do not apply to them.

The Union regulates member states' cooperation in the defence and protection of intellectual property rights in accordance with the requirements of international law (Section XXIII). Moreover, the Treaty gives national treatment throughout the entire Union to persons possessing rights to the intellectual property of EAEU countries.

Member states form and implement industrial policy independently on the principles of equality, non-discrimination, good-faith competition, and mutual benefit, with coordinating and advisory support from the EEC (Section XXIV of the Treaty). The EEC and member states have developed a document entitled "Main Areas of Industrial Cooperation within the Eurasian Economic Union". According to the document, industrial cooperation among EAEU countries focuses on, among other things, import substitution, increasing the export potential of the manufacturing industry, creating innovative industrial sectors, modernizing enterprises, and so on. Appendix No. 27 to the Treaty stipulates the EEC's powers associated with advisory support and coordination of member states' activities in industrial cooperation. For example, these include assisting the development and implementation of joint (interstate) programmes and projects, involving small- and medium-sized businesses in industrial cooperation, developing recommendations on the formation of Eurasian technological platforms, and other elements of innovative infrastructure for the Union.

Thus, in its coordinating role, the Commission has at present created 12 Eurasian technological platforms. They support the conditions necessary for cooperation among the industrial enterprises, scientific institutions, state bodies, and public organizations of member states in scientific, innovative, and industrial matters. These platforms focus on ensuring the Union's global competitiveness by building up and realizing its innovative, technological, and export potential in 12 specific sectors (space engineering and geoinformatics, biotechnology and photonics, ecodevelopment technologies, agriculture, metallurgy, etc.).[5]

As for industrial goods and services related to their production, the EAEU has common rules on granting industrial subsidies, which took effect on 1 January 2017. Disputes associated with industrial subsidies are settled through negotiations and consultations involving the EEC and, if necessary, are referred to the Court of the EAEU. Appendix No. 28 to the Treaty stipulates prohibited, permitted, and specific subsidies and the procedure for examination and application of countervailing and response measures.

Finally, member states pursue an agreed (coordinated) agroindustrial policy, which is regulated by Section XXV. Intergovernmental interaction in this area is intended to promote conditions in the Union's common agricultural market that are favourable for balanced growth of production and markets for agricultural and food products, good-faith competition among producers, and protection of their interests in internal and external markets. Appendix No. 29 to the Treaty stipulates measures of state support for agriculture in the EAEU, as well as the list of products subject to the common rules on such support, rules on calculating the amount of support, and other matters.

Section XXVI is dedicated to member states' cooperation to coordinate regulations on labour migration. It describes the mechanisms for interaction among the relevant state bodies of EAEU countries. In general, this section of the Treaty guarantees the operation of a single labour market and, consequently, conditions favourable for citizens of member states to work throughout the entire Union. (The EAEU Treaty's particulars regarding regulation of the EAEU labour market are contained in Sect. 4.5 of this monograph, which is dedicated to labour migration.)

Part four of the EAEU Treaty—its final part—contains transitional and concluding provisions. For example, Section XXVII includes transitional provisions on preserving in the law of the Union the validity of international treaties concluded under the Customs Union and Single Economic Space, on the technical nuances of the operation of EAEU bodies, on member states' implementation of agreed policies, and so on. Section XXVIII unites concluding provisions that define, among other things, the social guarantees, privileges, and immunities of the EEC and Court of the EAEU, and specifies the Russian language as the working language of Union bodies, rules for obtaining the status of observer or candidate state, the procedure for candidate states to join the Union and for member states to withdraw from it.

The EAEU Treaty covers all key aspects of the routine and long-term economic interaction of member states, specifies areas for expansion of the EAEU, and reflects the full complexity of the integration process. Importantly, Article 6 of Section II establishes a hierarchy of EAEU regulations and stipulates that the provisions of the EAEU Treaty, its objectives, and principles are to be given priority over international treaties within the Union, including with third parties, and over the decisions and directives of the Union's bodies. However, the large number of stipulated restrictions, including with respect to the jurisdiction of Union bodies, long transitional periods for integration of national industrial markets, and the rather watered-down and at times contradictory wording of provisions leave member states with the ability to deviate from several of the Treaty's regulations, if necessary. This problem is gradually being solved by the EAEU bodies that will be discussed below.

3.2 Supreme Council, Intergovernmental Council, and EEC

Pursuant to Article 8 of the EAEU Treaty, the bodies of the EAEU are:

- Supreme Eurasian Economic Council ("Supreme Council" or "SEEC")
- Eurasian Intergovernmental Council ("Intergovernmental Council")
- Eurasian Economic Commission ("Commission" or "EEC")
- Court of the Eurasian Economic Union ("Court of the Union" or "Court of the EAEU")

In the next few sections, we consider these four main bodies of the Eurasian Union. In addition to the three institutions that make and carry out integration decisions (Sect. 3.2), the Court of the EAEU has a potentially significant role (Sect. 3.3). It has already begun to function, and we will illustrate its decisions and their underlying principles. Then we will speak of the two institutions that form the Union's "economic ecosphere": Eurasian Development Bank (EDB, Sect. 3.4) and Eurasian Fund for Stabilization and Development (EFSD, Sect. 3.5).

The powers and operating principles of the Union bodies are stipulated by Section III of the EAEU Treaty and international treaties concluded within the EAEU and regulating matters such as the geographical location of these bodies in member states. The working language of the Union bodies is Russian.

3.2.1 Eurasian Economic Commission

February 2012 saw the beginning of the work of the EEC, a supranational institution that is the Union's main regulatory body. The EEC's powers cover many areas: regulation of foreign trade; technical, customs, tariff, and non-tariff regulation; regulation of sanitary, veterinary, and phytosanitary measures; protection of intellectual property and consumer rights; industry regulation in the production of drugs and medical products, the power industry, and transportation; as well as regulation of the Union's labour market, financial and services, state (municipal) procurement; and much more. The EEC's main tasks are to ensure the conditions necessary for the operation and growth of the EAEU and develop proposals to achieve further integration. The key principles guiding the Commission's activities include the requirement that adopted decisions be economically sound, the need for mutual benefit, and consideration of the national interests of member states.

In exercising its powers, the EEC adopts decisions that are binding on member states (just as in the European Union) and also makes non-binding recommendations. For example, the Commission may make a decision that obligates the government of one member state to repeal a resolution that contradicts the laws of the EAEU and infringes on the interests of another member state. As early as 2012, an important precedent was set by the Board of the Commission's decision that repealed a resolution of the Government of the Russian Federation, which stipulated that worsted cloth for uniforms would be purchased exclusively from Russian factories, thus violating the principles of competition in the

EAEU.[6] In this case, the EEC's decision was binding and contributed to increased shipments of cloth from Belarus. At the same time, pursuant to clause 30 of Appendix No. 1 to the EAEU Treaty, member states have the right to file a motion to cancel or amend any decision of the Commission.

The *Council of the Commission*, which includes one deputy head of government from each member state, provides general leadership of the Commission's activities and general management of integration processes. The functions and powers of the Council of the Commission include organization of work to improve the legal regulatory of EAEU activities and determination of the main areas for advancing economic integration under the EAEU. We must make special mention of the Council of the Commission's right to consider motions to cancel or amend EEC decisions, which have been filed with the Board of the Commission by a member state or member of the Council of the Commission before the corresponding decisions have taken effect.

In its work, the Council of the Commission relies on the *Board of the Commission*, which is the EEC's executive body. The Board consists of representatives of member states, with each party being represented equally. Representatives (members of the Board) are appointed by the Supreme Council and head up the corresponding industry-specific departments of the EEC (Table 3.1).

Table 3.1 Organizational structure of the EEC

Council of the Commission	Five members of the Council of the Commission: one deputy head of government from each member state
Board of the Commission (representatives of member states, with each party being represented equally)	
Chairman of the EEC Board *Tigran Sargsyan*	Organizational Support and Protocol Department Finance Department Legal Department Administrative Department
Member of the Board—Minister in charge of Integration and Macroeconomics *Tatyana Valovaya*	Department for Macroeconomic Policy Statistics Department Department for Integration Advancement

(*continued*)

Table 3.1 (continued)

Council of the Commission	Five members of the Council of the Commission: one deputy head of government from each member state
Member of the Board—Minister in charge of Economy and Financial Policy *Timur Zhaksylykov*	Department for Financial Policy Department for Entrepreneurial Development Labour Migration Department
Member of the Board—Minister in charge of Industry and Agroindustrial Complex *Sergey Sidorsky*	Department for Industrial Policy Department for Agricultural Policy
Member of the Board—Minister in charge of Trade *Veronika Nikishina*	Department for Customs Tariff and Non-Tariff Regulation Department for Internal Market Defence Department for Trade Policy
Member of the Board—Minister in charge of Technical Regulation *Valery Koreshkov*	Department for Technical Regulation and Accreditation Department for Sanitary, Phytosanitary, and Veterinary Measures
Member of the Board—Minister in charge of Customs Cooperation *Mukai Kadyrkulov*	Department of Customs Legislation and Law Enforcement Practice Department for Customs Infrastructure
Member of the Board—Minister in charge of Energy and Infrastructure *Adamkul Zhunusov*	Department for Transport and Infrastructure Energy Department
Member of the Board—Minister in charge of Competition and Antitrust Regulation *Marat Kussainov*	Department for Antitrust Regulation Department for Competition and Public Procurement Policy
Member of the Board—Minister in charge of Internal Markets, Information Support, Information and Communication Technologies *Karine Minasyan*	IT Department Domestic Markets Operation Department

Source: Adopted from the website of the Eurasian Economic Commission, as of end 2017

Box 3.1 Chairpersons of the EEC Board

Since the Commission was established, the Chairman of the Board ("Kollegiya") of the Commission has been Viktor Khristenko, who previously occupied the position of deputy chairman and acting chairman of the Government of the Russian Federation, Minister of Industry and Energy, and Minister of Industry and Trade of the Russian Federation. In February 2016, the Board appointed Tigran Sargsyan as Chairman of the Board of the Commission. He was previously prime minister of Armenia and head of Central Bank of Armenia.

It is expected that the chairmanship will subsequently rotate alphabetically and that in 2020 the next chairman of the Board will be a representative of Belarus. The chairperson is appointed to a single four-year term without the right to extend.

Twenty-four departments operate within the EEC. Simultaneously, 20 advisory committees on key areas of integration operate under the Board of the Commission. They draft proposals for the Board of the Commission and advise member states' government bodies. Information on the various committees, subcommittees, and working groups is available on the Commission's official website and departmental websites. The EEC's departments support the activities of the Board and Council of the Commission. They prepare draft decisions, directives, and recommendations. Furthermore, their competence includes drafting the international treaties required for the operation of the EAEU, monitoring member states' compliance with the decisions and directives of Union bodies and international treaties that comprise the law of the Union, as well as several other functions.

The EEC actively interacts with both EAEU member states and governments of other countries and their unions to position the Commission and Union internationally and to attract new partners to collaboration with the EAEU and potential membership in the Eurasian integration project. Thus, the Commission works with member states on two levels: intergovernmentally with national bodies and in business communities. As part of their authority, Commission officials hold regular meetings and consultations with the heads of state of Union members and with representatives of national ministries and departments.

Box 3.2 EEC Interaction with the Business Community

The EEC works with business circles in the Union in various formats.

First, it interacts with the business community through meetings of the Advisory Committee on Business Matters, created under the EEC. The committee prepares proposals on organizing cooperation and improving information exchange between the business community and the authorized bodies of EAEU countries and on improving the business climate, eliminating excessive administrative barriers to business, and so on. The committee's chair, a member of the Board (a minister), guides its work on the economic and budgetary policy of the EEC and may invite representatives of the EAEU business community to attend meetings. Several others of the Commission's advisory committees also interact with the business community.

Second, the EEC cooperates with business circles through the EAEU Business Council. The Business Council is a standing coordinating and advisory body of member states' business communities. The EAEU Business Council includes the Armenian Union of Industrialists and Entrepreneurs (Employers), Confederation of Industrialists and Entrepreneurs (Employers) of Belarus, National Chamber of Entrepreneurs of Kazakhstan Atameken, Kyrgyz Union of Industrialists and Entrepreneurs, and the Russian Union of Industrialists and Entrepreneurs. At the end of 2016, the Advisory Committee on the Interaction Between the EEC and the EAEU Business Council was created and tasked with becoming a forum for discussing strategic and systemic questions of the EAEU's development together with the Union's business communities.

Third, we should specifically note the "Operation of the Internal Markets of the Eurasian Economic Union" web portal introduced by the Commission in October 2016. In practice, this is a tool for constant communication between business entities and the EEC. Its main task is to identify barriers and restrictions in mutual trade. This resource is available at https://barriers.eaeunion.org. A section of this website lets visitors report potential barriers to business activities within EAEU member states' Single Economic Space and describe the situations facing an entrepreneur or his or her organization. The EEC will send an opinion letter on the reported situation within 30 days to the specified reply email address. Additionally, this website lets you monitor the Commission's subsequent actions regarding the barriers and review ongoing work to eliminate them.

The Commission also works with third parties and international organizations in various formats: official visits aimed at establishing cooperation, work with embassies and representative offices in the Union's member states, and the Commission's own image-building events, exhibitions, and press conferences abroad; EEC representatives' participation in international events. The Union's key partners on the Eurasian continent are well known and discussed later in the monograph (Chap. 5).

The EEC makes all decisions collectively. However, the Council of the Commission makes decisions, directives, and recommendations by consensus, while the Board of the Commission does so by a qualified majority (two-thirds of the votes of all members of the Board), except for decisions on the list of sensitive issues, which are determined by the Supreme Council. The Board makes such decisions by consensus.

In conclusion, we add that the Commission is located in Moscow. More detailed information regarding the Commission is contained in Appendix No. 1 to the EAEU Treaty and in the EEC Regulations.

Box 3.3 Where Can Eurasian Institutions Be Located?

Currently, 1070 employees of the Eurasian Economic Commission work in Moscow, while the Court of the EAEU works in Minsk. In the future, a supranational financial regulator, whose creation is planned by 2025 according to the Treaty, is to be located in Kazakhstan. Recall that previously the EurAsEC Integration Committee was located simultaneously in Almaty and Moscow.

That said, this "Eurasian geography" is not fixed once and for all and may well change in the future. Where might Eurasian institutions be located in terms of political expediency? Various proposals have been put forward on this matter. For example, Nursultan Nazarbayev in the 1990s spoke about the possibility of locating Eurasian Union institutions in Kazan or Samara (large Russian cities on the Volga, ca. 1000 km east of Moscow), and in the late 2000s, he proposed Astana as a potential location. Sergey Glazyev also backed the Kazan option.[7] In our opinion, the Astana variant has a deep symbolism ("the EAEU is not the same as Russia"). It might also be rather practical, especially if EAEU membership expanded in Central Asia. The political expediency of this option would lie in the refusal to place Eurasian institutions in the Union's country with the largest population and GDP: Russia. However, the matter is not straightforward. We should also consider the experience of the European Union, which indicates that placing institutions in different places is ineffective (the European Parliament's pilgrimage between Brussels and Strasbourg comes to mind).

3.2.2 Eurasian Intergovernmental Council

The Eurasian Intergovernmental Council, consisting of heads of government of member states, carries out work under ten competences. We will make special mention of the following: ensuring monitoring of compliance with the EAEU Treaty and the decisions of the SEEC; at the request of the Council of the Commission, consideration of issues for which consensus could not be reached in decision-making at the level of the Council of the Commission; approval of the Union's draft budgets, as well as consideration of member states' proposals to cancel or amend decisions adopted by the Commission, which, if necessary, are referred to the Supreme Council. The Intergovernmental Council is authorized to make decisions to suspend decisions of the Board and Council of the Commission.

The Intergovernmental Council holds meetings at least twice a year. If necessary, extraordinary meetings may also be convened at the initiative of member states or the chairman of the Intergovernmental Council. The EEC creates the agenda based on EAEU member states' proposals.

3.2.3 Supreme Eurasian Economic Council

The Supreme Council is the EAEU's highest body and consists of the heads of the member states. The SEEC is responsible for reviewing fundamental matters concerning the Union's activities and determining its strategy, directions, and prospects for advancing integration. The Supreme Council holds meetings at least once a year. Extraordinary meetings can be convened to resolve urgent issues concerning the EAEU's activities, at the initiative of any of the member states or the chairman of the Supreme Council. As in the case of the Intergovernmental Council, the agenda of SEEC meetings is created by the EEC on the basis of proposals from member states.

Here we note that the EAEU Treaty provides for the member states' chairmanship in the Supreme and Intergovernmental Councils and the

Council of the Commission to rotate annually in alphabetical order according to the states' official names in the Russian language.

According to Article 6 of Section II of the EAEU Treaty, if conflicts arise between EAEU bodies, the decisions of the SEEC have priority over the decisions of the Intergovernmental Council and the EEC, and in turn the decisions of the Intergovernmental Council have priority over decisions of the EEC.

The Supreme Council and the Intergovernmental Council adopt decisions and directives by consensus that are binding on the member states *in accordance with their national laws*. This means that the decisions of both councils are not actually directly applicable within the EAEU. Instead, they require additional procedures to be implemented at the national level and thus do not have priority over national laws. The original draft of the EAEU Treaty assumed that the Union's legal acts would have direct affect within the EAEU, that is, they received priority over the national laws of member states. However, in the process of preparing the final version of the EAEU Treaty, many provisions of concern to individual member states were deleted or replaced with vaguer wording. But this is a separate topic beyond the scope of this monograph. One way or another, this problem must be accounted for when carrying out analysis and further research on Eurasian economic integration.

3.3 Court of the Union

The Court of the EAEU is the Union's judicial body. It considers disputes regarding the implementation of international treaties within the EAEU and decisions of Union bodies. It was created to ensure uniform application of EAEU law by member states and Union bodies. The Court of the EAEU acts on the basis of the EAEU Treaty, Statute of the Court of the EAEU (Appendix No. 2 to the EAEU Treaty), and Regulations of Court of the Union. It is the procedural successor of the Court of the Eurasian Economic Community (EurAsEC).

Box 3.4 Regulatory Framework of the Court of the EurAsEC/EAEU

The Court adopted the Statute of the Court of the EurAsEC, that is, the act that established the Court, in Decision No. 122 of 27 April 2003 of the EurAsEC Interstate Council. The Court adopted a new version of the Statute of the Court of the EurAsEC in 2010, which provides for the competence to review cases related to the formation of the Customs Union of Belarus, Kazakhstan, and Russia.

The EAEU established the Court in 1 January 2012. Prior to this time, its presence in the Eurasian Economic Community's legal framework was secured by the decision of 19 September 2003 of the Council of Heads of State of the CIS to assign to the Economic Court of the Commonwealth of Independent States the functions of the Court of the EurAsEC and by the CIS-EurAsEC Agreement to have the Economic Court of the Commonwealth of Independent States fulfil the functions of the Court of the EurAsEC (which was signed on 3 March 2004 and expired on 1 January 2012 in connection with the start of the independent operation of the Court of the EurAsEC). On 19 December 2011, the EurAsEC Interstate Council adopted Decision No. 583 "On the Formation and Organization of the Court of EurAsEC". On 1 January 2012, the Court of the EurAsEC began to operate independently, and its membership had already been determined. The Court of the EurAsEC's activities were terminated on 1 January 2015 on the basis of the Eurasian Economic Community's Termination Treaty and the EurAsEC Interstate Council Decision No. 652 on the termination of Eurasian Economic Community's activities (both documents are dated 10 October 2014).

Decisions of the Court of the EurAsEC continue with their same status in accordance with Article 3 of the Eurasian Economic Community's Termination Treaty.

In 2012–2014, the Court of the EurAsEC considered five cases on regulation of common customs and tariffs in the Customs Union, classification of goods according to the Harmonized System Code, other problematic issues related to the operation of the CU's common customs territory, and challenges to the EEC's actions (omissions). The list of the Court of the EurAsEC's judicial acts also includes about 10 cases related to various issues, including complaints filed by companies from third parties (India, China, Germany) against the Board of the Commission's decisions to apply anti-dumping measures to their goods.

The most notable of these includes Case No. 1-7/1-2013. After considering this case, the Court of the EurAsEC ordered the EEC to enforce its decision. The applicant, represented by Coal Company Southern Kuzbass OJSC, successfully challenged clause 1 of Decision No. 335 of 17 August 2010 of the Customs Union Commission ("On Problematic Issues Related to the Operation of the Common Customs Territory, and the Practice of Implementing the

(*continued*)

Box 3.4 (continued)
Mechanisms of the Customs Union"). This clause, which concerned customs declaration and control at the CU's internal borders, was recognized by the Court to be inconsistent with international treaties concluded within the CU and had to be repealed.

Also worth mentioning is Case No. 1-7/2-2013, brought by Novokramatorsk Machine Building Plant CJSC (Ukraine) to challenge Decision No. 904 of 9 December 2011 of the Customs Union Commission "On Measures to Protect the Economic Interests of Manufacturers of Forged Steel Rolls for Rolling Mills in the Customs Union". In particular, the Court of the EurAsEC's decision in this case led to the development of a rule that stipulates that if the Court of the EAEU finds that EAEU law is inconsistent with WTO law, then WTO law shall apply.[8] Thus, the Court of the EurAsEC has played a significant role in shaping the EAEU's current laws, including laying the foundations for the work of the Court of the EAEU.

Source: The official website of the Court of the Eurasian Economic Community (http://www.courteurasian.org/en/).

Unlike the Commission, which is located in Moscow, the seat of the Court of the Union is in Minsk. Two judges from each member state ensure equal representation in the Court of the EAEU. The Supreme Council appoints and dismisses judges from their posts. According to the Rules of Procedure of the Court of the EAEU, two judges from two different member states are elected to the positions of presiding judge, who guides the Court's activities, and deputy presiding judge for a period of three years. The Court reviews cases in the Grand Chamber of the Court (all judges), a Chamber of the Court (one judge from each member state), or the Appellate Chamber of the Court (deals with motions to appeal decisions of the Chamber of the Court in a case and is comprised of judges who did not participate in the consideration of the case).

According to clause 49 of Chapter IV of the Statute, the Court works with disputes that arise regarding the implementation of Union law, both at the request of member states and at the request of business entities.

The Court of the Union considers the following types of disputes *at the request of a member state*:

- Disputes regarding the compliance of an international treaty within the Union, or its individual provisions, with the EAEU Treaty
- Disputes regarding another member state(s)' compliance with the EAEU Treaty, international treaties within the Union, and (or) decisions of the Union's bodies
- Disputes regarding the compliance of an EEC decision or its individual provisions with the EAEU Treaty, international treaties within the EAEU, and (or) decisions of the Union's bodies
- Challenges to the actions (omissions) of the EEC

Disputes considered by the Court of the Union *at the request of a business entity* are exclusively limited to possible violations of the rights and legal interests of such an entity by the EEC. It should be understood that a business entity means both a legal entity and an individual registered as a sole proprietor.

The Statute of the Court of the EAEU does not explicitly state that the Court is competent to review cases related to the implementation of the Union's international treaties with a third party. It follows that member states and business entities cannot count on support from the Court of the EAEU if they discover violations of the law under these treaties. However, the Statute of the Court stipulates that member states "may assign to the competence of the Court other disputes whose resolution by the Court is explicitly provided for by the Treaty, international treaties within the Union, the Union's international treaties with a third party, or other international treaties between member states" (clause 40 of Chapter IV of Appendix No. 2 to the EAEU Treaty). For example, the free trade agreement between the EAEU and Vietnam does not contain a single reference to the Court of the EAEU. As a rule, a specially created tribunal (arbitration group) settles disputes under such agreements in accordance with WTO regulations.

One of the problems faced by the Court of the EAEU is national law's priority over the law of the Union if there is a conflict between them.[9] For example, at present, the priority of the provisions of EAEU law depends on conditions established by the Constitution of Russia and the Constitution of Kazakhstan and therefore is not absolute throughout the entire EAEU. The Constitution of the Russian Federation stipulates that the provisions of the Constitution shall apply if they provide a higher level of protection of a citizen's rights and freedoms than the provisions of international law or an international treaty.

The European Union had a similar situation where for roughly 20 years the constitutional courts of Germany and Italy gave priority to national law rather than the acts of the European Communities. Thus, Germany did not recognize the supremacy of European regulations until the EU Court expanded human rights within the entire integration union to a level comparable to that guaranteed by the German Constitution.[10] These are examples of cases where national can (and does!) improve supranational regulation.

At the same time, the duality of legal regulation in the EAEU can lead to additional difficulties. For example, business entities operating in the same field in different member states may be provided with different amounts and levels of benefits and preferences, or the requirements applied to individuals and legal entities in a particular member state may be more stringent than those established by the EAEU Treaty.

As an example, let us consider Court of the EAEU Case No. SE-1-2/2-15-KS. It has to do with the restriction of business entities' rights due to the failure to make the technical regulations directly applicable. A sole proprietor from Kazakhstan, who imported cars to Kazakhstan to transport goods, faced a situation where Kazakh customs authorities charged him excise tax when the goods were released. This happened because the authorities recognized the imported cars as vehicles manufactured on the chassis of a car, which, according to the Tax Code of the Republic of Kazakhstan, are excisable goods. The entrepreneur filed a claim with the EEC, alleging that these authorities violated the principles of uniform application and implementation of the international treaties that form the legal framework of the Customs Union. In its response, the EEC indicated that performing a legal assessment of the legality of the activities and decisions of the EAEU member states' customs authorities is outside its competence. Disagreeing with the Commission's arguments, the entrepreneur turned to the Court of the EAEU. In December 2015, the Chamber of the Court decided to dismiss the claim and declared the EEC's inaction to be consistent with the Treaty and international treaties within the Union and not in violation of the business entity's rights and lawful interests in business and other economic activities.

At the same time, in instances of legal uncertainty or regulatory duality, the Court of the EAEU and the supreme courts of member states can add to each other, acting complementarily and thus improving the Union's legal framework.[11]

We should also mention the Court of the EAEU's advisory function, the demand for which will only grow. According to the Statute, the Court of the Union clarifies the rules and regulations of EAEU law, as well as the provisions of the Union's international treaties with a third party, if so stipulated by these treaties, and issues an advisory opinion. For now, applications to receive an advisory opinion can be submitted either by member states (on issues related to Union law) or employees and officials of Union bodies (on labour relations).

3.4 Eurasian Development Bank

Eurasian Development Bank ("EDB" or the "Bank") and the Eurasian Fund for Stabilization and Development ("EFSD" or the "Fund") are key elements of the financial infrastructure for Eurasian integration. They fulfil the important function of financial support for Eurasian economic integration, economic development, and stability in member states. The Bank and the Fund unite the same six countries: all the countries of the Eurasian Union plus Tajikistan. These countries established both the Bank and the Fund in the 2000s—EDB in 2006 on a wave of rapid economic growth and the Fund in 2009 as a response to the challenges of the global economic crisis. However, the Bank and the Fund are not formally affiliated with EAEU organizations. They are independent structures with their own membership and management bodies.

EDB is an international financial organization tasked with promoting economic growth in its member states, expanding trade and economic ties between them, and advancing integration processes in the Eurasian space.[12] EDB was established at the initiative of President of Russia Vladimir Putin and President of Kazakhstan Nursultan Nazarbayev. Authorized representatives of Russia and Kazakhstan established the Bank on the basis of an interstate agreement signed on 12 January 2006.

In addition to the Bank's founders—Russia and Kazakhstan—its members are Armenia, Belarus, Kyrgyzstan, and Tajikistan, which joined EDB between 2009 and 2011. Thus, by 2011, EDB included all member states of the future EAEU, as well as Tajikistan.

EDB is open to new members. New states, as well as international organizations, may become members by decision of the Bank's Council after they have accepted the EDB founding agreement and duly paid for the acquired shares of the Bank. It is noteworthy that the Bank's potential circle of shareholders is not limited to the post-Soviet space. In 2016, following the relevant decision of the Bank's Council, work began with potential new shareholders from the vast expanses of the entire Eurasian continent. This list of potential shareholders largely coincides with the list of states with which the EAEU is negotiating or plans to negotiate the creation of free trade zones. This is not accidental: both processes pursue essentially the same goals—to intensify areas of economic cooperation that benefit the Bank's member states, to increase trade and investment flows, and to create favourable conditions for exports.

Box 3.5 The Unfulfilled Plan to Transform EDB into the Shanghai Cooperation Organization's Development Bank

In 2013–2014, there were discussions of the prospects of converting EDB into the Shanghai Cooperation Organization (SCO) Development Bank. For many years, this organization's members have discussed the idea of the SCO creating its own financial development institution to stimulate investment activities and strengthen economic cooperation within the SCO. There were two main options. First, create an international bank from scratch. Second, expand the functionality and membership of the already-operating Eurasian Development Bank. The second option proposed that SCO member states China and Uzbekistan join the EDB (for the rest of the member states, both organizations' membership is the same), making appropriate changes to the EDB's statutory documents and increasing the authorized capital. However, due to differences in the positions of individual SCO member states and, above all, due to the creation of the Asian Infrastructure Investment Bank and the New Development Bank of BRICS, nothing came of the urgency of forming the SCO Development Bank, including by transforming the EDB.

The Bank's management structure is quite simple. The Bank's Council is EDB's supreme governing body, providing overall operational guidance. Each of the Bank's member states appoints one authorized representative and one deputy to the Bank's Council. The Bank's Council elects one of the authorized representatives to the post of chairman of the Bank's Council. As of 2017, the Bank's Council is represented mainly by the finance ministers of the Bank's member states and is headed by prime minister of Kazakhstan B.A. Sagintayev.

Day-to-day activities are entrusted to the Bank's Management Board, headed by a chairman, who is elected and approved by the Bank's Council. Igor Finogenov (formerly a successful commercial banker) was the founding Chairman of the Management Board from 2006 to February 2015. Since February 2015, Dmitry Pankin (former deputy finance minister) has headed the Bank. Andrey Belyaninov (former head of the Federal Customs Service) has replaced him in December 2017.

The EDB conducts its operations in accordance with the principles of political neutrality, social responsibility, transparency, and accountability, applying the world's best practices and complying with universally recognized rules of international law. The Bank's head office is located in Almaty. The Bank has offices in Astana, Bishkek, Dushanbe, Yerevan, Minsk, Moscow, and St Petersburg.

Becoming member states of the Bank and contributing to its capital, countries assume that combining their efforts and strengthening trade and economic cooperation will help each member to cope with the consequences of the global financial crisis and the challenges of globalization and to take its rightful place in the international division of labour. The main result of EDB's first decade of work is the establishment of the Bank as a recognized international institution of financial development with a mandate to develop regional economic integration.

Noteworthy among EDB's main activities is the financing of projects to develop energy, transportation, and municipal infrastructure in member states. At the same time, projects which generate a positive *integration effect* would be given priority. The term "integration effect" means the generation of mutual trade and mutual investments under financed projects, as well as the creation of effective value chains in the Eurasian region. For example, a top-priority client for EDB would be a Russian company investing in a new plant in Kazakhstan, for which components from Russia will be supplied to Kazakhstan, and finished products will find demand in all the countries of the EAEU. A transport corridor that creates new opportunities for trade and reduces transport costs is a priority project. Projects generating mutual trade and investment growth account for about 50% of the Bank's investment portfolio from year to year.

The Bank is active internationally. It is an observer in the UN General Assembly and has concluded a number of memorandums on cooperation with leading international organizations and development banks. It also collaborates actively with the EEC. For example, since 2014, the Bank and the Commission work together to forecast the socioeconomic development of the Union's economies using an up-to-date set of macroeconomic models. The Bank and the Commission have implemented a number of other projects related to the most complex integration-building issues requiring comprehensive analysis, including large-scale projects to analyse non-tariff barriers and the potential coordination of macroeconomic and monetary policies.[13]

Box 3.6 Why Are Regional Development Banks Created?

There are dozens of regional and subregional development banks in the world. The largest and most widely known are the European Bank for Reconstruction and Development, Asian Development Bank, the Inter-American Development Bank (which unites the countries of South, Central, and North America), Islamic Development Bank, African Development Bank, and Nordic Investment Bank (which unites Scandinavian countries). Andean Development Corporation and the Black Sea Trade and Development Bank are smaller but closer to the EDB in terms of their priorities. They are generally given tasks related to economic development, combating poverty, building infrastructure, and promoting regional integration.

According to EDB's Charter, its main mandate is to promote economic growth and expand economic and trade relations between member states (Article 1 of the Charter). Analytical support for regional integration processes and consultations on issues related to economic development, expansion of economic and trade relations, and public and international finance are singled out as special tasks (Articles 2 and 11 of the Charter). In general, EDB is a bank for advancing economic integration.

The Bank's paid-up capital is $1.5 billion. The Bank's investment portfolio, taking into account the projects implemented at the end of 2016, was $5.4 billion, and the current investment portfolio is ca. $2.4 billion.

Most of the projects in the Bank's current investment portfolio are in Kazakhstan (45%), Russia (33%), and Belarus (18%). At the end of 2016, the Bank's current investment portfolio consisted of 69 projects in six member states. The Bank issues the largest number of loans in the energy and transport sectors (infrastructure facilities) and in the financial sector (these are mainly special-purpose lines of credit to commercial banks to provide trade financing between EAEU countries), and in 2016 the share of projects in the mining industry increased (from 5.2% to 15.4%). In total, roughly 50% of the portfolio represents infrastructure. Examples of projects being implemented with EDB's involvement: financing the construction of the Polotsk Hydroelectric Power Plant on the Western Dvina (Belarus), financing the construction of an interregional power transmission line from North Kazakhstan to the Aktyubinsk Region (Kazakhstan), financing the production of new Sukhoi Superjet 100 civil aircraft, construction of the new Pulkovo airport terminal, construction of the Western Rapid Diameter (Russia), and so on.

3.5 Eurasian Fund for Stabilization and Development

The EFSD was established by Armenia, Belarus, Kazakhstan, Kyrgyzstan, Russia, and Tajikistan in 2009 in order to overcome the effects of the crisis in the economies of countries participating in the Fund, ensure their long-term economic and financial stability, and promote integration. In response to the global financial crisis of 2008, which accelerated the search for new economic risk minimization models and sustainable development, the member states established the EurAsEC Anti-Crisis Fund (renamed the Eurasian Fund for Stabilization and Development in 2015 due to the liquidation of the EurAsEC).

The EFSD's highest governing body is the Council of the Fund, which is comprised of member states' finance ministers and chaired by one of the ministers. EDB is administering the Fund technically (staff, office space, project administration, financial modelling, etc.), but the final decisions are made by the Council.

To date, the EFSD has established itself as an active regional finance mechanism. It has financial resources amounting to $8.5 billion at its disposal. The EFSD's assets consist of member states' contributions. Ten per cent of this amount was transferred in cash to the Fund's account, 90%—in the form of simple, non-negotiable, and interest-free notes from member states. Contributions are distributed as follows: Russia, $7.5 billion; Kazakhstan, $1 billion; Belarus, $10 million; Armenia, Kyrgyzstan, and Tajikistan $1 million each. Total contributions amount to $8.513 billion. Thus, Russia and Kazakhstan act as donors to the Fund, while the remaining countries are its beneficiaries.

The EFSD offers two basic types of credit—financing of stabilization (anti-recessionary) programmes and financing of members' investment projects through a number of financial tools.

First, the Fund provides *financial loans* to the governments of member states to support anti-crisis and stabilization programmes designed and implemented by the borrowers themselves. At the same time, an important condition on granting a loan is a guarantee that the financed programme includes measures to achieve macroeconomic stability and improve the business climate of the borrowing state, and to ensure long-term development, and fiscal and debt sustainability. As a result, each decision to grant a loan involves a complex process to coordinate a "matrix of economic reforms" that the borrowing state must carry out using the money issued by the Fund. The minimum loan amount is set at $10 million.

An example is financial assistance to Belarus. In 2011, the Council of the Fund approved the allocation of $3 billion to support the Belarusian Government's stabilization programme aimed at stabilizing the balance of payments and improving the competitiveness of the country's economy. In 2016, the Council of the Fund approved another loan to Belarus in the amount of $2 billion to support the reform programme of the Government and National Bank of Belarus, aimed at creating the conditions necessary for the country to enter a path of sustainable growth by improving economic policy and carrying out structural reforms.

At the end of 2016, the Fund also approved loans to Armenia ($300 million to support a three-year reform programme aimed at improving the effectiveness of fiscal and monetary policies and creating an environment more favourable to growth in the private sector) and Tajikistan ($40 million to support a two-year reform programme aimed at improving management of public finances and the banking sector). We should add that these funds are not issued to governments all at once but instead in several tranches, as conditions are fulfilled by the borrowing countries.

Second, the Fund provides *investment loans*, primarily to support interstate investment projects that promote integration, as well as major national investment projects. Recall that an integration-promoting project is a large project that affects several of the Fund's member states and connects their production chains. Member states' governments and private companies implementing interstate investment projects can apply to receive investment loans. The Fund provides investment financing when a borrowing state or company is unable to obtain market financing to fully implement a project. As of the beginning of 2017, nine investment projects were in progress for a total of $570.2 million. These projects include the rehabilitation of the Toktogul Hydroelectric Power Plant, commissioning of the second hydroelectric generator at the Kambarata Hydropower Plant 2 in Kyrgyzstan, repair of the Nurek Hydropower Plant in Tajikistan, modernization of irrigation systems, and construction of the fourth stage of the North-South road corridor in Armenia and more.[14]

All EFSD loans must be returned with interest. When lending to low-income countries, the Fund follows IMF recommendations regarding the level of concessionality of the loans.

Finally, up to 10% of the EFSD's net profit each year can be used to provide *grants*, which do not need to be repaid. Grants are intended to finance member states' social projects in areas such as education, health care, public administration efficiency, and social security and protection, including food security.

Box 3.7 EFSD: A "Regional IMF"?

We have already mentioned that the member states established EFSD in the wake of the global financial crisis. This is not a coincidence. The dramatic events of 2008–2009 exposed global financial institutions' inability to ensure that national finances remain stable in crisis conditions. The crisis highlighted the urgent need for a regional development bank (which at that time already existed) and a regional financial support system.

Is the EFSD the regional equivalent the International Monetary Fund? Yes and no. On the one hand, the Fund issues loans to provide budgetary support to member states, making it easier to implement anti-crisis and stabilization programmes. In doing this, its serves the same function as the IMF. On the other hand, EFSD also issues investment loans on preferential terms for major government and interstate projects, which goes beyond the mandate of the IMF.

Notes

1. EAEU Treaty (2014). The document is available on the Eurasian Economic Union's Legal Portal at https://docs.eaeunion.org/en-us.
2. The EAEU Statistics: http://www.eurasiancommission.org/en/act/integr_i_makroec/dep_stat/union_stat/Pages/default.aspx.
3. EEC (2015).
4. EEC (2016).
5. More detailed information is available on the EEC's official website at http://www.eurasiancommission.org/en/act/prom_i_agroprom/dep_prom/Pages/default.aspx.
6. EEC (2014).
7. Glazyev (2016).
8. Neshataeva (2016).
9. Chayka (2016).
10. Chayka (2016).
11. Chayka (2016).
12. EDB (2006).
13. EDB Centre for Integration Studies (2015a, b) and Demidenko et al. (2017).
14. More detailed information about the Eurasian Fund for Stabilization and Development, its activities, and projects being implemented by the Fund is available on its official website at https://efsd.eabr.org/en/.

References

Chayka, K. (2016). Pressing Issues of the Integration Association Law and the Constitutional Law of Member States. Journal of Foreign Law and Comparative Law, 1, pp. 129–133.

Demidenko, M., Korshunov, D., Karachun, O., Miksyuk, A., Pelipas, I., Tochitskaya, I., Shimanovich, G. (2017). Monetary Policy of EAEU Member States: Current Status and Coordination Prospects. Joint Report of the Eurasian Economic Commission and Eurasian Development Bank. Moscow: EEC; Saint Petersburg: Eurasian Development Bank. Available at: https://eabr.org/en/analytics/integration-research/cii-reports/monetary-policy-of-eaeu-member-states-current-status-and-coordination-prospects/.

EDB Centre for Integration Studies (2015a). Assessing the Impact of Non-Tariff Barriers in the EEU: Results of Enterprise Surveys. Report No. 30. Saint Petersburg: Eurasian Development Bank. Available at: https://eabr.org/en/analytics/integration-research/cii-reports/assessing-the-impact-of-non-tariff-barriers-in-the-eeu-results-of-enterprise-surveys/.

EDB Centre for Integration Studies (2015b). Estimating the Economic Effects of Reducing Non-Tariff Barriers in the EEU. Report No. 29. Saint Petersburg: Eurasian Development Bank. Available at: https://eabr.org/en/analytics/integration-research/cii-reports/estimating-the-economic-effects-of-reducing-non-tariff-barriers-in-the-eeu/.

Eurasian Development Bank (EDB) (2006). Charter of the Eurasian Development Bank. Annex to the Agreement Establishing the Eurasian Development Bank dated 12 January 2006. Available at: https://eabr.org/upload/iblock/c91/foundation-documents.pdf.

Eurasian Economic Commission (EEC) (2014). Eurasian Economic Union. Questions and Answers. Figures and Facts. Moscow: EEC. Available at: http://www.eurasiancommission.org/ru/Documents/eaes_voprosy_otvety.pdf.

Eurasian Economic Commission (EEC) (2015). On status of elimination of the barriers for mutual access which prevent functioning of the Eurasian Economic Union domestic market, as well as exemptions and restrictions with respect to the circulation of goods, services, capital and workforce. Analytical Report of the Eurasian Economic Commission. Moscow: EEC. Available at: http://www.eurasiancommission.org/en/nae/news/Pages/25-06-2015-3.aspx.

Eurasian Economic Commission (EEC) (2016). A further 18 sectors will be included in the single services market of the EAEU. July 5. Available at:

http://www.eurasiancommission.org/en/nae/news/Pages/2016-07-06-2.aspx.
Glazyev, S. (2016). Russia Should Play First Fiddle in the Large Eurasian Association (Interview Part 2). Business Online, September 30.
Neshataeva, T. (2016). The Court of the Eurasian Economic Union in Action. Eurasian Law Journal, 9 (100), pp. 11–14. Available at: https://www.eurasialaw.ru/index.php?option=com_content&view=article&id=8484:2016-11-15-10-10-35&cati.
Treaty on the Eurasian Economic Union (EAEU Treaty) (2014). Moscow: Legal Department of the EEC.

4

Common Markets Within the Eurasian Economic Union: Movement of Goods, Services, Labour, and Capital

4.1 Common Customs Area and Common Customs Tariff

The foundation of Eurasian economic integration is the Customs Union (CU). At its core, this is a common customs area in which the Common Customs Tariff (CCT) is in effect. Inside the CU, customs duties and economic restrictions do not apply, except for safeguards and anti-dumping and countervailing measures.

The CU took off in two stages. On 1 January 2010, the three countries' CCT entered force. Beginning 1 July 2011, all customs control moved from the member states' internal borders to the CU's external border.

The CCT is a collection of import customs duties applied to goods imported into the EAEU's customs territory from third parties, systematized in accordance with the single HS Code. At its core, the CCT is an instrument of the CU's trade policy.

The CCT's main objectives are to (1) rationalize the commodity structure of goods imported into the common customs territory of the member states, (2) maintain a rational ratio of goods exports and imports in the common customs territory of the member states, (3) create conditions

E. Vinokurov, *Introduction to the Eurasian Economic Union*,
https://doi.org/10.1007/978-3-319-92825-8_4

for progressive changes in the structure of production and consumption of goods in the CU, (4) protect the CU's economy against the adverse effects of foreign competition, and (5) support the conditions necessary for the CU to effectively integrate with the world economy.

When importing goods into the common customs territory, tariff preferences may be applied in the form of an import customs duty exemption or rate reduction. Tariff preferences may be applied to (1) goods imported under customs control under relevant customs regimes established by customs law, (2) goods imported as a foreign founder's contribution to the authorized (share) capital within the time frames established by the constituent documents on the formation of this capital, and (3) goods imported as part of international cooperation pertaining to space research and exploitation.

The CCT does not have to cover all goods. The parties may agree to exclude some tariff lines from the CCT. As a rule, this happens due to incompatible obligations with respect to a World Trade Organization tariff line. One of the major consequences of Russia's accession to the WTO in 2012 was several rounds of declining CCT rates. Virtually all Russian obligations have already been implemented. As for Kazakhstan, at the time it joined the WTO at the end of 2015, there were exemptions for 1347 tariff lines. By the end of 2016, the number of exemptions increased to 1914. Seven hundred and seventy-five positions are exempt for Armenia, while for Kyrgyzstan the number was 169.[1] Recall that Belarus is the only member of the Union that is not yet a WTO member.

Customs duties are collected in a "single pot". From there, they are distributed based on national budgets in accordance with an approved apportionment: Russia 85.32%, Kazakhstan 7.11%, Belarus 4.56%, Kyrgyzstan 1.9%, and Armenia 1.1%.

Member states finally brought the outdated customs legislation up to date in 2017. The new EAEU Customs Code took several years to be brought to life. The member states discussed more than 1500 amendments to the initial draft. The Customs Code was approved definitively only on 16 November at a meeting of the Eurasian Intergovernmental Council. The Supreme Eurasian Economic Council adopted the Customs Code Treaty on 26 December 2016. However, the Belarusians did not participate in the Supreme Council's meeting. On 28 December 2016, Belarus issued a presidential decree, indicating that the Belarusians had decided to continue work under the EAEU Customs Code.[2] As a result, Belarus signed the document on 12 April 2017. The Customs Code Treaty will take effect on 1 January 2018 after all EAEU member states sign and ratify it.

We will point out two major advantages of the new Customs Code. The first is the codification and simplification of a huge number of regulatory acts that at present often conflict with each other. The second is the simplification of customs procedures (e.g., "one-stop shop", electronic declaration methods, etc.).

As member states drafted the EAEU Customs Code, they audited all previously concluded international treaties governing customs relations. The states rethought existing customs procedures and technologies, including by making changes to the use of relevant information technology. Thus, the states designed the EAEU Customs Code to be an improved version of current legislation, adding several new regulations.

The EAEU Customs Code's innovations include electronic customs declaration and automation, which remove customs officers from the customs clearance procedure, the ability to submit customs declarations without supporting documents, and improvement of the institution of an authorized economic operator, which will simplify the process of getting goods through customs. The EAEU Customs Code also creates the conditions for a "one-stop shop" designed to speed up document processing. In all, the new code confirms that electronic customs declarations are to be preferred to paper declarations.

The EAEU Customs Code's new regulations include the institution of authorized economic operators. They will establish themselves as organizations with the ability to conduct foreign economic activities under simplified customs procedures. As a result, authorized economic operators will save considerable time and resources, and the customs office will be able to concentrate on those areas where there are real risks. In addition, the new code grants the right to authorized economic operator status to all parties involved in foreign economic activity (not just importers); this status will be recognized throughout the entire EAEU.

The EAEU Customs Code assumes that additional powers will be transferred to the supranational level. The number of customs administration issues to be decided by the EEC will increase from 30 to 60.

However, the member states' creation of the EAEU Customs Code was not without conflict between the member states. To reach a compromise and pass the document, it retains the principle of residence, which stipulates that the declarant can only file a goods declaration with the customs authorities of its own country, and not with the customs authorities of all EAEU countries. The original idea was to abolish this principle. This would mean that an EAEU resident would be able to perform the customs clearance procedure in any member state. However, in the end, a significant part of customs regulatory authority remained at the national level.

The new Customs Code is a document that reflects the current stage of Eurasian integration. Its adoption is a significant step forward. The importance of this document is evidenced by the politicization of its approval process. At the same time, the "babies" who had to be thrown out with the bath water in order to secure the document's approval, as well as the long period of work on the Customs Code, are evidence of the current relationship difficulties among EAEU members and the imperfection of existing mechanisms for coordinating positions.

4.2 Dynamics of Mutual and Foreign Trade

As a whole, the dynamics of EAEU member states' export volumes by value reflect a deterioration of the economic situation in recent years and especially the fall in oil and gas prices. In addition, countries' foreign trade operations negatively affected the financial market instability (resulting in the "parade of devaluations") in 2014–2015. By value, mutual trade volumes fell the most in 2015, when EAEU member states' export operations amounted to $45.6 billion, or 74.5% of the 2014 level in dollar terms (Table 4.1).

However, a positive process is taking place simultaneously—a qualitative change in the very structure of EAEU countries' foreign trade. For example, statistics on EAEU countries' mutual trade as a percentage of

Table 4.1 Mutual trade volumes of EAEU member states, 2011–2016, $ million

Member states	2011	2012	2013	2014	2015	2016
EAEU, total	63,100.9	67,856.4	64,520.0	61,183.3	45,605.3	42,536.4
Armenia	–	–	–	324.0	256.2	392.1
Belarus	15,182.9	17,116.3	17,708.4	16,179.0	11,007.8	11,255.1
Kazakhstan	7103.3	6228.7	5933.6	7155.0	5120.3	3917.6
Kyrgyzstan	–	–	–	637.6	399.8	417.5
Russia	40,814.7	44,511.4	40,878.0	36,887.7	28,821.2	26,554.1

Source: EEC

total foreign trade showed an increase from 12.3% in 2014 to 14.2% in 2016.[3] The balance of trade within the EAEU is changing. For example, Belarus' mutual trade deficit with the EAEU decreased from $10.4 billion in 2011 to $4.1 billion in 2016, and this trend is fairly stable.

However, powerful short-term fluctuations do also occur. For example, the devaluation of the Russian ruble in late 2014 mirrored a structural shift in mutual trade between the Russian Federation and the Republic of Kazakhstan and temporarily strengthened Kazakhstan's status as a raw material exporter in the EAEU.[4] The situation lasted about nine to ten months until the Kazakh tenge transitioned to a floating exchange rate regime in August 2015.

Consider how mutual trade exports have changed as a percentage of the EAEU's total exports (Table 4.2). In the EAEU's first year, this indicator grew 9.5% in 2014 to 10.8% in 2015. At the end of 2016, it reached 12.1%. In other words, in terms of value, the drop in export volumes between EAEU countries was less severe than the drop in total exports from the Union's economies.

A similar situation is unfolding with respect to EAEU import operations. Mutual trade imports as a percentage of the EAEU's total imports amounted to 18% and 17.3% in 2015 and 2016, respectively, compared to 15.8% in 2014 (Table 4.3). This trend again suggests that mutual trade among EAEU countries has grown in importance.

Almost 90% of total export and 70% of total import within EAEU are attributed to Russia and Belarus. This said, mutual trade with EAEU member states is crucial for Belarus—the country generates just 4% of EAEU GDP; meanwhile it contributes to more than a quarter of EAEU total export and more than one-third of EAEU total import (see Fig. 4.1).

Table 4.2 Mutual trade exports as a percentage of the EAEU's total exports, %

Member states	2010	2011	2012	2013	2014	2015	2016
EAEU, total	9.7	9.8	10.3	9.9	9.5	10.8	12 1
Belarus	42.2	36.7	37.2	47.6	44.5	41.2	48.1
Kazakhstan	10.0	8.4	7.2	7.0	8.1	10.7	10.7
Russia	7.7	7.9	8.4	7.7	7.2	8.4	9.2

Source: EEC

Table 4.3 Mutual trade imports a percentage of the EAEU's total imports, %

Member states	2010	2011	2012	2013	2014	2015	2016
EAEU, total	15 9	16 2	16 6	15 7	15 8	18.0	17.3
Belarus	53.5	56.0	59.6	53.4	55.0	56.8	55.7
Kazakhstan	41.4	43.2	38.1	38.3	35.3	36.1	38.4
Russia	6.8	7.0	7.1	7.1	7.5	7.7	7.8

Source: EEC

In the mutual trade among EAEU countries, mineral products represent the largest share (27.1% of mutual trade in 2016). But the second-largest commodity group is machines, equipment, and vehicles (17.5% of mutual trade in 2016). Food products and agricultural raw materials account for 16.1%. Thus, mutual trade within EAEU differs qualitatively from foreign trade by its much higher, and increasing, share of non-commodity goods. For example, mineral product exports amounted to more than 60% of total exports to third parties in 2016, while such exports represented 27.1% of mutual trade amount EAEU countries. At the same time, food products and machinery accounted for only 9.7% of total exports to third parties in 2016 (and 33.6% of mutual trade).

Statistics on value volumes provide only a small fraction of information about the processes at work inside the Union and are often cited as an argument by the EAEU's opponents. In our view, the qualitative transformations are the most important: how the mutual trade structure of hydrocarbon exporting countries (Russia, Kazakhstan) is changing and how much mutual trade depends on the economic development of a country's trading partners in the Union (Belarus). For example, domestic consumption dynamics in Russia almost entirely determine the dynamics of Belarusian exports to EAEU member states. In the years of Russia's economic slump,

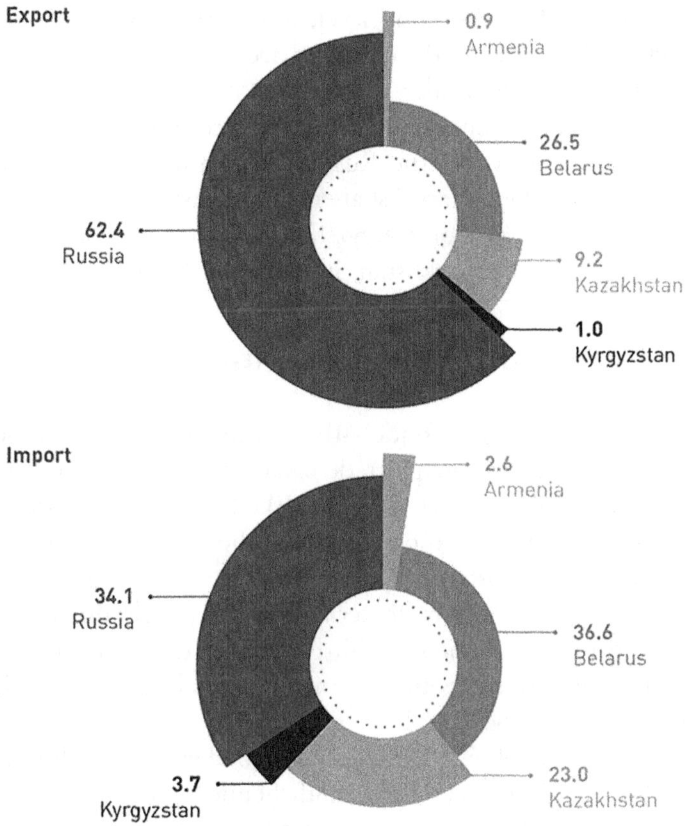

Fig. 4.1 Geographic structure of exports and imports within the EAEU, %. (Source: EEC)

exports of Belarusian products to the Russian market declined. Similarly, the stabilization of the Russian economy in 2016 positively impacted the dynamics of mutual trade between the Belarus and Russia: Belarusian exports to Russia grew by 4%. Belarusian exporters' success in the Russian market compensated for the drop in exports to other member states (for 2016, Belarusian exports to EAEU countries grew by 2.2%).

Comparing the year 2014–2016, we see that shares of mutual trade changed as follows. The Russian Federation's contribution to mutual exports increased from 60.3% to 62.4%. For Belarus and Kyrgyzstan, the indicator remained at the same level, amounting to 26.5% and 1%, respectively. In Kazakhstan, the indicator decreased from 11.7% to 9.2%. For Armenia, the indicator increased from 0.5% to 0.9%. Armenia's contribution to product purchases (imports) in the common market increased from 1.8% to 2.6%, while the Russian Federation's contribution rose from 32.9% to 34.1%. Belarus' share changed insignificantly, increasing from 36.5% to 36.6%. For Kyrgyzstan, the indicator decreased from 4.3% to 3.7%, and for Kazakhstan, it fell from 24.5% to 23%.

4.2.1 Structure of EAEU Foreign Trade

All key indicators of foreign trade—the volume of exports, imports, foreign trade turnover, and foreign trade balance—decreased in 2016 compared to 2015. Still, in 2016, the EAEU had foreign trade surplus, meaning that the value of exports exceeded the value of imports.

At present, the exports of the EAEU as a whole and of individual member states are mainly raw materials and are poorly differentiated. A significant portion of exports to third parties is due to trading mineral product: in Kazakhstan, about 75%; in Russia, about 66%; in Belarus, about 47% of total exports.

Mineral products (60.6% of the EAEU's total exports to third parties), metals and metal products (10.5%), and chemical products (6.7%) dominate the structure of commodity exports from EAEU member states to third parties. Russia is the main exporter of these goods to foreign markets (roughly 80%).

The EAEU's export structure has changed in certain ways. Since 2014, non-primary goods have dominated EAEU exports (see Fig. 4.2). In 2011–2013, more than half of the EAEU's commodity exports (in value terms) were raw materials, but in 2014 the balance tipped in favour of non-primary goods. Until 2015, the share of non-primary exports in the EAEU's total export volume had steadily increased. In 2016, there were no significant changes relative to 2015. At the end of 2016, non-primary goods represented 56.9% of the EAEU's export volumes by value, and raw materials represented 43.1%.

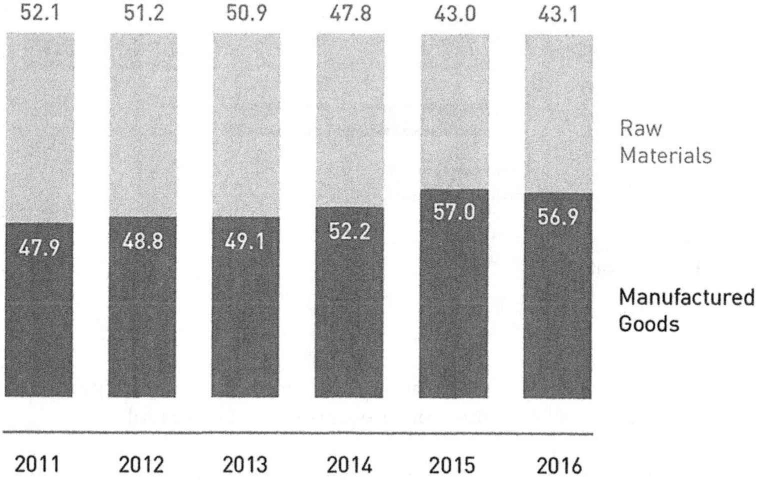

Fig. 4.2 Structure of EAEU exports: raw materials and manufactured goods, %. (Source: EDB Centre for Integration Studies 2017a)

The largest EAEU imports from the third parties are machinery, equipment, and vehicles (43.3% of total imports in 2016), chemical products (18.5%), foodstuffs and agricultural raw materials (13.2%). As in the case of exports, Russia is responsible for roughly 80% of purchases of these goods outside the EAEU.

In terms of products categorized according to their purpose (investment, intermediate, consumer), the situation is as follows. In 2016, the main share (84.7%) of EAEU member states' exports came from intermediate goods, of which energy products account for 58.9%, while other intermediate goods represent 25.8%. Intermediate goods dominate imports (41.6% of total imports) and consumer goods (32.4%). Investment goods represent 22.3% of EAEU imports.

In terms of geography, EU countries lead among the EAEU's trading partners: in 2016 these countries accounted for 46.5% of the EAEU's foreign trade turnover. APEC countries also have a significant share: 31.5% of the EAEU's foreign trade in 2016. Compared to 2015, in 2016 EU countries' share of the EAEU's foreign trade decreased by 2.3 percentage points, while APEC countries' share increased by 1.8 percentage points (Fig. 4.3).

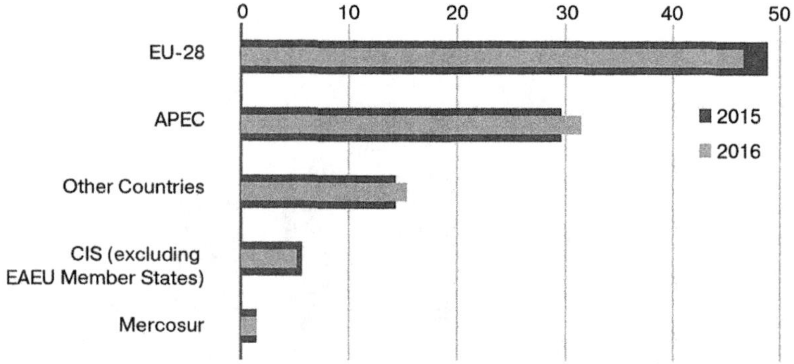

Fig. 4.3 Structure of the EAEU's foreign trade turnover with third parties in 2015 and 2016, %. (Source: EDB Centre for Integration Studies 2017a)

The significance of mutual trade within the EAEU is different for each member state. EAEU member states represent a small percentage of Russia's total imports and exports (roughly 8%). At the same time, Belarus depends heavily on both raw mineral imports from Russia and goods exports to Russia. Kazakhstan's exports are mostly directed outside the EAEU, but Russia's share in Kazakhstan's imports reached 40% in 2011.

As for the EAEU's current general export structure, high-tech products are almost entirely absent. This negatively affects the innovative activities of domestic enterprises.

Priority sectors in the economies of EAEU countries largely coincide, which makes it easier to coordinate foreign trade policy regarding supporting exports, attracting foreign direct investment in these sectors, and simplifying the process of importing components. In one way or another, all of the countries established the goal of boosting business productivity, increasing scientific and high-tech industries' share of GDP and attracting investment in manufacturing, transportation infrastructure, energy, and energy efficiency; using resources effectively; supporting exports in high value-add industries; and developing small business. In addition, Russia, Kazakhstan, and Kyrgyzstan face serious problems due to their orientation towards raw material exports and their need for economic diversification.

4.3 Building Out the EAEU's Common Markets: Drugs and Medical Products, Electric Power Industry, Finance, Oil, Gas, and Oil Products

Further development of Eurasian integration depends on how successful true "bottom-up integration" is, that is, growth of mutual trade in goods and services, cross-border investment, and civilized labour migration. This will require both the creation of unified "rules of the game" throughout the EAEU economy and the elimination of exemptions from the common market. The ultimate goal through 2025 should be to bring the common market's coverage as close as possible to 100%. The phrase *as close as possible* is key: there will always be exemptions both at the level of the Union and at the level of individual member states. The goal is to minimize the number of exemptions at both levels.

Eliminating single market exemptions is necessary and important for the modernization and cooperation of EAEU economies. The EAEU Treaty sets deadlines for major markets in critical sectors of the economy that still lack common markets. Figure 4.4 depicts the approximate timelines.

Progress is difficult. For example, the parties initially agreed to establish a *common market for drugs and medical products* before 1 January 2016 (the Treaty stipulated this deadline). However, organizing the common market and unifying the rules for drug manufacturers, especially the issue of certification, have proven to be very difficult. As a result, only on

Fig. 4.4 Stages for "building out" the EAEU's common markets. (Source: EDB Centre for Integration Studies)

16 November 2016, at a meeting of the Eurasian Intergovernmental Council, did members of the Council of the Commission sign the set of unified documents necessary for the launch and full operation of the common drug market within the EAEU.[5]

The approval process required sacrificing rapid enactment of key provisions of the common market for drugs. This was the price of compromise and progress. Until 31 December 2020, drug manufacturers have the right to choose which rules (national rules or uniform union rules) to follow when registering drugs. Drugs registered under national rules before 31 December 2020 must be reregistered under the unified EAEU rules before 31 December 2025. The rules leave the national pharmaceutical regulators with the issues of price-setting, licensing the activities of organizations engaged in retail sales, and drug advertising.

Preparations are already under way for the phased creation of a *common electricity market* based on electricity-generating systems operating in parallel. The actual creation of the market is planned for 2019. The details are still being discussed. The limited option is a common spot electricity market combined with the technical mechanisms for transboundary energy transfer. This option could be called "Nordpool-minus", based on the common electricity market successfully operating in Scandinavia, which largely serves as a standard and also operates a futures market.

The work to create a common electricity market is based on the following key documents: the EAEU Treaty, Framework for the Formation of the Common Electricity Market of the Eurasian Economic Union (approved 8 May 2015), and the Program for the Formation of the EAEU's Common Electricity Market (approved on 10 October 2016).

The activities outlined in the programme must be implemented before mid-2018, and in 2019 an international agreement on the formation of the EAEU's common electricity market is to be signed. The programme calls for the creation, by July 2019, of conditions for the organization of centralized electricity trading and for trading under free bilateral treaties. An electronic system to trade electricity under fixed-term contracts and on the day-ahead market may be created, as well as an information system for the Union's common electricity market.

Such a market will give EAEU countries several advantages. First, it will make their energy systems more stable: if one state experiences tech-

Box 4.1 Electric Power Industry of EAEU Member States

EAEU member states' electric power systems are quite developed, including various types of electric power stations, including thermal power plants (condensing power plants and cogeneration plants), hydropower plants and pumped-storage hydropower plants, nuclear power plants, power plants based on renewable energy sources, as well as electric grids (power lines and DC lines) of different voltages, including 750 kV and below.

Generating capacity is distributed as follows: thermal power plants produce 69% of electricity, hydropower plants produce 22%, and nuclear power plants produce 9%. In most countries, with the exception of Kyrgyzstan, thermal generation dominates. Hydropower plants' representation in the generating capacity of Armenia (33%) and Russia (21%) is also significant. Obviously, the development of hydropower plants in these countries is conditioned on the availability of domestic hydropower resources. Among EAEU member states, only two countries (Armenia and Russia) possess nuclear power sources.

External power grids linking EAEU countries with each other (with the exception of Armenia's power system) are also quite developed.

Each country has a different structure of power-generating capacity and production, reflecting the presence (or absence) of the corresponding types of energy resources within the country. Kyrgyzstan—with its electricity-generating capacity and production dominated by hydropower plants and with very limited electricity exchanges with other Central Asian countries of late—has a seasonal imbalance in energy generation and consumption. Other EAEU member states, where mainly thermal power plants generate basic electricity, e.g. Belarus and the Russian Federation's exclave territory (Kaliningrad Region), face the problem of covering the variable part of the daily load schedule.

nical problems, it will be easier to supply electricity from another state. Second, transboundary energy transfers will increase due to lower costs and greater transparency and accuracy in technical record-keeping and financial calculations. Third, export potential will expand.

Currently under discussion is the creation by 2022–2025 of *Union's Common Financial Market*, along with appropriate regulation and oversight. Once EAEU countries' laws regarding financial markets have been harmonized, a supranational body will be formed to regulate the Union's financial market. According to the EAEU Treaty, this body will be located in Almaty. Nobody is talking about a single central bank or common currency.

Integration processes influence a very wide circle of financial market participants' activities. It includes banks, leasing companies, insurance companies, microfinance organizations, stock exchanges, brokers, depositories, and so on.

Common financial markets should be formed by 2025. This long time frame is intentional: financial markets are complex, diverse, and sensitive to regulatory impact. Their regulation, especially at the supranational level, must be handled carefully. This is better than setting knowingly unattainable goals that will remain merely "paper integration".[6]

A road map, entitled the "Framework for the Establishment of the EAEU's Common Financial Market", was published in 2017. To accelerate this process, an agreement on exchanging information, including confidential information, in the financial sphere has already been adopted and took effect on 21 October 2016, in order to create financial markets conditions to ensure the free flow of capital. Moreover, members of the Council of the Commission have already approved the Agreement on the Harmonization of the Financial Market Legislation of EAEU Member States, which specifies the areas and procedures for harmonizing rules and requirements stipulated by the national laws of the countries of the Union. Work is under way to create and approve drafts of the Agreement on Coordinated Approaches to Regulation of Currency Relations and Liberalisation Measures, Agreement on Admitting Brokers and Dealers of One Member State to the Exchanges (of Trade Organizers) of Other Members of the Union, and Agreement on EAEU Countries' Cooperation Regarding Exchanging Credit History Information.

For EAEU member states, financial market integration implies significant economic advantages that will increase the potential for non-inflationary growth, improve the effectiveness of monetary policy, increase markets' ability to tolerate crises, make financial markets more efficient, and reduce costs.

A *single market for oil, oil products, and gas* should appear by 2025. This long time frame is associated with the oil and gas sector's extreme importance in creating national budgets. The relevant work will be carried out under two separate frameworks and, consequently, two different "road maps"—one for oil and oil products, one for gas. As of today, member states have approved both frameworks.

The Framework for the Formation of Common Oil and Oil Products Markets notes the following stages of work:

- Phase I (2016–2017)—development and approval of a programme to form the common markets for oil and oil products
- Phase II (2018–2023)—implementation of programme activities, development of unified rules for accessing oil and oil product transportation systems located in the territory of the Union's member states
- Phase III (2024)—conclusion and enactment of an international treaty, within the Union, on the formation of common markets for oil and oil products

The Framework for the Formation of a Common Gas Market also provides for three stages of development:

- Phase I (until 2020)—harmonization of member states' legislation regarding gas market regulation, ensuring the availability and full disclosure on information on the availability capacity of gas transportation systems, unification of gas regulations and standards, creation of a system to exchange information (on domestic consumption, pricing, etc.), development of unified rules for accessing gas transportation systems, establishment of procedures for the exchange-based gas trading in the Union's common gas market, formation of the Union's prospective gas balance, identification of infrastructural constraints in the transportation of gas within the Union, and development of proposals to eliminate these constraints
- Phase II (until 2021)—ensuring the operation of one or more commodity exchanges for trading gas, ensuring that participants in the Union's common gas market have non-discriminatory access to exchange-based gas trading on the Union's commodity exchanges, ensuring that participants in the Union's common gas market have access to gas transportation systems, support of various mechanisms for developing the capacity of the Union's gas transportation systems, expansion of investment activity in the Union's common gas market, implementation of joint infrastructure projects, consultations on transporting and supplying gas to third parties

- Phase III (no later than 1 January 2025)—enactment of an international treaty within the Union on the formation of the Union's common gas market of the Union, ensuring available gas supplies, support for market prices, member states' adoption of an agreed decision on the transition to equally profitable gas prices within the Union's member states

In general, regulation of common markets for oil, oil products, and gas will include regulation of the activities of natural monopolies in the transportation of these goods, anti-monopoly regulation, customs and tariff regulation, tax regulation, regulation of the derivatives market (exchange and over-the-counter markets), technical regulation, regulation of exchange-based trading of these products.

The efforts to create the common drug market, common electricity market, financial markets, and common oil and gas markets are elements of a single process to eliminate exemptions from the EAEU common market. In practice, this process is complex and rather contentious. It is logical to assume that the final decisions will be the result of a compromise.

Trade and economic conflicts in the common market are almost inevitable. The key factors in resolving these conflicts are the availability of regulatory tools and a willingness to listen to and compromise with the other party.

4.4 Technical Regulation and Combating Non-tariff Barriers

In the past two or three decades, restrictions on the free movement of goods and services globally have, with increasing frequency and prominence, taken the form of non-tariff barriers (NTBs, also known as non-tariff measures). This is due to the reduction of import tariffs as part of rounds of WTO negotiations and numerous trade agreements. NTBs can nullify the positive effects of lifting tariff restrictions, adversely affecting foreign trade flows, making it difficult for new products to enter the market, preventing the emergence of new trading partners, and hampering development and cooperation above all in technology industries.

Box 4.2 Conflicts in the EAEU Common Market

The events of 2015–2016 show that forming a single market will not be an easy feat. EAEU member states face several sensitive issues that serve as breeding grounds for conflicts. Let's present some examples.

The first example is connected with Russia's desire for other EAEU member states to join its sanctions against Ukraine. EAEU countries, except Russia, continue to engage in foreign trade with Ukrainian companies. Russia has provided no official recommendations regarding joining the sanctions. Nor has this issue been brought to the level of the EEC. However, there is, if not a legal conflict of interest, then a substantive conflict of interest, between Russia's foreign policy and the foreign economic relations of other EAEU countries.

Our second example is related to Belarusian manufacturers' and trading companies' reexportation from the EU of goods, against which Russia has imposed sanctions (mainly food products). For example, "Belarusian" bananas and oysters appeared on the Russian market. Accordingly, Russian authorities initiated inspection of the next shipment into Russia to verify that the transported goods corresponding to their actual origin. This resulted in significant shipping delays, lines at the Belarusian-Russian border, as well as the discontent of Belarusian authorities. In the end, the issue was settled by introducing a strict labelling procedure that involves specifying the country of origin of goods and by increasing Belarusian exporting companies' liability.

A third example relates to the conflict between Russia and Ukraine. In 2016, Ukrainian activists began blocking vehicles from Russia that were moving through Ukraine. In response, Russia introduced countermeasures against Ukrainian vehicles. This situation significantly complicated the work of Ukrainian exporters, who were trying to transport goods through Russia to Kazakhstan (a significant portion of shipments to Kazakhstan were probably actually intended for the Russian market). The issue found a partial solution through the EAEU shipment information system.

The EAEU Treaty states that member states are not to apply non-tariff regulatory measures in the internal market. The document also provides for exceptions to this rule: NTBs can be established to protect public morals and the rule of law; to protect life and health, the environment, animals and plants, and cultural values; to fulfil international obligations; and to ensure defence and security. However, they must not be used as a means of discrimination or a hidden trade restriction. Member states have established common principles, processes, rules, and procedures for the technical regulation and application of sanitary, veterinary-sanitary, and phytosanitary quarantine measures. However, the gradual unification and (or) abolishment of NTBs to trade in goods and services are some of the most important tasks of Eurasian economic integration. If they are not addressed, the common market will be inefficient and never realize its inherent potential.

Today there are literally hundreds of non-tariff measures in effect, and they are continuously scrutinized by the EEC and those responsible for the economic development and trade of the ministries and departments of EAEU member states.

For convenience, NTBs can be divided into two groups. The first group includes natural NTBs, including protective barriers, which can be gradually harmonized between EAEU member states. These are sanitary and phytosanitary measures, technical barriers to trade, and non-automatic licensing, as well as quotas, bans, and quantitative control measures that are not part of sanitary and phytosanitary measures and technical barriers.

The second group of NTBs includes price controls and financial measures that affect competition (the institute of "special importers", restrictions on sales and public procurement, subsidies, etc.). These are the so-called unproductive costs, figuratively referred to as *sand in the wheels*. Theoretically, NTBs in this group should be completely eliminated by focusing major efforts here,[8] because "sand in the wheels" has the most negative impact on mutual trade. In practice, however, doing this is much more difficult than reducing the influence of NTBs in the first group.

Estimates suggest that exporters face very high costs due to NTBs. On average, the largest costs were recorded by Kazakhstan (about 40%)[9] and Russia (12.4%) in trade with Belarus. For Belarus, the impact of NTBs was most significant when exporting to Kazakhstan (16.3%). As you can see, the negative impact of NTBs is *higher* than the actual tariff barriers abolished under the CU.

NTBs are especially harmful to industries with high added value, including the tech industries with the greatest prospects for growth. NTBs' most significant impact on the value of exports has been observed in the chemical industry and the production of rubber and plastic prod-

Box 4.3 Technical Regulation

Technical regulation issues are extremely important for business, though they rarely make headlines. These issues include a substantial part of non-tariff barriers, which in practice impede the movement of goods and services. Additionally, EAEU countries face the system-wide task of replacing obsolete state standards and modernizing technical regulation. It is desirable to increase compatibility with international standards (e.g., the International Electrotechnical Commission) and EU regulations.

The Eurasian Economic Commission has received considerable authority to develop technical regulations. As of 1 July 2017, the Commission has drafted 42 regulations, and 35 of them have taken effect. We will use the Commission's activities in 2016 to illustrate how this work is carried out in practice:

- The Commission performed work on the procedure for forming and maintaining the Unified Product List, for which mandatory safety requirements are established in the EAEU. The Unified Product List is one of the fundamental methodological documents forming the Union's common policy on technical regulation.
- The Commission adopted five new EAEU technical regulations on the safety of hydrocarbon gases, fertilizers, fish and fish products, rides, and restriction of hazardous substances and electrical products and radio electronics, which are aimed primarily at protecting the public life and health.
- Numerous changes were made to the EAEU's previously adopted technical regulations: "On the safety of roads", "On requirements for mineral fertilizers", "On the safety of packaging", "On the safety of perfume and cosmetic products", "On the safety of wheeled vehicles", "On the safety of railway rolling stock", "On the requirements for energy efficiency of energy-consuming devices", "On safety of light industry products", "On the safety of chemical products", and "On the safety of grain".
- Work to form unified approaches to measurements is complete. The document is intended to ensure mutual recognition of work regarding state regulation to guarantee uniform measurements by measuring devices manufactured in the EAEU.
- The Commission adopted an important document regarding sanitary measures—the Process for the Development, Approval, Modification, and Application of Uniform Sanitary, Epidemiological, and Hygienic Requirements and Procedures. It provides for specific stages, procedures, and timelines, ensuring the necessary level of transparency and legal specificity in the development and application of uniform sanitary requirements.
- The Commission adopted regulatory acts necessary for electronic auto passport systems to begin operating.[7]

ucts and then in mechanical engineering, textiles and clothing, food, footwear, and leather goods.[10]

According to research conducted by the EDB Centre for Integration Studies, the benefits of fighting against NTBs are considerable. If NTBs were reduced 50% among EAEU member states, Belarus would benefit the most: in the medium term, real GDP would grow by 2.8%, and wealth would rise by 7.3%. Kazakhstan's gain would be smaller: wealth would increase in the medium term by 1.3% cumulatively, while real GDP growth would increase by 0.7%. For Russia, these figures will be even smaller: household wealth would grow by 0.5% cumulatively, while real GDP would rise by 0.2% (this is due to the Russian economy's large size and the lesser importance of the markets of EAEU trading partners). Our calculations showed that reducing NTBs would most favourably affect Belarusian mechanical engineering, namely, the production of machinery and equipment, as well as chemical production, production of rubber and plastic products, and metallurgy. Among Kazakhstan's key industries, mechanical engineering and vehicle production stand to gain the most. In Russia, the top beneficiaries would be the food industry, production of leather and leather products, production of footwear, and agriculture.

A survey of goods exporters showed that *technical barriers* are among the main barriers restricting trade within the SES. Of these, product testing and certification requirements, as well as the need to comply with industrial standards, are paramount in terms of their influence. The respondents believe the solution lies in mutual recognition of procedures for assessing the conformity of products not covered by the technical regulations of the CU, the use of international standards, and the harmonization of the rules and regulations for labelling, packaging, and tagging within the CU. Other barriers noted by respondents regardless of the area of trade include price controls, including additional taxes and fees in the country of destination (especially those related to the payment of VAT), and measures that affect competition (the institution of "special importers"). In addition, exporters from Kazakhstan and Russia are concerned with the restrictive effect of preshipment inspections and other formalities, conditional trade protective measures, and financial measures in the form of regulation of import payment conditions in the country of destination or conditions on obtaining and using credit to finance imports.

Public procurement restrictions in Kazakhstan and Russia constrain exports from Belarus. Armenia also complains about these restrictions.[11] International cargo shipments are particularly sensitive to NTBs. For example, during focus groups Belarusian transport companies argued that abolishing the permit system would double the volume of freight traffic in three years.[12]

4.5 Single Labour Market and Labour Migration

The EAEU's common labour market is often lost amid topics such as trade dynamics, changes in customs tariffs, or negotiations on free trade zones. Meanwhile, for some member states, removing barriers in the labour market is even more important than free movement of goods, services, and capital. Moreover, in terms of international comparisons, creating a common labour market is a huge achievement: there are only two of them in the world—in the EU and in the EAEU.

Amid a shortage of jobs, high unemployment, and poverty, labour migration and remittances sent home by migrant workers are the most important factors for the economy of Kyrgyzstan and are very important for the economy of Armenia. According to Euromonitor estimates, after the collapse of the USSR, more than one million Armenians moved to other countries (about 70% moved to Russia). Only in 2013–2014 did Armenian immigration rise slightly, but since 2015 this trend has reversed due to the worsening socioeconomic situation in the country. Among the countries of the Union, Armenia has the highest unemployment rate in relation to the working age population at about 18%. Kyrgyzstan takes second place at 7.6%. These two countries also have the highest poverty levels in the Union: in Kyrgyzstan, 32% of the population lives below the poverty line, while in Armenia, this figure is almost 30% (in 2015).[13] In Russia, 13.3% of the population had incomes below the subsistence level in 2015.

At the same time, the average monthly nominal wages in EAEU member states in 2016 were as follows: in Kyrgyzstan, $207 (in the capital,

$270); in Armenia, $393 (in the capital, $425); in Belarus, $361 (in the capital, $510); in Kazakhstan, $416 (in the capital, $613); and in Russia, $549 (in the capital, $1065).[14] We note that in comparison with 2015, statistics show a decrease in average monthly nominal wages in Belarus (on average by $52) and Kazakhstan (by $149 for the country and by $249 in the capital). In general, dollar-denominated salaries are converging between EAEU countries as a result of an exchange rate adjustment.[15] It has also come to light that in Russia the wage gap between the average Russian citizen and the average migrant worker is gradually shrinking.[16]

Countries in need of labour resources and offering more attractive conditions attract the able-bodied population of countries with fewer opportunities for employment and earnings. First and foremost, this is Russia.

According to the Ministry of Internal Affairs of the Russian Federation, in 2016 826,600 citizens of Kyrgyzstan, 631,700 citizens of Armenia, 545,600 citizens of Kazakhstan, and 345,800 citizens of Belarus registered as immigrants in Russia.[17]

Labour migration allows citizens who leave their native country to work to support their families and households back home through money transfers (remittances). In some countries, the volume of cross-border transfers becomes significant nationally. These remittances are often the only source of income for hundreds of thousands of citizens. Thus, according to the World Bank, remittances to Kyrgyzstan represented

Box 4.4 Importance of Labour Migration and the Common Labour Market for Kyrgyzstan

The World Bank estimates that remittances from migrant workers represent about 30% of Kyrgyzstan's GDP. The republic's government regards labour migration as a positive factor that serves to reduce unemployment and social tension. The words of the President of Kyrgyzstan A. Atambayev, at the signing ceremony for the EAEU Treaty confirm this position: "Integration implies the free movement of labour in the Eurasian space. Migrant workers from our country will find it much easier to live and work in Russia and Kazakhstan."[18]

30.3% of the country's GDP in 2014, to Armenia—19.1%.[19] According to the Central Bank of Armenia, 35% of the country's population receives foreign remittances. In 2012–2013, remittances exceeded 20% of GDP. Most of the transfers come from Russia, accounting for more than 73% of proceeds in 2012–2014. At the same time, the citizens of Armenia are sending considerable funds—roughly 0.8–0.9 billion dollars a year—from the country, and Russia's share here was also great (in 2008–2015 it averaged 26%, and in 2016 it exceeded 40%).

In 2015, according to the EDB Centre for Integration Studies, the volume of remittances in Kyrgyzstan decreased to 25.7% of GDP and in Armenia to 15.5% of GDP. This negatively impacted the household consumption and economic growth of the two countries.[20] In 2016, remittances to Armenia amounted to roughly 14.5% of GDP. The Central Bank of Russia's data on remittances from Russia to Armenia and Kyrgyzstan, which declined sharply in 2015 (see Table 4.4), confirm this. The main reason is the devaluation of the Russian currency, which foreign workers receive for their wages and then convert into dollars to send money transfers. However, money transfers from Russia ceased to decline in 2016.

The CIS Intergovernmental Committee's data for 2016 shows that the EAEU's highest share of self-employed people is found in Kyrgyzstan and Armenia (respectively, 45% and 43% of the total number of people employed).[21] Here we mean employers, freelancers, employees of family businesses who work without pay, and members of production cooperatives. Moreover, according to data for 2015, in Armenia, 29% of workers

Table 4.4 Amount of money transfers and remittances from individuals from Russia to Armenia and Kyrgyzstan in 2014–2016, $ million

Country	Year	Amount of money transfers from individuals	Amount of remittances from individuals
Armenia	2014	1416	1550
	2015	682	941
	2016	346.2	711.4
Kyrgyzstan	2014	2026	2062
	2015	1083	1383
	2016	976	1742.5

Source: Central Bank of Russia (2017)

have a higher education, and 20% have a secondary vocational education, in Kyrgyzstan—21% and 10%, respectively.[22] Both states could exploit this feature of the labour markets to their advantage, especially considering the EAEU's need to increase the level of business activity among their populations. In the EAEU's other member states, the vast majority of workers are employees: in Kazakhstan, 74%, and in Belarus and Russia—93%.

Here we should mention additional advantages and disadvantages of labour migration. The benefits include the fact that upon returning to their homeland, migrant workers bring with them a host of new skills, abilities, knowledge, and business ties, which may subsequently become an additional driver of growth for the national economy. One disadvantage is the outflow of skilled labour. But creating new jobs and attractive working conditions and reorienting the education system to train cutting-edge workers for high-potential sectors of the national economy that have the greatest need for growth can solve this problem.[23]

4.5.1 What Opportunities Does the EAEU Unlock for Its Member States' Workers?

According to the EAEU Treaty (Section XXVI), member states' workers have the right to work in any state of the Union and to receive basic social guarantees for themselves and their family members. The ground for staying in another member state is an employment agreement or civil law contract concluded with the employer. The term of the agreement or contract determines the period in which the worker and members of his or her family may temporarily stay in the country. No additional documents need to be registered, and procedures required for citizens of countries that are not part of the Union do not apply.

The Treaty gives workers from EAEU member states 90 days from their date of entry into another member state to settle all matters of employment (in other words, they are given 30 days before being registered as an immigrant and another 60 days after), while the Treaty gives the citizens of other countries only 30 days for everything. However, EAEU countries are obligated to not apply restrictions to protect their national labour market, unless doing so is dictated by the need to ensure national security and public order. The absence of such restrictions is also beneficial to employers, who are free to recruit workers from any EAEU member state. However, there are still instances when employers themselves impose restrictions, for example, by refusing to hire citizens of certain nationalities. This is a violation of the law.

Those wishing to get a job in the neighbouring country of the Union are no longer required to have their education documents recognized in a special procedure—they are mutually recognized by member states. Workers engaged in pedagogical, legal, medical, and pharmaceutical activities are an exception. The documents of these specialists are subject to the recognition procedure.

We note here that educational and medical activities, like other socially oriented work, unfortunately remain the least attractive for the EAEU as a whole. According to the EEC, in 2015 the average monthly salary of health and education workers in EAEU member states was 20–40% less than the average worker's salary.[24] Thus, the additional employment restrictions established within the Union with respect to these professions do not promote the development of socially oriented sectors, even with all of their strategic importance for the EAEU.

The EAEU Treaty also specifies a number of other rights and obligations of workers and their family members who have come from another country of the Union. In particular, they must comply with the laws of the host state (including the duty to pay income taxes) just as its citizens and respect the culture and traditions of its peoples. EAEU states mutually guarantee them rights, equal with their citizens, to receive free medical assistance for them and their family members (including urgent and non-urgent care), education for their children, and other rights. Furthermore, this period of employment is added to their total record of service for social security purposes, including pension benefits.

Pension mobility, the issue of pension provision for migrant workers from Union countries, will be resolved within the framework of the EAEU. The Board of the Commission approved a draft of the relevant international agreement in December 2016.[25] This agreement will govern how workers from other member states gain pension rights and the procedure for these workers to be assigned and receive pension payments after they reach retirement age and return to their homeland. In particular, the mechanism set forth in the pension provision agreement calls for (once the agreement enters into force) the state in which the worker was employed to pay his or her pension for the period of employment in its territory.[26] The Council of the Commission must approve the document, after which the Council will send it to EAEU countries to undergo the internal government procedures necessary to sign it. The Council of the Commission, at its meeting on 28 April 2017, decided to continue to form the rules and regulations governing pension calculations and the procedure for exporting pension liabilities and recording the length of employment in another state of the Union. In addition, the parties will have to decide how to determine the individual pension coefficient used to calculate the size of a pension.[27]

All these measures are expected to help improve working conditions in the Union and promote the legalization of migration flows, since all the advantages mentioned above are only available to workers under official employment agreements or civil law contracts. Ultimately, this is beneficial to the states providing employment: legalization of migrant workers means additional state revenues from the workers' payment of income taxes.

4.5.2 What Do the Citizens of EAEU Member States Think About Labour Migration?

In 2012, 650 migrant workers who travelled from Kyrgyzstan to Russia and Kazakhstan participated in a survey.[28] The results showed that 44% of Kyrgyz citizens have long-term plans to work in Russia, while 18% have relatively short-term plans (these figures are, respectively, 33% and 8% for Kyrgyz citizens working in Kazakhstan). The majority of respondents expressed their intention to eventually return to Kyrgyzstan.

Recall that, as part of the EDB Integration Barometer, annual surveys of the population of several CIS countries have been conducted since

2012 on a wide range of issues. In 2016, the Barometer revealed the following[29]: 70–87% of the citizens of EAEU member states (depending on the country) support the freedom to move, receive an education, obtain employment, and reside within the Union.

4.6 Mutual Investments in the EAEU

The EAEU's common markets provide investing companies with a number of advantages in doing business, as well as the ability to more actively build cross-border value-added chains. Thanks to the region's shared historical and economic past and geographic and linguistic proximity, the corporate sector is highly aware of the specifics of doing business in EAEU member states. Today, EAEU countries have already seen positive results in investment activities. But there are limitations that impact or may potentially impact business activity within EAEU countries.

The success of economic integration can be seen not only in increased mutual investment but also in its ability to "absorb" negative trends. In this regard, one of the EAEU's achievements is that, amid a slowdown in the global economic growth, member states have retained a relatively stable level of mutual investment. For example, since 2008, mutual FDI stock in EAEU member states has been more stable than in the CIS as a whole (Fig. 4.5). According to data from monitoring mutual investments in CIS countries, in the four years after the peak of 2012, the mutual FDI stock of EAEU countries fell by 14.3%, while the same indicator for CIS countries decreased by 26.1%.[30] Against the background of a twofold devaluation of national currencies, this is a relatively good sign.

In 2016, mutual investment activities in the EAEU have started to recover. Moreover, mutual FDI by EAEU member states grew twice as fast as CIS countries' total mutual FDI stock, increasing by 15.9% to $26.8 billion. Among the key mutual FDI growth factors are strengthening of the Russian ruble and recovery of economic activity in Russia. As a recipient of EAEU FDI, in 2016 Russia posted record-breaking growth rates, with direct investment stock skyrocketing by 77% to $5 billion. Still, Russia came only third after Belarus ($8.6 billion) and Kazakhstan ($8.2 billion).

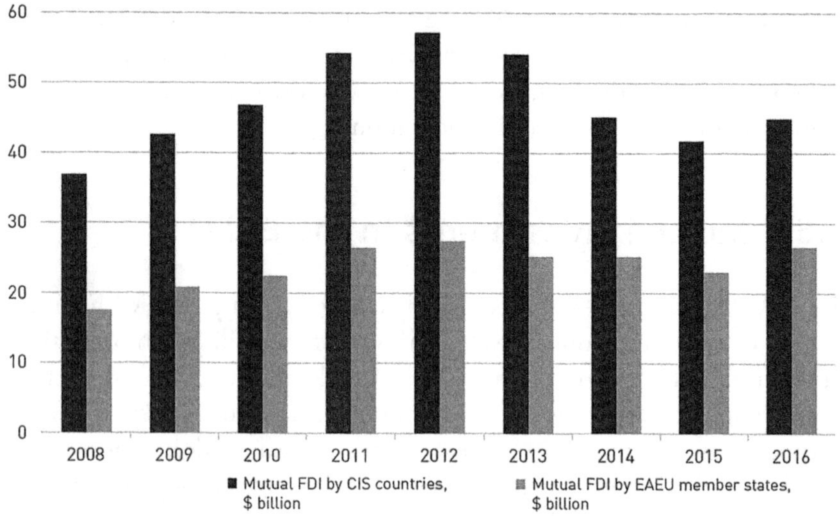

Fig. 4.5 Mutual FDI stock of CIS countries and EAEU member states. (Source: EDB Centre for Integration Studies 2017b)

Box 4.5 Why Do We Need to Use a "Bottom-Up" Approach to Monitor Cross-Border Investments?

The "Monitoring and Analysis of Mutual Investments in the CIS and Eurasia" project, being implemented by the EDB Centre for Integration Studies in conjunction with the Primakov National Research Institute of World Economy and International Relations (IMEMO), is a valuable addition to the official direct investment statistics maintained by central banks using balance of payments data. It overcomes the shortcomings of investment project accounting performed by the central banks and state statistical agencies of the post-Soviet space. Researchers are turning directly to companies' financial statements and supplementing them with several secondary sources. The result is that monitoring "sees through offshore companies", giving a more accurate picture of the ultimate owners. In addition, data on the reinvestment of profits received abroad are more accurately reflected. Monitoring is performed as part of a two-level industry classification—15 sectors comprising more than 90 industries.

Russian companies are the largest exporters of capital in the EAEU, accounting for more than 78% of FDI exports. Moreover, Russia is the only net exporter of mutual FDI originating from EAEU member states. This is largely due to the scale of the Russian economy, which accounts for more than 85% of the EAEU's GDP. Additionally, Russian transnational companies (TNCs) were among the first in the post-Soviet space to start a large-scale foreign expansion. Kazakhstan has been the second-largest FDI exporter to other EAEU states, with 13.5% of total exported mutual investments. Belarus goes third, with 7.8% of exported FDI. Armenia and Kyrgyzstan lag significantly behind the EAEU largest economies (Table 4.5).

The distribution of mutual direct investments within the EAEU space is quite diverse with respect to economic sectors.[31] However, Russia's traditional specializations—oil and gas and non-ferrous metals—dominate. According to the EDB Centre for Integration Studies, at the beginning of 2017, these sectors represented 43.8% and 10.9% of mutual direct investments, respectively. The next largest sectors are communication and IT (9.6%), chemicals (8.1%), finance (6.1%), transport (4.2%), and agriculture and food products (3.7%).[32]

Russian companies are the most active and the largest investors in the EAEU. For them, the countries of the EAEU, as well as the CIS as a

Table 4.5 Mutual direct investments by EAEU member states at the end of 2016

	Investor countries' FDI stock, $ million					
Recipient country	Russia	Kazakhstan	Belarus	Armenia	Kyrgyzstan	All five countries
Russia	X	2948	2054	8	0	5010
Kazakhstan	8212	X	34	0	0	8246
Belarus	8522	57	X	16	2	8597
Armenia	3441	0	0	X	0	3441
Kyrgyzstan	858	605	3	0	X	1466
All five countries	21,033	3610	2091	24	2	26,760

Source: EDB Centre for Integration Studies (2017b)

Note: In accordance with the methodology underlying the Monitoring of Mutual Investments in CIS Countries (EDB Centre for Integration Studies), the database includes projects with FDI stock of $3 million or more whole, are the most comfortable location for foreign activities. The development and deepening of integration within the EAEU play a positive role. As a result, the sectoral structure of Russian direct investment is most diversified in countries of the Union, including in the areas of production with high added value.[33] However, Russian FDI in Kyrgyzstan (and Tajikistan) is not as significant, as in other countries. Russian companies' expansion into these countries should be given special attention. It is of fundamental importance for small economies.[34]

Predictably, 52.7% of Russian FDI stock in EAEU countries is in the oil and gas. Non-ferrous metals, communication and IT, and finance have attracted 12.6%, 11.5%, and 6.7%, respectively. FDI holds a significant position in wholesale and retail trade and infrastructure networks.[35]

A limited circle of companies provides the high figures for Russia. The leading Russian oil and gas TNCs (Gazprom, LUKOIL, Transneft), as well as the telecommunications company MTS and the mining company Polymetal, carried out the largest projects. This trend of transnationalization is very typical for Russian business, where super-large companies prove to be the most stable. There are several reasons for this (from excessive monopolization of the Soviet economy and privatization model to the specific relationships between business and government). FDI by the 25 largest Russian companies investing in EAEU member states accounts for 71% of total EAEU mutual FDI stock. The 25 largest projects implemented by Russian companies account for about 61% of total EAEU mutual FDI stock (according to the monitoring of mutual investments by the EDB Centre for Integration Studies; the MIM CIS database contains data on almost 1300 projects). Thus, a limited circle of large companies supply the FDI. Medium-sized business has yet to go abroad.

Kazakhstan is the second-largest exporter of capital in the EAEU. Kazakhstan's stock of direct investments in the region amounted to $3.6 billion by the end of 2016. Like Russian investors, in 2016, Kazakh companies demonstrated a recovery of FDI growth to EAEU states. The bulk of Kazakhstan's direct investment within the EAEU is concentrated in Russia and Kyrgyzstan.

The sectoral structure of Kazakh FDI stock in EAEU countries differs markedly from the structure of Russian FDI. The agriculture and food products industry ranks first in terms of attracting Kazakh investments (20.8%). Second place is taken by the tourism (19.7%), and transport is third (19.1%). Oil and gas, non-ferrous metals, finance, and construction also stand out.

For 2016, Belarus stays the leader in terms of attracting direct investment from EAEU countries ($8.6 billion) (Table 4.5). This leadership is mainly due to several major transactions by Russian TNCs: Gazprom's purchase of Beltransgaz, which supported the export of natural gas from Russia to Poland and other EU countries (now called "Gazprom Transgaz Belarus"), telecommunications company MTS's investment in a subsidiary structure, Transneft's acquisition of trunk pipelines, Slavneft's acquisition of a stake (42.6%) in the Mozyr Oil Refinery.

Meanwhile the year 2016 was a remarkable one for Belarus as an investor in the EAEU: its FDI stock increased more than sixfold to exceed $2 billion. Such a sharp increase of Belarusian FDI stock is attributable to the acquisition of a 20% stake in PJSC Uralkali by a Belarusian company Yuras Oil.

In general, the structure of Belarusian FDI stock is not too diverse when compared with Russian and Kazakh FDI. Starting from 2016, the leading sector is the chemicals (84%). Oil and gas have a considerable share (8.5%) in FDI stock, although Belarus is not an oil and gas power. Agriculture and food products and mechanical engineering go next, by the end of 2016 accounting for 3.3% and 2.8% of Belarusian companies' FDI, respectively.

Armenia's cooperative investment with its partners in the EAEU essentially comes down to Russian capital flowing into its economy. At the beginning of 2017, the volume of Russian FDI stock here exceeded $3.4 billion (Table 4.5). Russian TNCs invest mainly in communication and IT, oil and gas, non-ferrous metals, and finance. At the current stage, Armenia's partnership with other EAEU countries is weak. Belarusian and Kazakh companies do have projects that are small in terms of investment volume. As for Armenia's outgoing investments, they are mainly directed at the agriculture and food products industry.

Kyrgyzstan has a great potential to attract foreign capital to extractive industries. Not surprisingly, Russian and Kazakh TNCs dominate among entities from EAEU countries investing in Kyrgyzstan. Moreover, by the

Table 4.6 EAEU countries' mutual FDI and the outside world's FDI in the EAEU

	2011	2012	2013	2014	2015
EAEU countries' mutual FDI stock, $ billion	26.6	27.6	25.1	25.4	23.6
Incoming FDI stock in EAEU countries, $ billion	537.0	580.7	622.2	442.3	404.4

Sources: UNCTAD for the outside world's incoming FDI; the "Monitoring of Mutual Investments in the CIS and Eurasia" project by EDB Centre for Integration Studies with respect to mutual FDI

end of 2015, Russia has already surpassed Kazakhstan, which had previously led in terms of FDI in Kyrgyzstan, largely due to the "neighbourhood effect" (Table 4.5). As a whole, Kyrgyzstan's investment positions look very weak, again due to the lack of necessary investment resources and the technological backwardness of the country.

EAEU countries' mutual FDI is a small fraction of the outside world's FDI stock in the EAEU: there is a 17-fold difference (Table 4.6). However, in 2014–2015, the outside world's FDI in the EAEU dropped far more precipitously. In 2014, the decline in FDI in the EAEU was 29%, and in 2015 the indicator fell by another 9% to $404 billion. The decrease in EAEU countries' mutual FDI was not so significant: in 2014 it grew by 1%, and in 2015 it decreased by 7% to $23.6 billion. Thus, the Eurasian Union absorbed the shock of the fall: companies in EAEU countries did not curtail their investments in neighbouring countries.

In the coming years, we expect the structure of investment flows in the EAEU to experience a partial transformation. The main factor behind this transformation is the active development of relations within EAEU. The deepening of Eurasian integration in the EAEU and its single market provides new opportunities for business collaboration to investors in the "middle echelon". The fact is that cross-border barriers are less painful for big business: they are effectively overcome with resources (e.g., the largest companies are represented on foreign investor councils that advise presidents). But companies in the "middle echelon" are limited in their money, administrative resources, and clout. The single market provides them with a wider range of opportunities to build value chains and simply scale up their business operations.

We assume that there is a significant potential for mutual investments in industries where cross-border investment activity is currently low: agriculture and food products, retail trade (food items and industrial goods), construction of commercial and residential real estate, tourism, and information technology. Given the EAEU's relatively young age, we should not expect an immediate large-scale increase in FDI. Growth will happen when medium-sized enterprises go abroad. Based on the above data, we can speak of an emerging foundation of corporate relations.

4.7 Steps Towards the Coordination of Macroeconomic, Exchange Rate, and Monetary Policies

Coordination of macroeconomic policy in the EAEU is a very complicated issue, but in the long term, it is critically important. The EAEU Treaty provides for ensuring macroeconomic stability, the formation of unified principles for the functioning of the economy, and harmonization of key indicators in order to increase stability and deepen integration between member economies. One of the key tasks for the progress of the EAEU is to ensure the full coordination of member states' macroeconomic policies, primarily monetary policy. Over the long-term, deepening monetary integration may bring tangible benefits to the EAEU's three "small" economies, primarily by "importing" economic stability through reducing long-term interest rates.[36]

The EAEU Treaty sets forth three indicators to comply with: the debt-to-GDP ratio, the level of inflation, and the budget deficit. However, at the moment the EAEU has no well-defined mechanism for using these criteria in practice. The Eurozone in its time faced a similar problem: the criteria to ensure the stability of foreign sovereign debt and the deficit were not observed. The result was regrettable: in the absence of strict fiscal policy and with uncontrolled growth in government spending, the rise in debt became dangerous, resulting in a revision of risk premiums and the sovereign debt crises. The most famous of these is the Greek sovereign debt crisis. The EAEU may face the very same situation. In the first two years since the Treaty took effect, each of the three criteria has been violated by at least one of the parties. This is a serious long-term problem that has yet to be solved. The solution promises to be difficult: we need a mechanism to "gently coerce" the parties to bring their macroeconomic policies into compliance with the criteria specified by the EAEU Treaty.

Several unresolved problems prevent a transition to deeper levels of monetary policy coordination. These problems are high and volatile inflation in individual countries, significant dollarization of the economy, member states' different monetary policies, and the high volatility of mutual exchange rates.[37] In fact, these problems constitute the EAEU's agenda for the next five to ten years. They need to be addressed regardless of whether member states will face the task of deepening monetary coordination. Settling these matters will reduce the costs of mutual trade, increase its volume, and open the way for sustainable growth in mutual long-term investments.

The very first measures needed in this area are, first, a decrease in the level of dollarization of economies and, second, a reduction in member states' inflation with the emergence of similar long-term trajectories for inflation.[38] High and volatile inflation makes it difficult to pursue monetary policy because of the prolonged effects of shocks on the real economy. The average inflation volatility index in the EAEU is currently more than 15 percentage points higher than in the EU in 1996–2000. As for dollarization, its high level significantly distorts the monetary transmission mechanism and diminishes the effectiveness of monetary policy. All this increases the probability that the integration association will experience asymmetric shocks. Coordination of actions in currency regulation will allow countries to avoid imbalances arising from exchange rates changing at a different speed (in a different direction) and react to external shocks in a synchronized manner.

In addition to monetary policy coordination, EAEU countries face other challenges in the financial sector: liberalization of banking sector services, equalization of conditions for capital account operations, liberalization of access to the securities market, reduction of restrictions on brokerage and depositary activities, and others.[39]

As forms of deep coordination, exchange rate mechanisms and currency unions promote the economic convergence of countries and stimulate trade within the region. However, this requires a high level of monetary policy coordination and involves significant costs associated with harmonizing monetary policy. Therefore, a number of regional initiatives related to currency unions, such as the introduction of a single currency, have not been implemented in practice. At the same time, exchange rate stability under a regional economic agreement is the most important prerequisite for the success of any of the aforementioned forms of monetary coordination.

As of 2016, exchange rate and monetary policy regimes in EAEU member states vary significantly.[40] Russia, Belarus, and Kyrgyzstan implemented a flexible exchange rate, while Armenia actually uses a stabilized USD exchange rate, limiting the dram's fluctuations within a two-percentage-point corridor. Kazakhstan for a long time used an exchange rate target with a crawling peg, but in 2015 it devalued the tenge and announced the move to an inflation targeting regime with a floating exchange rate.

As noted above, effective integration of financial markets requires greater monetary policy coordination among EAEU member states. Countries' general plans to move to inflation targeting with a flexible exchange rate may serve as the basis for this deeper coordination. Moreover, the announced medium-term inflation targets largely coincide (see Table 4.7).

A prerequisite for successful monetary coordination is convergence between countries and strong business cycle synchronization. Analysis has shown that EAEU countries are experiencing real, nominal, and institutional convergence. However, these processes are progressing unevenly and are not affecting all countries of the Economic Union simultaneously.

Table 4.7 Medium-term inflation targets in EAEU member states, %

Armenia	Belarus	Kazakhstan	Kyrgyzstan	Russia
4 ± 1.5	5	3–4	5–7	4

Source: Data from the central (national) banks of EAEU member states
Note: For Belarus, Kazakhstan, and Kyrgyzstan, the medium-term targets are not permanent and may change over time

There is a real convergence between Belarus, Kazakhstan, and Russia. This is the catch-up convergence: per-capita GDP (PPP) in Kazakhstan and Belarus is steadily approaching the figure seen in Russia. Armenia is also gradually reducing its lag behind Russia in terms of per-capita GDP (PPP), but this is happening extremely slowly. Kyrgyzstan is not currently demonstrating convergence with the EAEU's leaders, having very low per-capita income to start with (Fig. 4.6).

Consumer price indices in EAEU countries are converging. The economic association exhibits so-called club convergence, where indicators converge in all countries. Moreover, this convergence is absolute, meaning that indicators are truly tending towards the same magnitude (recently Belarus has been an exception: inflation is still high there, although in 2015 the prerequisites for falling inflation began to take shape). This finding suggests that it may be possible to use a single inflation target within the EAEU to coordinate the monetary policies of member states.

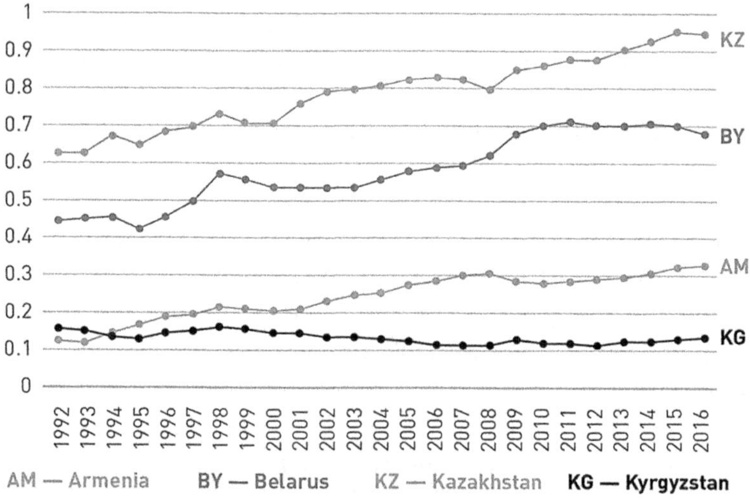

Fig. 4.6 Ratio of per-capita GDP (PPP) in the EAEU countries to per-capita GDP (PPP) in Russia, ratio. (Note: Per-capita GDP (PPP) in Russia is taken to be 1. Source: Authors' calculations)

In summary, the Treaty sets forth the tasks necessary to effectively coordinate macroeconomic, exchange rate, and monetary policies, but they have not yet been addressed in practice. The degree of real coordination will determine the effectiveness of the common markets and how often trade conflicts will arise. The essential prerequisites and most important tasks along this path are a significant reduction in the dollarization of economies and the achievement of similar, low, and stable levels of inflation.

Notes

1. Edovina (2017).
2. National Legal Internet Portal of the Republic of Belarus (2016).
3. Hereinafter, mutual and foreign trade statistics are based on the EEC data supplemented by the authors' calculations.
4. Alpysbaeva et al. (2015).
5. EEC (2016a).
6. Golovnin (2010). Pp. 201–202.
7. EDB Centre for Integration Studies (2017a). Pp. 18–19.
8. EDB Centre for Integration Studies (2015a, b).
9. Estimates concerning Belarus obtained from a survey of Kazakh exporters should be treated with caution. This is because the percentage of Kazakh firms exporting to Belarus is relatively small, and the corresponding estimates are less statistically reliable compared to the other country pairs.
10. EDB Centre for Integration Studies (2015b).
11. News Agency Sputnik (2017).
12. EDB Centre for Integration Studies (2015a).
13. CIS Statistical Committee (2016a).
14. EEC (2017b).
15. EDB Centre for Integration Studies (2017a).
16. Denisenko and Chernina (2017).
17. Ministry of Internal Affairs of Russia (2017).
18. Cited in: Aliev (2016).
19. World Bank Group (2016).
20. EDB Centre for Integration Studies (2017a).
21. CIS Statistical Committee (2016c).
22. CIS Statistical Committee (2016b).
23. EDB Centre for Integration Studies (2015c).

24. EEC (2016b).
25. EEC (2016c).
26. Aliev (2016).
27. EEC (2017a).
28. EDB Centre for Integration Studies (2013).
29. EDB Centre for Integration Studies (2016a).
30. EDB Centre for Integration Studies (2016b).
31. EDB Center for Integration Studies (2015d, 2016b).
32. EDB Centre for Integration Studies (2017b).
33. Kuznetsov (2014); EDB Centre for Integration Studies (2016b).
34. Heifetz (2011). P. 228.
35. EDB Centre for Integration Studies (2017b).
36. Vinokurov et al. (2017).
37. Demidenko et al. (2017).
38. Demidenko et al. (2017).
39. Mishina and Khomyakova (2014).
40. Demidenko et al. (2017).

References

Aliev, S. (2016). Labour Migration and Social Security for Workers in the Eurasian Economic Union. Moscow: Eurasian Economic Commission. Available at: http://www.eurasiancommission.org/ru/Documents/spreads.pdf.

Alpysbaeva, S., Kenzhebulat, M., Kamzin, A., Kaskeev, S. (2015). Structural Changes in the Mutual Trade of Kazakhstan and Russia in Conditions of External Shocks and Differences in Monetary Policy. Eurasian Economic Integration, 2 (27), pp. 41–51. Available at: https://eabr.org/upload/iblock/c1e/eei_2_2015_alpysbayeva_etc.pdf.

Central Bank of the Russian Federation (CBR) (2017). Cross-Border Transfers of Individuals (Residents and Nonresidents). Available at: http://www.cbr.ru/eng/statistics/Default.aspx?Prtid=tg.

CIS Statistical Committee (2016a). Basic Socioeconomic Indicators of Poverty in CIS Countries. Database "Statistics of the CIS". Available at: http://www.cisstat.com/2base/frame00.htm.

CIS Statistical Committee (2016b). The Labour Market in the Commonwealth Countries in 2015. Database "Statistics of the CIS". Available at: http://www.cisstat.com/2base/frame00.htm.

CIS Statistical Committee (2016c). The Socioeconomic Situation of the Countries of the Commonwealth of Independent States in 2016. Database "Statistics of the CIS". Available at: http://www.cisstat.com/2base/frame00.htm.

Demidenko, M., Korshunov, D., Karachun, O., Miksyuk, A., Pelipas, I., Tochitskaya, I., Shimanovich, G. (2017). Monetary Policy of EAEU Member States: Current Status and Coordination Prospects. Joint Report of the Eurasian Economic Commission and Eurasian Development Bank. Moscow: EEC; Saint Petersburg: Eurasian Development Bank. Available at: https://eabr.org/en/analytics/integration-research/cii-reports/monetary-policy-of-eaeu-member-states-current-status-and-coordination-prospects/.

Denisenko, M. and Chernina, E. (2017). Labour Migration and Earnings of Migrants in Russia. Voprosy Ekonomiki, 3, pp. 40–57.

EDB Centre for Integration Studies (2013). Labour Migration and Human Capital of Kyrgyzstan: Impact of the Customs Union. Report No. 13. Saint Petersburg: Eurasian Development Bank. Available at: https://eabr.org/en/analytics/integration-research/cii-reports/labour-migration-and-human-capital-of-kyrgyzstan-impact-of-the-customs-union/.

EDB Centre for Integration Studies (2015a). Assessing the Impact of Non-Tariff Barriers in the EEU: Results of Enterprise Surveys. Report No. 30. Saint Petersburg: Eurasian Development Bank. Available at: https://eabr.org/en/analytics/integration-research/cii-reports/assessing-the-impact-of-non-tariff-barriers-in-the-eeu-results-of-enterprise-surveys/.

EDB Centre for Integration Studies (2015b). Estimating the Economic Effects of Reducing Non-Tariff Barriers in the EEU. Report No. 29. Saint Petersburg: Eurasian Development Bank. Available at: https://eabr.org/en/analytics/integration-research/cii-reports/estimating-the-economic-effects-of-reducing-non-tariff-barriers-in-the-eeu/.

EDB Centre for Integration Studies (2015c). Labour Migration and Labour-Intensive Industries in Kyrgyzstan and Tajikistan: Possibilities for Human Development in Central Asia. Report No. 31. Saint Petersburg: Eurasian Development Bank. Available at: https://eabr.org/en/analytics/integration-research/cii-reports/labour-migration-and-labour-intensive-industries-in-kyrgyzstan-and-tajikistan-possibilities-for-huma/.

EDB Centre for Integration Studies (2015d). Monitoring of Mutual Investments in CIS Countries — 2015. Report No. 32. Saint Petersburg: Eurasian Development Bank. Available at: https://eabr.org/en/analytics/integration-research/cii-reports/monitoring-of-mutual-investments-in-cis-countries-2015/.

EDB Centre for Integration Studies (2016a). EDB Integration Barometer – 2016 (Fifth Wave of the Survey). Report No. 40. Saint Petersburg: Eurasian Development Bank. Available at: https://eabr.org/en/analytics/integration-research/cii-reports/integratsionnyy-barometr-eabr-2016/.

EDB Centre for Integration Studies (2016b). Monitoring of Mutual Investments in CIS Countries 2016. Report No. 39. Saint Petersburg: Eurasian Development Bank. Available at: https://eabr.org/en/analytics/integration-research/cii-reports/monitoring-of-mutual-investments-in-cis-countries-2016/.

EDB Centre for Integration Studies (2017a). Eurasian Economic Integration – 2017. Report No. 43. Saint Petersburg: Eurasian Development Bank. Available at: https://eabr.org/en/analytics/integration-research/cii-reports/eurasian-economic-integration-2017/.

EDB Centre for Integration Studies (2017b). Monitoring of Mutual Investments in CIS Countries 2017. Report No. 45. Saint Petersburg: Eurasian Development Bank. Available at: https://eabr.org/en/analytics/integration-research/cii-reports/monitoring-of-mutual-investments-in-cis-countries-2017/.

Edovina, T. (2017). We must pay for the opening of partner countries' markets by lowering duties. EEC Minister in charge of Trade Veronika Nikishina on plans to expand free trade. Kommersant, February 10. Available at: http://www.kommersant.ru/doc/3214431.

Eurasian Economic Commission (EEC) (2016a) A package of documents on the launch of the EAEU's common pharmaceutical market was signed. November 16. Available at: http://www.eurasiancommission.org/en/nae/news/Pages/16-11-2016-5.aspx.

Eurasian Economic Commission (EEC) (2016b). On the Labour Market in the Eurasian Economic Union. 2015. Analytical review October 31. Available at: http://www.eurasiancommission.org/ru/act/integr_i_makroec/dep_stat/econstat/Documents/labourmarket_2015.pdf.

Eurasian Economic Commission (EEC) (2016c). The Board of the Commission approves a draft of the Agreement on Pension Provision for Workers of EAEU Member States. December 20. Available at: http://www.eurasiancommission.org/ru/nae/news/Pages/20-12-2016-4.aspx.

Eurasian Economic Commission (EEC) (2017a). Outcomes of the EEC Council: the EAEU new Customs Code will enter into force on January 1, 2018. April 28. Available at: http://www.eurasiancommission.org/en/nae/news/Pages/28-04-2017-3.aspx.

Eurasian Economic Commission (EEC) (2017b). The Eurasian Economic Union in Figures: Brief Statistical Compilation. Moscow: EEC. Available at: http://www.eurasiancommission.org/ru/act/integr_i_makroec/dep_stat/econstat/Documents/Brief_Statistics_Yearbook_2017.pdf.

Golovnin, M. (2010). Interaction of Financial Systems of the CIS Countries. Saint Petersburg: Aletheia.

Heifetz, B. (2011). Russian Business in EurAsEC Countries: The Modernization Factor. Moscow: Ekonomika.

Kuznetsov, A. (2014). Russian Direct Investment as a Factor of Eurasian Integration. Voprosy Ekonomiki, 8, pp. 58–69.

Ministry of Internal Affairs of the Russian Federation (Ministry of Internal Affairs of Russia) (2017). Statistical Information on the Migration Situation in the Russian Federation for 12 months of 2016 with a Breakdown by Countries and Regions. January 30. Available at: https://xn--b1aew.xn--p1ai/Deljatelnost/statistics/migracionnaya/item/9359228/.

Mishina, V. and Khomyakova, L. (2014). The Integrated Currency Market of the Eurasian Economic Area and Calculations in National Currencies: Myths or Reality? Vorposy Ekonomiki, 8, pp. 41–57.

National legal Internet portal of the Republic of Belarus (2016). Decree No. 499 of the President of the Republic of Belarus of 28 December 2016 "On the Draft of the International Treaty". December 31, 1/16815. Available at: http://www.pravo.by/document/?guid=12551&p0=P31600499&p1=1.

News Agency Sputnik (2017). Aramian: Privileges with regard to Goods from EAEU Countries can be Revoked. February 6. Available at: https://ru.armeniasputnik.am/armenia/20170206/6305003/aramyan-privilegii-v-otnoshenii-tovarov-iz-eaes-mogut-bit-otmeneni.html.

Vinokurov, E., Demidenko, M., Korshunov, D. (2017). Potential Costs and Benefits of Monetary Integration in the Eurasian Economic Union. Voprosy Ekonomiki, 2, pp. 75–96.

World Bank Group (2016). Migration and Remittances: Recent Developments and Outlook. Migration and Development Brief 26, April. Available at: http://pubdocs.worldbank.org/en/661301460400427908/MigrationandDevelopmentBrief26.pdf.

5

Eurasian Economic Union: Foreign Economic Relations

5.1 The Emerging Network of Free Trade Areas

The rules of world trade are undergoing serious transformation, often in ways that do not favour EAEU countries. In addition to the sanctions currently harming the trade and economic ties of the EAEU's largest member, Russia (and other member countries through Russia), the prospect of eroding WTO rules is alarming. The threat to WTO rules stems from the nascent trend towards mega-agreements that do not involve the EAEU. Though the Trans-Pacific Partnership and Transatlantic Partnership have not yet materialized, if they do, there will be increased risk not only that WTO rules will be partially replaced by other regulations but also that the Eurasian Union will be isolated in terms of trade. What actions should its member states take in these circumstances? How should it build relationships with external partners? How can it achieve the best conditions for non-commodity exports and for integrating into global production chains?

We must acknowledge that today the EAEU—with its nominal GDP of $1.5–2 trillion, GDP at purchasing power parity of $4.5 trillion, and population of 183 million people—is not a self-sufficient market, at least

E. Vinokurov, *Introduction to the Eurasian Economic Union*,
https://doi.org/10.1007/978-3-319-92825-8_5

Box 5.1 EAEU and WTO

Currently, four out of five EAEU member states belong to the WTO. It took almost two decades for Russia and Kazakhstan to complete the negotiations (2012 and 2015, respectively). As the "trio" conducted their negotiations on the Customs Union in 2007–2009, they seriously discussed the idea of simultaneously pursuing WTO membership. This was actually quite reasonable, since Belarus, Kazakhstan, and Russia were to negotiate their own CCTs. Unfortunately, due to inconsistent positions as well as the negative response from the United States and EU, this idea did not come to life.

Armenia and Kyrgyzstan became members much quicker (2003 and 1998, respectively), but this came at the cost of surrendering their markets (a much easier decision for small economies than for large ones). Belarus is still not a member.

As Kazakhstan joined the World Trade Organization in 2015, it unilaterally made 1347 exemptions from the EAEU CCT (i.e., 1347 tariff lines have become exempt). By the end of 2016, this number had grown to 1914. Russia, though unhappy about the weakening of the CCT, agreed to it. When these goods enter the customs territory in Kazakhstan and then re-exported in the EAEU, customs levy higher import duties.

In fact, Kazakhstan is not the only state that exempted a number of tariff lines from the CCT. Armenia has 775 exempted lines and Kyrgyzstan 169.[1] As Kyrgyzstan's average import tariff has been a mere 5.1%, completion of the CCT is in a transition period until 2020. Likewise, a wide nomenclature of goods is subject to the transition period until 2022 in Armenia.

The CCT should become uniform by 2021–2022.

In the long term, it would probably be wise for EAEU member states to push for collective membership in the WTO, following the European Union's example.

as concerns many higher-value-added goods. This represents just 3.2% of global GDP! Any attempt to build a "Eurasian fortress" would be suicidal. The EAEU's economy would be forever doomed to play catch-up technologically. Opportunities to export non-primary goods would be missed. Consumers, cut off from competitive imports, would lose. Domestic producers, protected from competition, would grow overly lax: why exert yourself if the domestic market is guaranteed to be yours? Perhaps the main disadvantage of such a future is the inability to achieve economies of scale (reducing costs per unit of output by increasing production) on most high-tech goods. At the same time, a certain level of EAEU market protection is acceptable in order to create a comfortable "springboard" for national producers. However, in the long term, there is no alternative to integration into world markets and international production chains.

Free trade agreements with countries outside the EAEU began to be cultivated even before the Treaty on the Eurasian Economic Union officially emerged in 2015. A free trade area (FTA) is a classic mechanism for building mutually beneficial relations with foreign trading partners. In the last couple of decades, FTAs are increasingly transforming into full-fledged trade and economic agreements. In addition to reducing or eliminating trade duties, they govern numerous mutual agreements on investment conditions, capital flows, technical regulation, dispute resolution procedures, rules for determining the country of origin of goods, and other important issues pertaining to market access. Therefore, such an arrangement often goes under the title "FTA+". Like mushrooms after rain, other terms are springing up—"deep and comprehensive free-trade area", "comprehensive trade and economic agreement", and so on. This evolution is natural and justified in terms of promoting the economic interests of the contracting parties.

As already noted, the EAEU's main negotiator with third parties is the EEC. The Commission approaches cooperation with each partner through a thorough comprehensive evaluation of all its advantages and risks for all member states and its alignment with the Eurasian integration association's goals and principles. For example, before commencing formal negotiations with a country regarding a free trade agreement, the Commission forms a joint research team with that country, including experts from the EEC's industry departments and member states' national government bodies. The research team conducts an in-depth systematic analysis of the possible economic effects of establishing a free trade regime between the potential partners, including for areas of trade and sensitive industries that might be regulated by the agreement. The Commission uses this analysis to make recommendations regarding the expediency of concluding the agreement. Once this has happened, official negotiations can begin based on a decision of the Union's Supreme Council. Importantly, as of today in its negotiations to establish a free trade area with third parties, the EEC only has a mandate to discuss a trade bloc for goods, while the issues of investment and trade in services, which provide an FTA's greatest economic effect, remain strictly within the competence of the member states. This often hinders the negotiation process.

The Eurasian Union's first free trade agreement could well have been an agreement with New Zealand. However, it broke down in 2014 due to the escalation of the crisis in relations between Russia and the West. As a result, the free trade agreement with Vietnam, ratified in November 2015, was the first to establish not only a trade deal but also an investment arrangement. Later we will provide more detailed information on this and several other free trade agreements currently being developed.

What might be the solutions to the current relationship crisis between Russia and the West?

In 2013, in one of its reports, the EDB Centre for Integration Studies announced the expediency of developing and implementing a programme of the EAEU (which at that time was being formed) under the name "Eurasian Partnership" in order to promote various forms of deep integration with neighbouring countries and for multilateral continental cooperation.[2] The Centre proposed a flexible approach to form external relations with the possibility of both bilateral and multilateral cooperation. However, it was pointed out that it would be desirable to *emphasize bilateral agreements* that account for both the specifics of a particular partner and the interests of all parties. Cooperation could be realized not only through treaties but also through joint action plans (as with the European Neighbourhood Policy) and participation in joint programmes.

In 2016, the EEC declared its interest in forming its own trading blocs. In this light, the work carried out by the Union and its member states to build a network of free trade agreements and trade and economic cooperation agreements has become known as the formation of the Eurasian Partnership. President of the Russian Federation V. Putin said at the St Petersburg International Economic Forum in 2016, "We with our partners believe that the Eurasian Economic Union can become one of the centres for forming a broader integration area. <…> We propose to think about creating a large Eurasian Partnership involving the Eurasian Economic Union, as well as countries with which we already have close relations—China, India, Pakistan, Iran, and, of course, I am referring to our partners in the CIS—and others interested states and associations."[3] A little later, at the Eastern Economic Forum, First Deputy Prime

Minister Igor Shuvalov clarified that the great Eurasian Partnership is an open forum for continental cooperation that above all presumes the elimination of trade barriers between the EAEU and its partners in accordance with WTO principles.[4]

As long as work on such mega-projects occurs mainly in the political arena, the most realistic way for the EAEU to promote its foreign economic interests is to form a network of bilateral free trade agreements between the Union and its partners on the continent. The network of free trade agreements is designed to expand and simplify the access of producers and exporters of goods and services from the EAEU to other countries' markets, help Union members integrate into regional and global production chains, and attract investments. Ultimately, such agreements aim to accomplish two tasks—to further increase exports and to increase investments—which are considered to be drivers of economic growth.

Roughly 50 countries and associations expressed some interest in cooperating with the EAEU.[5] In 2015, the EAEU and Vietnam reached an agreement on free trade. It entered into force in October 2016 (Table 5.1). In 2016, the negotiation process accelerated noticeably. Free trade agreements are negotiated between the EAEU and Egypt, Israel, India, Iran, and Singapore. Negotiations are under way to establish a single preferential trade regime between all EAEU member states and Serbia, and so are negotiations on a non-preferential agreement with the PRC. Other potential partners include South Korea, Chile, Thailand, South Africa, and so on.

What are the most important details of the EAEU's free trade agreements, concluded and under negotiation, with third parties? There is a unique story about how each specific agreement between the parties evolved, although the EAEU gradually standardized its procedures. For example, the first discussions on deeper cooperation with Vietnam began in 2009, while such discussions with Egypt began in 2014. At the time, the talks covered these countries' bilateral cooperation with Russia. Later, the format expanded first to include the three countries of the Customs Union and then the five countries of the EAEU.

On the technical side, once the presidents of EAEU countries take a decision to start negotiations, they proceed along two tracks: the Commission and member states will negotiate trade in goods, and mem-

Table 5.1 Areas of current work on EAEU trade and economic agreements as of 1 July 2017

Ratified FTA	Vietnam (the agreement came into force in October 2016)
Mandates received for negotiation tracks; negotiations/consultations are in progress	China (in May 2016 a mandate to negotiate a non-preferential trade and economic agreement)
	Iran (a "limited" FTA)
	India
	Israel
	Singapore
	Egypt
	Serbia (a single FTA between the EAEU and Serbia will replace the bilateral FTAs that Serbia has concluded with Belarus, Kazakhstan, and Russia)
Potential candidates (working groups, expressions of interest, memoranda)	South Korea
	Cambodia
	Mongolia
	Peru
	Chile

Source: EDB Centre for Integration Studies

ber states will negotiate trade in services and investments, with Russia providing overall coordination of the negotiation process. This "two-track" scheme will probably become the main approach in negotiating FTAs of the Eurasian Union. Then, a high-level negotiating team is appointed. It consists of the EEC representatives and three deputy ministers (economics or foreign affairs, industry, and agriculture) from each side.[6]

5.1.1 FTA with Vietnam

The free trade area between the EAEU and Vietnam, concluded by the parties in May 2015 and enacted in October 2016, provides for markets to gradually open on both sides.[7] According to EEC estimates, the establishment of an FTA between the EAEU and Vietnam has the capacity to more than double their trade turnover in the next few years. Thus, the EAEU countries' exporters could save about $40 million on duties in the FTA's first year of operation. After all transitional periods expire, the abolition of customs duties should yield a positive effect of $55–60 million annually. According to the EEC's calculations, by 2025, EAEU countries' average import tariff will decrease from 9.7% to 2% and Vietnam's from 10% to 1%. Moreover, in 2017, Vietnam is abolishing customs duties on 59% of mutual trade positions. At the end of the transition period (less than ten years), this figure will reach 88%. Only 12% of the commodity nomenclature is not covered by Vietnam's cancellation of import customs, and EAEU countries lack any export interest in the majority of these excluded items.[8]

It is assumed that the EAEU's FTA with Vietnam will have a positive effect in both the agricultural and industrial sectors. For example, the documents signed by the parties provide for Russian companies' ability to conduct business in Vietnam on the same terms enjoyed by local companies. This affects the joint projects of automakers (GAZ, KAMAZ, UAZ) and investments in power generation, transportation infrastructure, and oil refining. As for the sensitive sectors of EAEU countries' economies, such as light industry or agriculture, significant protection levels will remain.[9] Thanks to the agreement, EAEU producers received fundamentally better conditions for supplying goods to the Vietnamese market, and their goods become more competitive. In addition, the agreement allows the Union's producers and suppliers to access Vietnam's established supply chains in the Asia-Pacific region.

We will note some useful information on each of the other countries the EAEU is working with to conclude free trade agreement. Just to remind, the information is actual as of 1 July 2017.

5.1.2 FTA with Israel

The EAEU and Israel are working on a full-fledged free trade agreement pursuant to a decision adopted by the Supreme Eurasian Economic Council in October 2015. According to the EEC, such an agreement would lead to trade growth: Israel's trade with the EAEU countries may grow by 6–8%, while for Russia the growth may be only tenths of a per cent.[10] Intensified investment and technological cooperation between the parties may offset such imbalances, so the FTA should include provisions that help reduce investment barriers.

5.1.3 FTA with Serbia

According to a decision of the Supreme Eurasian Economic Council of 31 May 2016, the Union is negotiating with Serbia for the uniformity of Serbia's trade conditions with the EAEU's member states.[11] To this end, a free trade agreement is proposed between the EAEU and Serbia, which should replace the current three bilateral FTA with Russia, Belarus, and Kazakhstan (Armenia and Kyrgyzstan have no such agreements with Serbia).

5.1.4 FTA with Singapore

At the end of December 2016, after completion of a joint study, the Council of the Commission recognized that it would be advisable to initiate negotiations on an FTA with Singapore.[12] At present, the parties are considering such issues of cooperation as technical regulation and application of sanitary, phytosanitary, and quarantine measures; mutual investment issues; and forms of cooperation in the energy sector and industry. Singapore generally maintains insignificant tariffs on goods exported by the Eurasian Union, so an FTA would be sure to have a positive effect if the agreement extends to investment and trade in services. An FTA with Singapore would have particular value due to opportunities that provide EAEU countries with better access to the markets of states and associations with which Singapore has preferential agreements.

In December 2016, the Supreme Eurasian Economic Council decided to start negotiations on EAEU free trade agreements with Egypt and India and on an interim agreement leading to the creation of a free trade area with Iran.[13]

5.1.5 FTA with Egypt

In 2015, EAEU countries and Egypt reached their first agreements regarding the creation of an FTA and the work of a joint research team. The parties have scheduled substantive work on the EAEU-Egypt FTA agreement to begin in autumn of 2017. According to the EEC's preliminary estimates, the formation of this FTA could increase EEC countries' exports to Egypt by 14.5% and imports from Egypt by 34%. EAEU countries have serious potential to increase their exports of food products, vegetable oils and fats, vegetables, leather goods, coal, ferrous metals, and certain types of machinery and equipment to Egypt. Exports of Egyptian vegetables, fruits, nuts, certain types of chemical products, clothing, and textiles would increase. The EAEU may receive additional benefits from member states' use of the Russian industrial zone created within the Suez Canal Economic Zone. Certain opportunities for EAEU countries are also opening up in connection with the network of free trade agreements concluded by Egypt with a number of countries in North Africa.[14]

5.1.6 A Limited-Scale FTA with Iran

As with Egypt, the EEC's first contacts with Iran and the formation of the joint research team on a potential FTA took place in 2015. The EAEU recognizes that an agreement with Iran would be beneficial. The EAEU first plans *a limited FTA* (conclusion of a temporary agreement by the end of 2017 and a narrow list of goods to stimulate mutual trade, valid for three years), followed by the launch of a full-scale FTA during a certain transition period. According to the joint research team's analysis, if the EAEU creates a full FTA, EAEU countries' exports to Iran could grow by 73%.[15] Moreover, 83% of the total projected increase in the shipments will be due to goods such as medicines, paper, clothing, steel products, various types of machinery and electrical equipment, and cars. Infrastructure development projects can increase mutual trade volumes. Above all, this pertains to the problem of transportation access between the EAEU and Iran, which makes trade more difficult. The solution may be to organize effective railway transit through Georgia and Armenia or through Azerbaijan.

5.1.7 FTA with India

The work of the EAEU's and India's joint research team began in 2015. In June 2017 at the St Petersburg International Economic Forum, it was announced that formal negotiations had begun to conclude an FTA between the EAEU and India.[16] According to the EEC's estimates, mutual liberalization of the trade regime will boost GDP in all EAEU countries and India. In particular, total GDP in EAEU countries would grow $1.5 billion in the short term and up to $3 billion in the long term.[17] However, India may compete with Belarus in some niches of the Russian market, for example, in agriculture. At the same time, mutual trade between the EAEU and India could grow by 18–20%. For example, Belarus' exports to India may increase by 20% over the current volume, while Russia's exports by 18%, Kazakhstan's exports by 12%. The most promising sectors and commodity positions are grain, food products, vegetables, beverages, fertilizers, transportation, turbojet engines, and steel products.

According to the EEC, if there is a transition to a free trade regime, trade turnover between the EAEU and India may grow by 30–40% (compared to the current level), depending on the level of tariff liberalization achieved following negotiations. The upcoming talks will cover a wide range of trade regulation topics, including customs administration, defence and protection of intellectual property rights, reduction of tariff and non-tariff barriers in mutual trade, and so on. However, the willingness of India, like Iran, to reduce the non-tariff barriers successfully regulated by these markets is a key condition essential to the full realization of the FTA's potential benefits.

Among other countries we will mention the **Republic of Korea** and Mongolia. On the basis of the Memorandum of Cooperation signed in November 2015 between the EEC and the Ministry of Industry, Trade, and Energy of the Republic of Korea, a team of scientists from Russia and Korea conducted a joint study in order to develop an optimal formula for deepening cooperation between the EAEU and Korea.[18] This study revealed substantial threats to the Russian automobile and electronics industries. The work is currently in the on-hold mode.[19]

As for **Mongolia**, the work with the country built on the Memorandum of Cooperation signed in June 2015 between the EEC and the Government of Mongolia.[20] Pursuant to mutual agreements, EAEU countries and Mongolia are developing trade and economic cooperation in the agroindustrial complex, competition policy, technical regulation, and application of sanitary, veterinary-sanitary, and phytosanitary quarantine measures. The parties established a joint research team to promote economic dialogue between the Union and Mongolia. In June 2017, at the St Petersburg International Economic Forum, the Prime Minister of Mongolia announced the country's willingness to conclude an FTA with the EAEU.[21]

There are good prospects for starting the negotiation process between the EAEU and its major trade and economic partners—the EU and the PRC. In this case, the EAEU's best policy may be formulated in the spirit of a Chinese dazibao: "Stand on two legs". An Italian children's riddle also comes to mind: "Why does the heron stand on one leg? Because it knows that if it lifts both feet, it will fall down." The Eurasian Union is not a heron—it simply must stand on both legs for stability. Long-term sustainable development will ensure close-knit cooperation with both the European Union and China. There is already a certain movement in this direction. The EAEU and the PRC have begun a dialogue to work out an agreement on trade and economic cooperation. We will consider relations with the EU and China in more detail in Sects. 5.3 and 5.4, respectively.

Finally, as noted, the EAEU actively works to establish trade and economic ties outside the Eurasian continent. For example, the EEC concluded several memorandums of understanding and cooperation with Chile, Peru, and the Andean Community.[22] But the obvious priority is the Eurasian continent, especially those countries with which growth in mutual trade and investment is realistic and potentially profitable.

5.2 Will New Member States Join the EAEU? Is It Possible for Member States to Leave the Union?

On 1 January 2015, the Treaty on the Eurasian Economic Union took effect. Belarus, Kazakhstan, and Russia, the three founding states, initially signed its text. On 2 January, Armenia joined the integration union, and in May Kyrgyzstan signed an agreement to join (the document took effect in August 2015). Will the Eurasian Union continue to expand? Which countries are realistic candidates and why?

This issue often causes confusion. At various times, the media has reported about the accession of Turkey and India to the EAEU. We must immediately clarify that these reports are about concluding a free trade agreement or other agreements on trade and economic cooperation. Membership in the organization is an entirely different matter with respect to both rights and obligations.

We believe that Tajikistan is the only realistic mid-term candidate for joining the EAEU. The reasons are as follows.

Economically, Tajikistan maintains close ties with the Russian and Kazakh economies. Institutionally, it is an active participant in a number of Eurasian entities, including the CSTO and Eurasian Development Bank. In 1998, Tajikistan joined the Treaty on Deepening Integration in the Economic and Humanitarian Fields.

Tajikistan has considered the feasibility of joining the EAEU since 2015. In general, Tajikistan is in no hurry to join the EAEU. We see no drama in the fact that is not being forced. Quite on the contrary, it is a sign of political maturity on the side of Russia. Neither Tajikistan nor the EAEU countries has the political goal to join at any cost. The pros and cons of such a decision should be clear from the onset.

One reason for Tajikistan's slow pace is its desire to assess the practical advantages and disadvantages of participating in the integration by looking at countries that have recently joined—Armenia and, especially, Kyrgyzstan. After rather long deliberations by the working group under the Ministry of Economy and Trade of the Republic of Tatarstan, the matter was referred to the republic's government for consideration in the autumn of 2016. Russia and Kazakhstan are not forcing the issue either. All parties desire to understand the particulars of the process and create acceptable solutions.

Will Tajikistan accede to the EAEU? What are this decision's pros and cons for Tajikistan, Russia, and other countries of the integration association?

Tajikistan is a small country with a population of about 8.6 million people. Agriculture, mining, and remittances from migrant workers are the foundations of its economy. Its geography provides a generally poor "starting point" for building a strategy for long-term sustainable growth: isolation from the existing global transportation infrastructure, lack of access to the sea, mountainous terrain (communications within the country are also problematic and require increased investment), and considerable distance from the main markets. In 2015, GDP was $7.9 billion, which is less than $1000 per capita and about $2700 per capita at purchasing power parity.

What opportunities will joining the EAEU give Tajikistan? We see two main advantages: *increased investments in the republic* and *increased remittances from migrant workers*. According to our estimates, GDP growth potential due to investments will provide an additional 1.6 percentage points of GDP growth per year. The investment potential from remittances will add another 1 percentage point of GDP growth per year. Attracting foreign direct investment may change aggregate economic productivity through technology transfer and increased competition, producing additional growth by 0.5 percentage points. The increased capital will help GDP grow by 0.4 percentage points thanks to the involvement of new labour resources. Thus, the total effect will potentially be up to 3.5 percentage points per year if, first, an accession would trigger large-scale investments and, second, all benefit of the common labour market would be used in full.[23]

Tajikistan's population is rapidly increasing, while the number of jobs is not growing quickly enough. Employment in non-agricultural sectors is growing very slowly. At present, up to 66% of the workforce finds employment in agriculture. By comparison, this figure is 10% in Russia and Belarus.

When discussing Eurasian issues, the topic of the common labour market tends to fade into the background relative to the common markets for goods and services. Meanwhile, it was the formation of a single labour market that produced significant results for Kyrgyzstan in 2015–2016. The statistics for 2015 confirm the fact that the labour market has begun working: the number of Kyrgyz migrant workers in Russia increased by 1.6%, and the number of Tajik migrant workers decreased by 13.7%. This is a direct consequence of the fact that Kyrgyzstan is part of the EAEU, and Tajikistan is not.

The Tajikistan's accession to the EAEU would change this situation. Tajik migrant workers will pour into the common labour market, and the volume of remittances will rise again. This may be the main channel through which the republic will benefit from joining the Union, and it will work quickly, literally within a year. Migrants' wages will partially catch up with the wages of citizens of the Russian Federation and Kazakhstan. Estimates of wage growth for migrants following Tajikistan's accession to the EAEU range from 9% to 28%. We also estimate that remittances will increase by 15–25%.[24]

The second channel is investment. If joining the EAEU creates a more favourable environment for Russian and Kazakh investments (specifically, the Russian Federation and Kazakhstan are the largest investors in the CIS region), the consequence will be increased state revenues and additional jobs. The latter is particularly important to control migration and maintain social stability in the country.

For Tajikistan to join in the smoothest and least painful way, it may be necessary to employ several mechanisms to provide external support to the Tajik economy. The first is budgetary support. The second area is support for investment projects in Tajikistan to augment the state budget and create jobs.

The fact that Tajikistan's population supports the idea of the republic joining the EAEU is also positive. The EDB Integration Barometer has consistently confirmed this since 2012. According to the latest data for 2016, 68% of the population are in favour of joining; a negative opinion is expressed only by 4%; 20% are indifferent to the topic. Such public sentiment is quite conducive to making crucial political decisions.

For Tajikistan, the balance of costs and benefits of joining the EAEU will be positive. But what is of interest here for Russia and Kazakhstan, potential donors in Tajikistan's accession to the EAEU?

First, investment opportunities: they are present in four sectors—mining, hydropower, agroindustry, and light industry. The Tajik economy is currently capable of absorbing investment resources in excess of $2.5 billion per year. Tajikistan's entry into the common Eurasian market will likely also entail new prospects, especially in agroindustry and light industry. Low labour costs create opportunities for higher-yielding investments. Second, the preferential trade regime, which secures conditions favourable to Russian exports (products of mechanical engineering and other sectors). Third, the long-term sustainable growth of the Russian economy requires labour resources to grow, which is difficult due to the demographic situation in Russia. More organized conditions on the use of labour resources in the Russian economy will benefit Russian GDP. Fourth and most significantly, Tajikistan's accession to the EAEU will have a beneficial effect on political stability in the country and the region as a whole. The alternative—destabilization in the country and region (especially since the country borders Afghanistan)—may prove to be extremely costly for the EAEU, especially for Kyrgyzstan, Kazakhstan, and Russia. EAEU countries are interested in a stable and prosperous Tajikistan.

In considering the issue of Tajikistan's accession to the EAEU, Russia, Kazakhstan, and Tajikistan itself must proceed from an understanding of the economic nature of the Eurasian Union. The EAEU is one tool for building a strategy for long-term sustainable growth. Political and military-political issues will continue to be resolved bilaterally within the framework of the CSTO.

Are there any other candidates for joining in the short and medium term?

In fact, there are few of them. Uzbekistan has shown moderate interest in joining the EAEU, but only informally, at the level of analytical centres that have evaluated the possible effects of such a political decision. Uzbekistan has a complicated history of interaction with Eurasian integration entities (in 2004, the country joined the Eurasian Economic Community but withdrew in 2006). We may also count among the negatives Uzbekistan's contentious relations with Kyrgyzstan and Tajikistan with respect to the management of water and energy resources in the region and with respect to the problems of territorial settlement, including in the enclaves of the Fergana Valley. Still, we do not rule out the possibility of Uzbekistan's accession to the EAEU in the long-term future.

There is also a small long-term probability that Azerbaijan, Georgia, and Moldova will join. Ukrainian membership in the Eurasian integration bloc makes profound economic sense,[25] but the events of recent years prevent us from taking this possibility seriously.

In general, we should never perceive the expansion of the Eurasian Union as an end in itself. The Union must carefully analyse each new country with respect to the decision's economic and political effects (the balance of potential costs and benefits for all EAEU countries and the candidate itself), as well as its "stress tolerance". Our research shows that expansion of regional organizations generally has a negative effect on their effectiveness: the wider the membership, the more likely it is for the organization to morph into a "discussion forum" or "zombie".[26]

Nor should we forget about the existence of a full-fledged alternative to accession, that is, the development of close relations under various trade and economic agreements (both with the EAEU as a whole and with its individual members) regulating access to the markets for goods and services, capital flows and people, large cross-border infrastructure projects, and so on.

We end this section with an "uncomfortable" question: *is it possible for one of the five current members to withdraw* from the integration association? Legally, such a step is possible and regulated by Article 118 of the EAEU Treaty—the final article in the Eurasian Union's principle document. It provides for the right of any member state to withdraw from the Union. To exercise this right, a diplomatic notification should be deployed. This begins a mandatory 12-month period, after which the state withdraws from the association. There is an obligation to resolve all financial issues and settle various other obligations.

Thus, a member of the Union may withdraw. The EU experience (Brexit) suggests that the EAEU should not completely rule out such a scenario. Of course, this step may prove to be painful, both economically and politically. Various aspects of the common market—from the common customs territory to the general labour market—are gradually being absorbed into the flesh and blood of the economies of the Eurasian association's member states.

5.3 Prospects of the EAEU's Relations with the European Union

Relations between Russia and the West have been in crisis for several years. The political crisis stands in the way of fundamental decisions on economic cooperation between the European Union and the Eurasian Union.

Deep economic integration with the EU is extremely important for the Eurasian countries. First, the EU is Russia's and Kazakhstan's largest trading partner: it accounts for 50.3% of total exports and 40.8% of total imports of EAEU countries. But bear in mind that according to the results of 2016, the EAEU imported 1.5% more goods from APEC countries (42.3%, due to the growth of supplies from China, South Korea, and ASEAN countries) than from the European Union. Second, Europe could be an important source of capital. Third, the EU could play an important role in helping to modernize EAEU countries and could serve as a source of technological renewal.

We note that, according to the EDB Integration Barometer, in 2016, 68–82% of the population of EAEU member states expressed support for even the prospect of concluding an agreement on free trade and investments between the EAEU and the EU.[27]

The European Union's significance for the EAEU is also confirmed by the size of the European market, whose GDP at current prices is $16.4 trillion and at PPP is $20 trillion (versus $1.5 and $4.5 trillion, respectively, in the EAEU), while the EU is 2.8 times more populous (see Table 5.2).

According to the EDB Centre for Integration Studies, capital investments in the European Union account for 62% of all Russian FDI and 90% of all Kazakh FDI in the countries of Eurasia. Thus, despite the objectively growing importance of the Asian economic vector, trade and investment ties with the EU are key to the EAEU.

Although EAEU countries still give priority to European capital, they are increasingly looking for alternative sources of foreign investment. European investors must understand that the risk of losing the EAEU markets is growing due to the inflow of capital from leading Asian economies. The European Union is also fundamentally interested in the EAEU,

Table 5.2 GDP and population in the EU and EAEU in 2016

	EU	EAEU
GDP in current prices, $ trillion	16.4	1.5
GDP (PPP), $ trillion	20.0	4.5
Population, million people	510.3	183.0

Source: IMF, authors' calculations

which is its third trading partner after the United States and China. The 183-million-person market for European products is a good incentive for European business to support closer relations with Russia and its partners. At first glance, there is a strong dependence on the supply of oil and gas; we are actually talking about interdependence: Europe is interested in stable supply, and the EAEU wants stable demand. Of great importance is geographic proximity, which creates a lot of problems (and opportunities!) related to the movement of people, interaction between border regions, cross-border infrastructure, water resources, and environmental threats.

Thus, the economic foundation for mutual interest is present: geographic proximity, significant trade flows, the security of energy supply (for EU) and demand (for EAEU), EAEU countries' interest in the transfer of European technologies, the presence of joint common neighbourhood, and so on.

Here we need a make a technical comment. Member states have transferred more than a hundred competencies, including the authority to create a customs tariff and administer a common customs territory to the supranational level of the EAEU. Therefore, the discourse should actually proceed to reaching agreements between the Eurasian and European Union. Of course, EAEU member states retain their jurisdiction over a whole range of issues—such as the movement of capital (investment regime) and people (visa-free regime). Nevertheless, from a legal point of view, the relations between the two regional organizations are formally at the centre of this process.

In general, 2014–2017 will be remembered in the EU-Russia relations as a difficult and very unpleasant time. If there is a breakthrough in the EU-EAEU relations one day, what form could the development of EU-EAEU relations take?

We proceed from the premise that the resolution of the political crisis in Russia's relations with the West is an indispensable condition for ending the current confrontation. A certain level of trust must be restored first. To start an official dialogue between the two unions, it is important that the Europeans recognize the EAEU and EEC. This has not happened yet.

In addition to the short-term tasks, in the work to normalize and expand EU-EAEU relations, it is already important to formulate a long-term vision of a future agreement (more precisely, a set of agreements). The Eurasian Union is currently initiating a number of free trade agreements with smaller partners. In this context, we should see the EU as the main long-term partner.

It is essential the negotiations on concluding the agreement involve not Russia alone but the entire EAEU, which has the requisite supranational powers. The EAEU does not equal Russia. Accordingly, two unions should build the basic at the level of the supranational bodies, namely, the European Commission and the Eurasian Economic Commission. Tracks at the level of individual states on such issues as security, the investment regime, and the movement of people should supplement the supranational dialogue.

The EAEU countries are mainly interested in concluding a comprehensive agreement with the European Union that will cover a much broader range of issues than a standard free trade area. The motivation is simple: simply zeroing out or reducing import tariffs would be profitable for neither Russia nor Kazakhstan—both countries primarily export raw materials, for which the European Union's import duties are already very low or absent. Because of the existing trade structure, Russia and Kazakhstan are not interested in a narrow free trade regime with the EU (this is also true for Belarus, though to a lesser extent). The set of agreements should cover many areas of interaction—from trade in goods and services to freedom of movement of capital and labour resources, from a visa-free regime and the development of a cross-border and transit infrastructure to mutual recognition of technical standards and other issues.

It is likely that the prospective set of agreements will be a "mega-deal" due to the huge range of topics being raised.[28] Mutual concessions and compromises will be interlinked. Different topics are of varying importance to the parties. Yielding in one, a partner will ask for "something in exchange" related to another problem. An EU-EAEU mega-deal precisely represents the idea of an interregional integration agreement uniting the two blocs. This work is new and therefore especially difficult.

Whatever legal form the agreement takes, the party to the agreement will be not Russia but the EAEU in view of its supranational competence.

National representatives (relevant departments of the ministries of economics, foreign affairs, etc.) will, of course, be present and decisively influence the negotiation process and final agreements, but the EEC will formally negotiate trade issues.

EAEU member states will next be interested in not a free trade agreement alone but a deep, comprehensive agreement with the European Union. At the same time, obvious problems associated with concessions in trade should be compensated by benefits in other areas. Substantial progress in other areas of economic cooperation would support the admissibility of the free trade area.

The list of issues to be resolved in the context of EU-EAEU integration includes dozens of items. The list below is certainly not exhaustive. Nevertheless, it illustrates the complexity of the potential EU-EAEU agenda:

- Trade in goods (cancellation of import duties with an exhaustive list of exceptions to the general rule)
- Elimination/reduction of non-tariff barriers
- Regulation of cross-border electronic trading
- Trade in services
- Issues related to the operation of the labour market
- Liberalization of access to financial markets
- Freedom of movement of capital
- Technical regulation
- Regulation of the protection of intellectual property rights
- Development of international transportation infrastructure (road and railway corridors)
- Creation of a single EU-EAEU electricity market
- Environmental agenda (for various cross-border problems and standards)
- Regulation of limited mutual access to public procurement
- Rules of competition
- Dispute resolution mechanisms

In addition to this, there are a number of issues that fall within the competence of individual countries, especially in the EAEU. They include:

- Mutual recognition of diplomas and professional certificates
- A visa-free regime, including a set of agreements on readmission
- The special status of the Kaliningrad Region (investment, trade and investment, movement of people)
- Conditions of cooperation among border regions
- Large-scale exchange in the field of education
- Application of the EU's Third Energy Package to Russian gas export projects[29]

An important task for experts is to analyse potential disagreements related to building long-term relations with partners in the common neighbourhood—the countries located between the two unions (Ukraine, Moldova, Georgia, Azerbaijan). For example, preliminary calculations show that concluding an EU-EAEU FTA agreement would be beneficial to the Russian Federation and Kazakhstan in the long term but less profitable or unprofitable for Armenia, Georgia, Azerbaijan, Belarus, and Moldova.[30]

A report from IFO Institute (Munich)[31] on the possible economic effects of creating a free trade area between the EU and the EAEU makes additional arguments for a comprehensive agreement that is broader than a traditional FTA. In particular, the survey highlights an FTA agreement's significant positive impact on the economies of the countries of both unions. For example, we forecast exports from Russia to the EU to increase by 30% (primarily exports of natural resources) and real income growth in the Russian Federation to rise by 3.1%. According to research, income growth in Belarus will be even more significant, amounting to 4.9%, and growth rates in other EAEU countries will be positive. We also project exports from the EU to the EAEU to increase by 60% (primarily mechanical engineering and agricultural products), which will cause real incomes in eastern European countries to rise by 1.2–1.8%. At the same time, in Russia, metallurgy (+23%), mining (17% growth), and oil refining (15% growth) will benefit the most. However, IFO forecasts negative impact on the agricultural sector (falling up to 17%) and the automotive industry (decline of 37%). The EU's industry indicators will exhibit the opposite behaviour: agriculture and car manufacturing will receive the greatest advantages. In our opinion, this suggests that it would be disadvantageous for the EAEU to conclude an agreement with the EU that is limited solely to tariff-based market protection.

In summary, in the short and medium term, EAEU countries are gaining experience and competence by drafting and concluding free trade agreements with small trading partners, for example, Vietnam and Singapore. However, *in the long term, the Eurasian integration bloc cannot do without large comprehensive agreements with its two "super partners"—the European Union and China.*

5.4 Relations Between the EAEU and China: The State of Affairs and Prospects

China is the EAEU's second-most important foreign economic partner. This is a strategic and long-term partnership. In this section, we will describe the state of affairs in mutual trade and investment, give a description of the negotiations on the forthcoming economic cooperation agreement, and present the prospects for merging the EAEU's transportation strategies and policies with China's Belt and Road Initiative (BRI).

Today the PRC is second among foreign trade partners of EAEU countries (13.6% of total turnover), lagging considerably behind the collective EU (48.9%). Its share of foreign trade is growing rapidly. In general, China is a natural strategic partner for the EAEU.

The trade turnover between EAEU countries and China grew continuously through 2014. However, in 2015, as a result of the slowdown in global economic growth, shrinking domestic demand, weak external environment, and volatility in the financial markets, trade turnover decreased by 27.6% compared to 2014, amounting to $78.7 billion (see Table 5.3). Countries whose main commodity is energy carriers or other resources, that is, Russia and Kazakhstan, typically experienced the largest decline in exports (in value terms).

In 2016, prices for raw material exports partially recovered, and national currency trends improved, slowing the decline in EAEU countries' trade turnover with China. At the end of 2016, the value of trade between the EAEU and China remained virtually unchanged (−0.3%).

Table 5.3 Trade turnover between China and EAEU countries (2008–2016), $ billion

	2008	2009	2010	2011	2012	2013	2014	2015	2016
Russia	55.9	39.5	58.7	82.7	87.5	88.8	88.3	63.5	66.1
Growth, %	*41.3*	*−29.3*	*48.6*	*40.8*	*5.8*	*1.4*	*−0.6*	*−28.0*	*4.1*
Kazakhstan	12.2	9.5	14 1	21.3	24.0	22.7	17.2	10.6	7.9
Growth, %	*33.9*	*−22.7*	*48.9*	*51.3*	*12.5*	*−5.2*	*−24.5*	*−38.4*	*−25.4*
Kyrgyzstan	0.8	0.6	0.7	1.0	1.3	1.5	1.1	1.1	1.5
Growth, %	*85.1*	*−17.6*	*9.1*	*39.0*	*31.7*	*15.7*	*−23.1*	*−5.9*	*45.0*
Belarus	2.0	1.3	2.2	2.8	2.8	3.3	1.6	3.1	2.5
Growth, %	*56.0*	*−38.2*	*72.2*	*29.5*	*−0.8*	*18.4*	*−51.7*	*95.5*	*−19.5*
Armenia	0.4	0.3	0.4	0.4	0.4	0.5	0.6	0.5	0.5
Growth, %	*88.8*	*−19.9*	*43.0*	*−3.3*	*2.2*	*5.7*	*29.4*	*−17.9*	*−5.9*
EAEU, total	71.3	51.2	76.1	108.2	116.0	116.7	108.7	78.7	78.5
Growth, %	*40.9*	*−28.3*	*48.7*	*42.2*	*7.2*	*0.7*	*−6.9*	*−27.6*	*−0.3*

Source: Trademap.org

The structure of imports from China took shape as early as the 1990s. Consumers in EAEU member states above all value imports of Chinese electronics, household appliances, and light industry goods (e.g., footwear and clothing). Machines (equipment) account for significant volumes of imports.

China continues to increase its economic presence in EAEU countries, not only by expanding trade relations but also by constantly increasing *direct capital investment.* China leads Asian countries in terms of FDI stock in the region. According to the EDB Centre for Integration Studies, since 2008, Chinese companies' total FDI stock in the five EAEU countries has increased by 138% to become $25.7 billion (it was roughly $11 billion in 2008). Even amid the crisis of 2015, Chinese FDI stock in the EAEU declined insignificantly, by $0.6 billion, mainly due to the revaluation of assets.

Kazakhstan and Russia are the main recipients of direct investment from Chinese TNCs. Traditionally, the lion's share of Chinese FDI in EAEU countries has been concentrated in Kazakhstan. At the end of 2015, Chinese FDI stock in Kazakhstan amounted to $21 billion (82% of all Chinese FDI stock in the EAEU) (Fig. 5.1). For Chinese companies investing in the Kazakh economy, the most attractive areas are oil and gas

Fig. 5.1 Geographical structure of Chinese FDI in the EAEU, $ billion, as of end-2016. (Source: EDB Centre for Integration Studies)

(production) and transportation of hydrocarbons via trunk pipelines. Collectively, these industries have attracted approximately 98% of Chinese investment.

Other sectors of the Kazakh economy attract an insignificant amount of investment from Chinese TNCs. Finance, non-ferrous metals and wholesale and retail trade account for a total of about 1% of China's total direct investment stock in Kazakhstan.

It is a striking and largely unexpected fact that the Russian economy lags behind Kazakhstan by a factor of six in terms of Chinese FDI stock as of 2016 (the situation is changing only as of 2017 due to the several large investments in Russian oil and gas). Chinese investors are not entering the Russian market with the same urgency. According to the EDB Centre for Integration Studies, Chinese FDI stock in Russia amounted to only $3.4 billion in 2016. A significant portion of the major deals framed in recent years is still waiting to be implemented. Moreover, in a weak economic environment, Chinese investors often expect more favourable terms from Russia.[32]

In addition to Kazakhstan, Chinese investors are also very active in Belarus and Kyrgyzstan. By 2016, Chinese companies had increased direct investment stock in Belarus to $417 million. Belarus achieved such a significant figure thanks to literally ten projects distributed among three sectors: mechanical engineering (57%), tourism (24%), and construction (19%). Kyrgyzstan attracted significant FDI from the PRC for only two projects in two sectors of the economy: oil and gas (oil refining) and non-ferrous metals (development of a gold deposit). In total, Chinese direct investment stock in Kyrgyzstan had reached $912 million by the end of 2015. Of course, this figure is very significant for a small economy.

A new *agreement on economic cooperation*, which the EAEU and China began to negotiate in 2016, aims to stimulate mutual trade and investment flows. This topic is extremely complex, primarily for EAEU countries. There are two fundamental complications. First, EAEU countries are not yet ready to fully open their markets to Chinese imports. Too many industries would be the victim of such a decision. Second, EAEU countries have quite different interests in cooperating with the PRC. A common denominator should be found, which is very difficult to do.

Only in the second half of May 2016 was it possible to formulate an extremely general vision of the agreement's format and content and then submit it for approval to the Supreme Eurasian Economic Council in Astana on 31 May 2016. The Council then authorized the EEC to begin formal negotiations with the PRC. Negotiations started in August 2016.

At this stage, EAEU member states' position on the agreement with China is the following: a *non-preferential hybrid agreement with regulatory elements for transportation, industrial cooperation, and investments*. In general, the EU-EAEU agreement on trade and economic cooperation will primarily focus on creating the infrastructure for trade between the EAEU and China and regulating that trade. However, at the current stage of cooperation, trade liberalization, that is, making changes to actual import duties, is not on the table. EAEU member states are not yet ready to reduce duties and fully open markets.

An agreement on trade and economic cooperation between the EAEU and PRC *will not* be a free trade agreement in its substance or content. The purpose of the planned non-preferential agreement will be to create conditions favourable to cooperation in building infrastructure, industry, transportation, and investment activities, to expand parties' access to specific markets (financial market, services market), and so on.

We consider *policy coordination within the EAEU* as essential to the outcome of the negotiation process. Within the Union itself, it will be critically important to prioritize and identify the domains where member states see EAEU-Chinese cooperation as more profitable. An open dialogue is necessary not only to develop a single harmonized position regarding the PRC but also to prevent from splitting into separate, unrelated tracks, for example, Kazakhstan-China, Russia-China, and so on. In a number of areas (customs regulation, protection of domestic markets and producers, and eventual development of a common transportation and energy market), a negotiating position within the EAEU is more effective than a unilateral approach. It is also more effective for EAEU member states to jointly prioritize key projects and harmonize investment programmes. This will make it possible to avoid situation when the EAEU countries implement infrastructure projects in an unsynchronized manner. One current example: in implementing the Western Europe-Western China road project, Kazakhstan constructed a modern highway from its border with China to its border with Russia (China also completed construction of its section). Russian delays reconstruction and modernization of several sections of the road, which prevents the route from being used to maximum effect.

The *Belt and Road Initiative* is currently the PRC's convincing strategy for international cooperation and economic development in Greater Eurasia. From a practical point of view, the concept includes three basic tools: political cooperation, trade, and investment. China's main goal in expanding cooperation is to ensure energy security, diversify energy sources, and find markets for its numerous products. Another important goal of the project is to create the most favourable conditions for developing its internal regions, especially regions in the country's west, such as the Xinjiang Uygur Autonomous Region, which borders Kazakhstan and Russia.

The leaders of the Union's member states positively received the idea of developing the BRI in EAEU territory. The initiative will produce several positive effects, most importantly: utilization of EAEU countries' transit potential, strengthened cohesion between intracontinental states and regions (Central Asia, Siberia, the Urals, and countries in the Caucasus),[33] and the possibility for more rapid development of infrastructure and, above all, transportation capacity. The main beneficiaries of this process are Kazakhstan, Russia, and Belarus, since the transportation routes will go through their territory.

Cross-border transportation and logistical infrastructure projects are an absolute priority and the key to discovering cooperation's practical potential. The main question here is whether it will be possible to attract some international transit from sea routes to land routes. In terms of the strategic interests of Russia and Kazakhstan, there are two key tasks in this area. The first (but not most important) task is to stimulate some transit to switch from sea to land, so that goods moving from China to Europe and vice versa go through the EAEU. This will yield immediate economic gains. The second (and much more important) task is to develop logistical infrastructure in internal regions that lack access to maritime transportation. This is highly relevant for the Russian Urals, Siberia, and, of course, all the states of Central Asia, Kazakhstan in particular. The BRI transport corridors can "sew" the Eurasian macroregion together in theory, providing a link between resources, producers, and markets.

These grand ideas are still very far from being realized. The trade turnover of the EAEU and China is predominately supported by maritime transport. For example, in the flow of goods between Russia and China, maritime transport accounts for 77% of cargo, land transport through the Russian-Chinese and Russian-Mongolian borders 21%, and transit through Central Asia—only 2%. At the same time, 86% of goods traded between Kazakhstan and China are supplied by land transport (including trunk pipelines) crossing the border between the two states; the rest of the cargo goes through Russian ports and terminals (Vladivostok, Vostochny, and St Petersburg). Moreover, in most cases Chinese goods are exported to Kazakhstan via maritime transport through Russia.

Under the BRI, the development of two transport corridors seems promising: two routes of the Central Eurasian corridor going through Kazakhstan (China-Kazakhstan-Russia-EU) and the Northern Eurasian corridor passing through the Transsib (Shanghai-Vladivostok-Transsib-EU) (Fig. 5.2). These corridors have several advantages: they only use railway transport, pass through the fewest border crossings, and have already been developed; and the volume of container shipments in both directions is growing rapidly. Most importantly, these corridors are most competitive in price.[34]

Furthermore, statistics show that, starting in 2013, freight flows from China to Europe along railway routes have grown extremely rapidly (albeit from a low baseline), reaching 104,000 containers in 2016. In 2016, shipments through Dostyk (Kazakhstan) and Naushki (through Mongolia to the Trans-Siberian Railway) more than doubled, and shipments through Zabaykalsk (from the northeastern provinces of China to the Trans-Siberian Railway) increased by 42%. Robust container shipments through Khorgas (Altynkol station, Kazakhstan) have begun. In the opposite direction (from Europe to China), the flow of containerized cargo also almost doubled in 2016, reaching 52,000 containers per year.

Land routes can win in terms of shipping time, but this advantage still needs to be realized. This factor plays in favour of land transport but requires additional conditions. For example, logistics specialists say that trains should serve a specific line, that is, follow a fixed regular schedule. Only if this is true will the speed of delivery begin to work in favour of

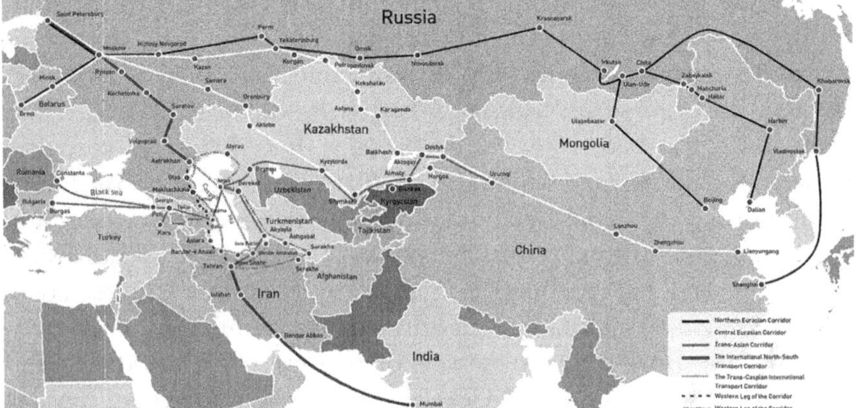

Fig. 5.2 Map of potential BRI transport corridors. (Source: Eurasian Development Bank)

land transportation. To use these corridors most effectively and attract additional cargo traffic, the following important issues (limitations) must be addressed: the need to increase corridor throughput by developing the transportation and logistical infrastructure, the need to increase the level of containerization.

Notes

1. Edovina (2017).
2. EDB Centre for Integration Studies (2013c).
3. TASS (2016).
4. RIA Novosti (2016b).
5. EEC (2017a).
6. Edovina (2017).
7. EEC (2016a).
8. EEC (2016a).
9. EEC (2016a).
10. Korostikov (2015).
11. RIA Novosti (2016a).
12. EEC (2016b).
13. President of Russia (2016).
14. Edovina (2017).
15. EEC (2017d).
16. EEC (2017b).
17. Interfax (2017).
18. EEC (2015b).
19. Edovina (2017).
20. EEC (2015a).
21. EEC (2017c).
22. http://www.eurasiancommission.org/en/act/integr_i_makroec/dep_razv_integr/memorandymi/Pages/default.aspx
23. EDB Centre for Integration Studies (2013b).
24. EDB Centre for Integration Studies (2013b).
25. EDB Centre for Integration Studies (2012, 2013a).
26. EDB Centre for Integration Studies (2016d).
27. EDB Centre for Integration Studies (2016b).
28. Vinokurov (2014).

29. Vinokurov (2014) and EDB Centre for Integration Studies (2016c).
30. EDB Centre for Integration Studies (2016c).
31. Bertelsmann Stiftung (2016).
32. EDB Centre for Integration Studies (2016a).
33. Karaganov (2015).
34. Vinokurov and Tsukarev (2018).

References

Bertelsmann Stiftung (2016). Free Trade from Lisbon to Vladivostok. A Tool for Peace and Prosperity: The Effects of a Free Trade Area between the EU and the Eurasian Region. Focus Paper. Available at: https://www.bertelsmann-stiftung.de/en/publications/publication/did/focus-paper-free-trade-from-lisbon-to-vladivostok/.

EDB Centre for Integration Studies (2012). Comprehensive Assessment of the Macroeconomic Effects of Various Forms of the Deep Economic Integration of Ukraine with Member States of the Customs Union and the Common Economic Space. Report No. 1. Saint Petersburg: Eurasian Development Bank. Available at: https://eabr.org/en/analytics/integration-research/cii-reports/a-comprehensive-assessment-of-the-macroeconomic-effects-of-various-forms-of-the-deep-economic-integr/.

EDB Centre for Integration Studies (2013a). Customs Union and Ukraine: Economic and technological cooperation in sectors and industries. Report No. 18. Saint Petersburg: Eurasian Development Bank. Available at: https://eabr.org/en/analytics/integration-research/cii-reports/customs-union-and-ukraine-economic-and-technological-cooperation-in-sectors-and-industries/.

EDB Centre for Integration Studies (2013b). Economic Impact of Tajikistan's Accession to the Customs Union and Single Economic Space. Report No. 14. Saint Petersburg: Eurasian Development Bank. Available at: https://eabr.org/en/analytics/integration-research/cii-reports/economic-impact-of-tajikistan-s-accession-to-the-customs-union-and-single-economic-space/.

EDB Centre for Integration Studies (2013c). The Customs Union and Neighboring Countries: Models and Instruments for Mutually Beneficial Partnership. Report No. 11. Saint Petersburg: Eurasian Development Bank. Available at: https://eabr.org/en/analytics/integration-research/cii-reports/the-customs-union-and-neighboring-countries-models-and-instruments-for-mutually-beneficial-partnersh/.

EDB Centre for Integration Studies (2016a). EAEU and Eurasia: Monitoring and Analysis of Direct Investments 2016. Report No. 41. Saint Petersburg: Eurasian Development Bank. Available at: https://eabr.org/en/analytics/integration-research/cii-reports/eaeu-and-eurasia-monitoring-and-analysis-of-direct-investments-2016/.

EDB Centre for Integration Studies (2016b). EDB Integration Barometer – 2016 (Fifth Wave of the Survey). Report No. 40. Saint Petersburg: Eurasian Development Bank. Available at: https://eabr.org/en/analytics/integration-research/cii-reports/integratsionnyy-barometr-eabr-2016/.

EDB Centre for Integration Studies (2016c). European Union and Eurasian Economic Union: Long-Term Dialogue and Perspectives of Agreement. Report No. 38. Saint Petersburg: Eurasian Development Bank. Available at: https://eabr.org/en/analytics/integration-research/cii-reports/european-union-and-eurasian-economic-union-long-term-dialogue-and-perspectives-of-agreement/.

EDB Centre for Integration Studies (2016d). Regional Organizations: Typology and Development Paths. Report No. 37. Saint Petersburg: Eurasian Development Bank. Available at: https://eabr.org/en/analytics/integration-research/cii-reports/regional-organizations-typology-and-development-paths/.

Edovina, T. (2017). We must pay for the opening of partner countries' markets by lowering duties. EEC Minister in charge of Trade Veronika Nikishina on plans to expand free trade. Kommersant, February 10. Available at: http://www.kommersant.ru/doc/3214431.

Eurasian Economic Commission (EEC) (2015a). Memorandum on Trade and Economic Cooperation between the Eurasian Economic Commission and the Government of Mongolia is Signed. June 17. Available at: http://www.eurasiancommission.org/en/nae/news/Pages/17-06-2015-2.aspx .

Eurasian Economic Commission (EEC) (2015b). The EAEU and South Korea Have Signed a Memorandum of Cooperation. November 30. Available at: http://www.eurasiancommission.org/en/nae/news/Pages/30-11-2015-5.aspx.

Eurasian Economic Commission (EEC) (2016a). Questions and Answers on the Free Trade Agreement between the Eurasian Economic Union and the Socialist Republic of Vietnam. Available at: http://www.eurasiancommission.org/en/act/trade/dotp/Pages/default.aspx.

Eurasian Economic Commission (EEC) (2016b). The Council of the Commission Recognizes the Wisdom of Negotiations on an FTA with

Singapore. December 23. Available at: http://www.eurasiancommission.org/ru/nae/news/Pages/23-12-2016-5.aspx.

Eurasian Economic Commission (EEC) (2017a). Congratulations on the third anniversary of signing the Treat y on the Eurasian Economic Union. May 29. Available at: http://www.eurasiancommission.org/en/nae/news/Pages/29-05-2017.aspx.

Eurasian Economic Commission (EEC) (2017b). EAEU and India began formal negotiations on a free trade agreement. June 3. Available at: http://www.eurasiancommission.org/en/nae/news/Pages/3-06-2017.aspx.

Eurasian Economic Commission (EEC) (2017c). Mongolia is Ready to Conclude an Agreement on a Free Trade Area with the EAEU. June 2. Available at: http://www.eurasiancommission.org/ru/nae/news/Pages/2-05-2017-3.aspx.

Eurasian Economic Commission (EEC) (2017d). The Interim Agreement on the Free Trade Area between the EAEU and Iran Will Be Operational by the End of the Year. June 1. Available at: http://www.eurasiancommission.org/ru/nae/news/Pages/1-06-2017-3.aspx.

Interfax (2017). EEC Minister in charge of Trade: Negotiations with Iran Should Pursue a Win-Win Solution. June 9. Available at: http://www.interfax.ru/interview/566008.

Karaganov, S. (ed.) (2015). To the Great Ocean – 3. The Creation of Central Eurasia: The "Silk Road" Economic Belt and the Priorities for Joint Development of the Eurasian States. Analytical Report of the Valdai International Discussion Club, June. Moscow. Available at: http://ru.valdaiclub.com/files/11300/.

Korostikov, M. (2015). Israel Plans to Establish a Free Trade Area with the EAEU. Kommersant, October 28. Available at: https://www.kommersant.ru/doc/2842046.

President of Russia (2016). Approved draft documents of the Supreme Eurasian Economic Council. December 26. Available at: http://kremlin.ru/supplement/5153 (official website of the President of Russia).

RIA Novosti (2016a). EEC: EAEU Countries Begin Negotiations with Serbia on the Free Trade Area. May 31. Available at: https://ria.ru/world/20160531/1441164875.html.

RIA Novosti (2016b). Shuvalov: The Greater Eurasian Partnership will not be a Counterposition to the TPP. September 5. Available at: https://ria.ru/economy/20160905/1476106027.html.

TASS (2016). Putin Calls for the Creation of a Greater Eurasian Partnership. June 17. Available at: http://tass.ru/pmef-2016/article/3376295.
Vinokurov, E. (2014). A Mega Deal Amid a Relationship Crisis: Why a European-Eurasian Integration Agreement Should Be Discussed Now. Russia in Global Affairs, 5, December 18. Available at: http://eng.globalaffairs.ru/number/A-Mega-Deal-Amid-a-Relationship-Crisis-17221.
Vinokurov, E. and Tsukarev, T. (2018). The Silk Road Initiative and the Interests of Transit Countries: An Economic Assessment of Transport Corridors. Area Development and Policy, 3 (1), pp. 93–113.

6

A "Normal" Regional Organization: Explaining Eurasian Integration

6.1 Roots and Ideology of Eurasian Integration

The term "Eurasian" originally appeared at the beginning of the nineteenth century in India, then a colony of the British Empire. It applied to the children of mixed marriages, almost always between a European father and an Indian mother. It was used as a politically correct euphemism that concealed its pejorative meaning: "half-blood". The term later spread to other parts of the British Empire and China. In China, closer to the end of the nineteenth century and especially at the beginning of the twentieth century, it applied to the offspring of marriages between a European mother and a Chinese father. It was specifically in China—Shanghai, Hong Kong, Macau, and Taiwan—that the word's initially negative connotation began to gradually disappear.[1]

As an ideological, scientific, and cultural school of thought, Eurasianism has a huge number of variations. It originates in the ideas of the first wave of Russian emigrants in the 1920s–1930s. The Soviet and post-Soviet periods are associated with the names of Lev Gumilev, Alexander Dugin, Alexander Panarin, Olzhas Suleimenov, and others. Currently,

E. Vinokurov, *Introduction to the Eurasian Economic Union*,
https://doi.org/10.1007/978-3-319-92825-8_6

Eurasianism has a strong political component. In practice, it is used for a variety of purposes. Marlene Laruelle provided a high-quality critical survey of the subject.[2]

The Eurasianism of the 1920–1930s is a tragic story of people who lost their homeland. Its most famous representatives are Peter Savitsky, Nikolai Trubetskoy, George Florovsky, George Vernadsky, Roman Jakobson, and Nikolai Alekseev. In the words of George Florovsky, the Eurasianism of that period does not necessarily give the right answers but gives "the truth of the questions".[3] One of the main starting points is the premise that Russians are "others"—either they are *not* Europeans and *not* Asians (i.e., logic from negation), or they are *both* Europeans *and* Asians (logic from synthesis). This is one of the truly truthful questions. It is a common thread throughout the history of the Russian Empire, USSR, and now of the post-Soviet space and the EAEU.

In Russia, modern Eurasianism also has many varieties. Some authors point to a special "Slavic" and "Orthodox" world that Russia is called on to lead. Others (like Lev Gumilev) perceive Russia as the result of a "synthesis" that includes the nomadic peoples of the Great Steppe. As a whole, Gumilev's views very significantly influence today's Eurasian discourse: his ideas are taught in universities, and a university in Astana bears his name. The study of Gumilev's views often acquires a quasi-religious character, when his opinions are accepted as the truth without requiring proof. A third variant (like A. Dugin) views Russia as a special "continental" power that opposes "island" states such as the United States. A fourth variant points to the shared historical destinies of Russia and the countries of Asia (in various combinations—India, China, Japan, and others), while a fifth points to the unity of Slavic and Islamic peoples. A certain variation of Eurasianism takes the form of the idea of Eurasia as a special "geographic world", that is, unity of nature and landscape, coupled with shared historical destinies. This concept played an important role for the original Eurasianism—its teachings are more cultural and geographical than economic in their origin.

Eurasianism has ceased to be an exclusively Russian phenomenon, and this happened long ago: in Russia, Eurasian rhetoric is most actively used in Tatarstan, Bashkortostan, and Yakutia. Shoqan Walikhanov, a Kazakh ethnographer and historian of the nineteenth century, who lived a short but extremely fruitful life, drew attention to this aspect, noting that Eurasia is not synonymous with Russia.[4]

Eurasianism—as a school of thought, rhetoric, and political ideology—is especially strong in Kazakhstan. Olzhas Suleimenov expresses it in his literary works, and Nursultan Nazarbayev voices it in the political realm in his speeches and political and economic strategy. Eurasian terminology is also used to describe the internal transformation of a country[5] and its foreign policy.

There are frequent references to Eurasia in the speeches of Kazakhstan's leadership, especially President N. Nazarbayev. However, in this case, the Eurasianism we are talking is different from the "Russian" variants. First, Russian Eurasianism (both in Russia itself and among emigrants) is generally treated as a philosophy, ideology, or even a scientific school, but, for Nazarbayev, Eurasianism is instead a system of foreign policy and foreign economic ideas and priorities for international cooperation. Second, this Eurasianism cannot be called "Russia-centric"; it is "Kazakhstan-centric". Third, for Kazakhstan, Eurasianism implies being unequivocally open to Europe. It is not hostile to modernization. On the contrary, it is entirely compatible with the policy of economic, bureaucratic, and societal modernization Kazakhstan has pursued for the last 25 years. In other words, "Kazakh Eurasianism" has nothing to do with the "classic Eurasianism" of the 1920–1930s.

What are the ideological underpinnings of the EAEU?

It is based on certain ideas about the long-term economic agenda. Accordingly, the EAEU's overall goal is to create an environment conducive to realizing the potential of economic ties within the region, modernizing national economies, and increasing global competitiveness. The centre, the core, of Eurasian integration is the single market for goods, services, capital, and labour.

In practice, the participating countries' goals and objectives partially overlap and partially differ.

Within the EAEU, practical goal-setting related to Eurasian integration consists of two components. The first component is political. For Russia, this is a desire to strengthen the political, economic, and sociocultural elements of its influence in Eurasia. For Kazakhstan, Belarus, Kyrgyzstan, and Armenia, it is important to strengthen alliances with Russia. Additionally, Kazakhstan is taking steps to become an intermediary in Eurasian countries' relations with other countries. The success of

Box 6.1 Two Eurasian Integrations

We should make a conceptual distinction between two parallel processes often referenced using the same term "Eurasian integration". The first process is integration in the post-Soviet space, primarily within the EAEU. The second process is the deepening of economic and political cooperation (not integration in the narrow sense of the term) throughout the entire Eurasian continent.

In addition to *post-Soviet Eurasian integration*, the process of *continental cooperation* has become a reality in the past decade. It is promoted primarily by the PRC through various initiatives (mainly the BRI) but also by countries of the post-Soviet space (Kazakhstan and Russia), for which continental economic cooperation is potentially extremely beneficial and strategically important. In a broad sense, by Eurasian continental integration, we mean the qualitative improvement of economic relationships between different subregions of the Eurasian supercontinent—Europe, East Asia, Western Asia, South Asia, and the post-Soviet space. Geographically, the latter may be called *Northern and Central Eurasia*.[6]

this strategy promises serious political dividends (and has already brought them in relation to Ukraine, Turkey, and Syria).

The second component is economic: a desire to use the infrastructural, economic, social, and cultural heritage accumulated during the period of shared history to create the basis for economic growth, expand the common market, and, from there, lay the foundation for global competitiveness. At the same time, each member state has specific reasons why Eurasian integration is natural and important. For Belarus, exports to Russian markets are most important. Improving export conditions within the Customs Union will have a positive impact on economic development. It is no coincidence that nearly all calculations of the macroeconomic effects from the CU and EAEU show Belarus as the biggest beneficiary, in relative terms. The common labour market is singularly important for Kyrgyzstan: remittances from migrant workers employed in the Russian Federation and Kazakhstan account for approximately 30% of the Kyrgyz gross domestic product (this same factor will be decisive for Tajikistan when deciding whether to join the EAEU). Armenia values the military-political component of cooperation (Russia guarantees Armenia's security), ensuring remittances from migrant workers (12–18% of GDP), attracting Russian investment (more than 40% of total investment[7]), providing comfortable living conditions for the Armenian diaspora, and doing business in Russia. Kazakhstan's economic motivation is the most nuanced: expanding exports to the common Eurasian market is significant. Cooperation between Russia and other EAEU countries, on the one hand, and between Russian and China in the context of BRI, on the other hand, is also important. Kazakhstan intends to (and in all likelihood will) become the biggest beneficiary of these processes.

The overall drive of Eurasian integration's regulatory framework and working institutions—the EEC, EDB, EFSD, and so on—is a pragmatic approach to building integration. Completely pragmatic political and economic goal-setting, not ideological content, occupies the central position in the wording of the EAEU Treaty and the logic of building institutions of Eurasian integration.

6.2 Holding-Together Integration

Classical regional integration theories were developed mainly in relation to Europe and the European Union. This has strongly influenced the general direction of scientific analysis. As a rule, this analysis has focused on a process in which historically independent states increase the connectedness of their economies and transfer some powers to the supranational level.

But Eurasian integration has clearly unique features: it is taking shape in a region that used to be a united and highly centralized state. We therefore have reason to ask: is the traditional approach sufficiently accurate? And how well suited is it to understanding the logic of Eurasian integration? The answers to these questions are especially important, since the assumption that the world consists of states that are, and always have been, independent may apply to modern Europe but is far from certain in many other parts of the world. Africa and Asia have relatively young states that gained independence from the larger entities, to which they previously belonged, for example, European colonial empires. We may assume that in these conditions regional integration would follow different logic than that which is considered in the widely accepted literature.

To explain the logic of regional integration arising within a previously existing entity, Libman and Vinokurov (2012) offer the theory of *holding-together integration*. *Holding-together integration* is regional integration initiated by a group of countries that until recently were part of a single political or economic union (a unitary state or a colonial empire) and maintain a high level of economic, political, and cultural ties. In this model, regional integration may serve a different purpose than in the traditional approach: a higher level of regional integrity is a question not only of the region's future but also of its past. In other words, both the starting point and the final goal of integration may differ from those inherent in the classical model, the European Union.[8]

Holding-together integration, first, helps maintain a certain level of economic and political cohesion between newly independent states—either indefinitely or for a limited period (thereby making the separation process less costly and painful). Second, holding-together integration may also imitate a U-turn: strong disintegration after dissolution of the unitary state, followed by reintegration based on interstate cooperation, various mechanisms, and, possibly, a revised set of members.

There are numerous differences between the classical European variant and the holding-together model of integration, which is more applicable to Eurasia and Africa. For example, the empirical and theoretical literature on regional integration frequently contains the following statement: the integration process is less likely to progress if the parties to the regional agreement experience significant external shocks, for example, the global economic crisis. Thus, the literature expects the level of trade and economic relations to decline during crises.

Holding-together integration follows a completely different path for a number of reasons. First, in this model, disrupting existing economic ties would be much more expensive than leaving them untouched. Second, the negative effect of disintegration can be especially noticeable if a national identity evolved at the same time. During periods of economic prosperity, countries can take symbolic steps to create a national identity, but an economic slump makes the costs of nation-building prohibitive. In general, holding-together regionalism may be an integration project necessitated by a crisis[9]: an economic downturn may spur cooperation between countries. In an unfavourable economic situation, deep economic ties between newly independent states are more likely to be strengthened than these states' links with third parties.[10]

The countries of the former Soviet Union showcase features that make the model of the second integration type very natural for them. First, they inherited extremely close economic and especially infrastructural ties (we discussed this in Chap. 2). Second, thanks to a centuries-old shared past, these states are close culturally. Third, for the same reasons, they have largely similar institutions. Despite the fact that this Soviet legacy was gradually eroded in the 1990s and 2000s, the ties between the countries remained strong.[11] One of the most significant similarities between the countries of the former Soviet Union is the general acceptance of the Russian language in these states. Even two decades after the collapse of the Soviet Union, political and economic elites of former Soviet countries converse freely in Russian. As for the younger generation, the picture is different, but more than 50% of children can communicate in Russian in every country of the former USSR. The Russian-language media (in particular, television) still have a great influence: more than 50% of the population of countries of the former Soviet Union regularly watch Russian TV shows.[12] Extremely close family ties also hold together the post-Soviet states: a significant proportion of their population has relatives in other newly formed independent states (for more details, see Sect. 2.3).

6.3 EAEU Among Other Regional Integration Organizations: Comparative Analysis

As concerns the "universe" of regional integration organizations, the EAEU is a new kid on the block. As such, it should be compared with other regional and subregional organizations. A correct and realistic assessment of its successes and problems is often impeded by its direct and exclusive comparison with the paragon of regional integration—the European Union. However, for a more objective analysis of the EAEU's structural features, successes, and failures, it is useful to compare it with other major regional integration associations—NAFTA, MERCOSUR, Cooperation Council for the Arab States of the Gulf, ASEAN, and the South African Customs Union (SACU).

Then everything falls into place. On the one hand, the EAEU is not a flawless "success story". After an initial phase of rapid growth, it hit a certain ceiling by 2016. On the other hand, it has managed to achieve quite a lot. The treaty and institutions are working. The common market for goods is functional, albeit with a number of exemptions. The common labour market is already operational—a huge and often underappreciated achievement. There has been substantial progress in developing common technical regulations and so on.

Overall, the EAEU should be viewed not as an exception to the rules but rather as one of the existing "customs unions +" with its own achievements and problems.[13] Its structural features are certainly important, but they are not unique—even those that seem so at first sight. Russia's economic dominance in the EAEU matches South Africa's weight in the South African Customs Union, which is even greater. Besides, the United States economically dominates NAFTA. Exports' orientation towards oil and gas is certainly pronounced in the EAEU, but the oil's role is even greater in Cooperation Council for the Arab States of the Gulf (GCC), and the exports from MERCOSUR are mainly raw materials. Trade conflicts began to appear within the EAEU, just like in MERCOSUR, ASEAN, or NAFTA. Hence, both the EAEU's achievements and its failures are comparable to other regional integration organizations. In the remainder of this section, we provide a few relevant comparisons.

In terms of GDP per capita, EAEU is in the mid-range of the reference group (Fig. 6.1).

The share of intraregional trade in total trade is indicative of the degree of interaction between member countries. It is often used to analyse the effects produced by the establishment of preferential trade agreements and by regionalization processes. Figure 6.2 demonstrates that the highest intraregional trade levels were achieved by the EU (61%) and NAFTA (40%). The lowest value of the indicator was observed in the GCC (7.6% in 2016). In the EAEU, the MERCOSUR, and the SACU, it stood at comparable levels of 14–15% (Fig. 6.2).

Low complementarity index values were, in turn, attributable to the structure of exports and to the high share of primary commodities in total exports (Fig. 6.3). A breakdown of available data by broad economic categories shows that the share of raw materials in total exports amounted to 37–39% in the EAEU and the MERCOSUR, 65% in the GCC, but

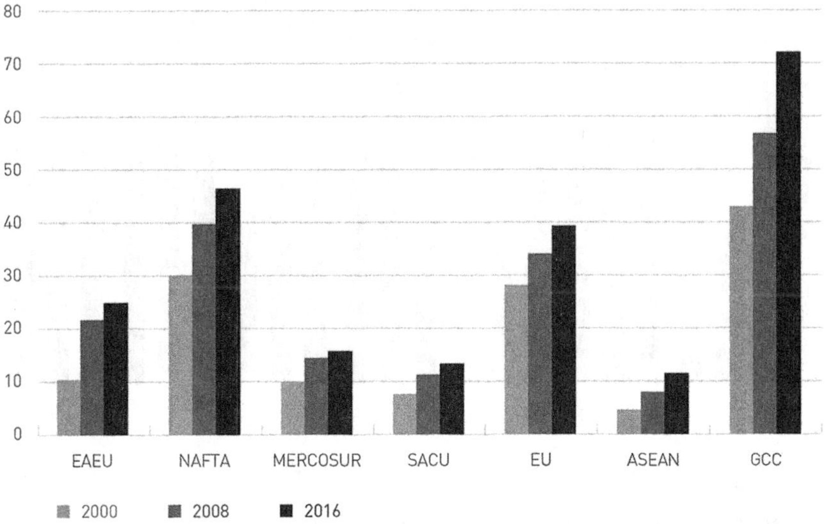

Fig. 6.1 GDP per capita at purchasing power parity, $. (Source*:* Calculations based on IMF data)

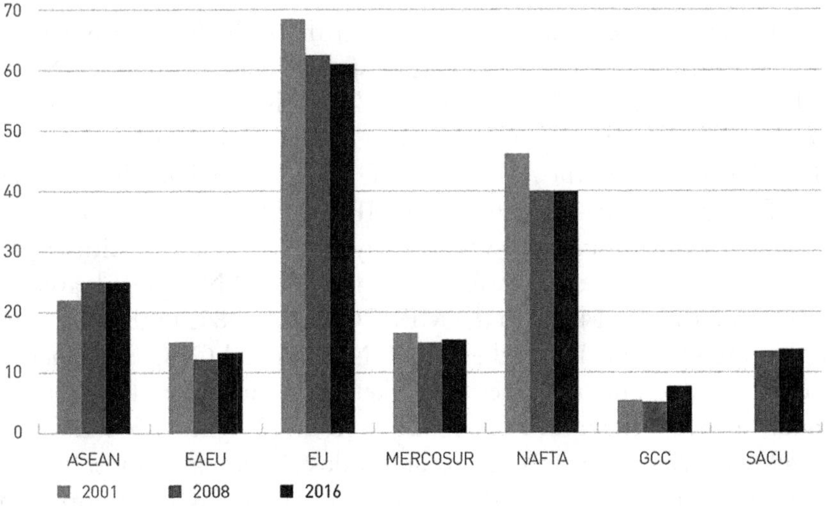

Fig. 6.2 Share of mutual trade in total trade turnover, %. (Note: ASEAN and NAFTA data for 2015, SACU data for 2010 and 2016. Source: Calculations based on Trade Map data)

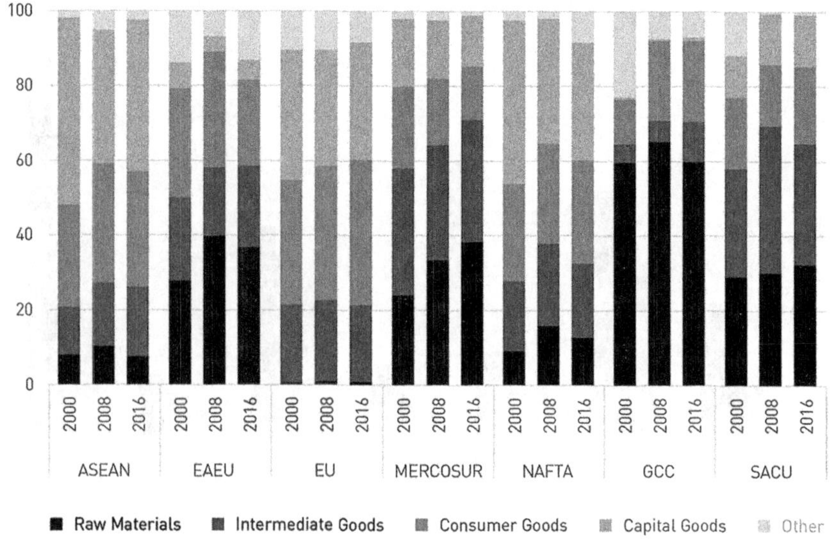

Fig. 6.3 Structure of exports with a breakdown by broad economic categories, %. (Source: Calculations based on COMTRADE)

merely 12% in the NAFTA and 7.5% in the ASEAN. Consumer and capital goods dominated the structure of exports from the ASEAN, the EU, and the NAFTA. For example, in 2016 the share of capital goods stood at 32% of total exports from the EU and the NAFTA and at 41% of total exports from the ASEAN. In the EAEU capital goods accounted only for 5.3% of total exports, in the MERCOSUR—for 13.8%.

Regional organizations (ROs) actively protect their agricultural producers. In 2016, the most favoured nation (MFN)-applied average-weighted tariff was 14.8% in the MERCOSUR, 10.8% in the EU, 9.3% in the SACU, and 8.1% in the EAEU. NAFTA and GCC implemented a drastic reduction of domestic market protections for this group of goods, reducing the tariff in 2000–2016 from 12.1% to 4.3% and from 13.4% to 3.2%, respectively. As regards industrial goods, in most regional associations under review, with the exception of the SACU, import tariffs have been going down, reaching 2–4% by 2016. In the EAEU, tariffs applied to consumer and industrial goods were more than halved in 2008–2016. The MERCOSUR was the only bloc where duties for those goods changed little (11.3%) (Fig. 6.4).

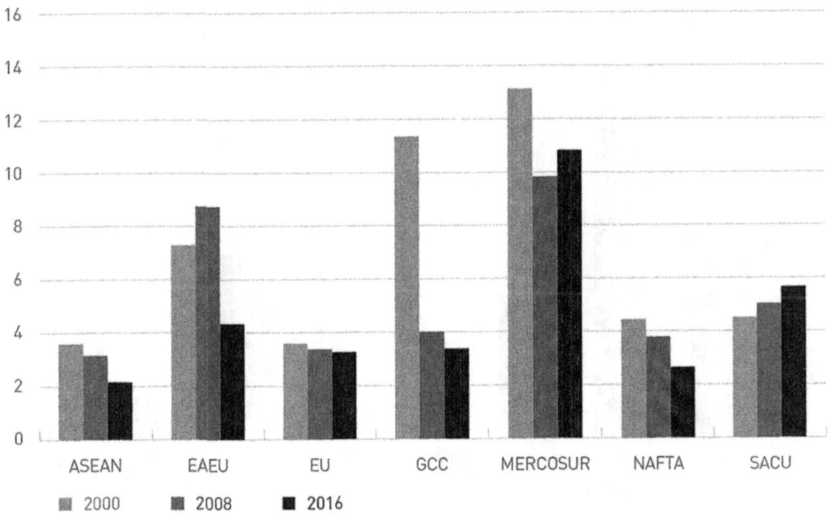

Fig. 6.4 MFN-applied average-weighted tariff. (Source: TRAINS)

EAEU, EU, and NAFTA are leading in terms of migration, labour migration, and remittances (Fig. 6.4; CIS is also added for the sake of comparison). In these integration associations, migration is fueled by existence, within the respective blocs, of countries with different levels of income and development. Also, in the EU and EAEU alike, these processes are facilitated by the respective common labour markets (in the latter, since 2015) (Fig. 6.5).

6.4 Conclusion

The EAEU is there to stay. It is certainly not a flawless "success story". After an initial phase of rapid growth, it hit a number of problems which will occupy the organization and its member states for several years. On the other hand, it has managed to achieve quite a lot. It is a viable and active organization. The treaty and institutions are working. The common market for goods is functional (albeit with a number of restrictions).

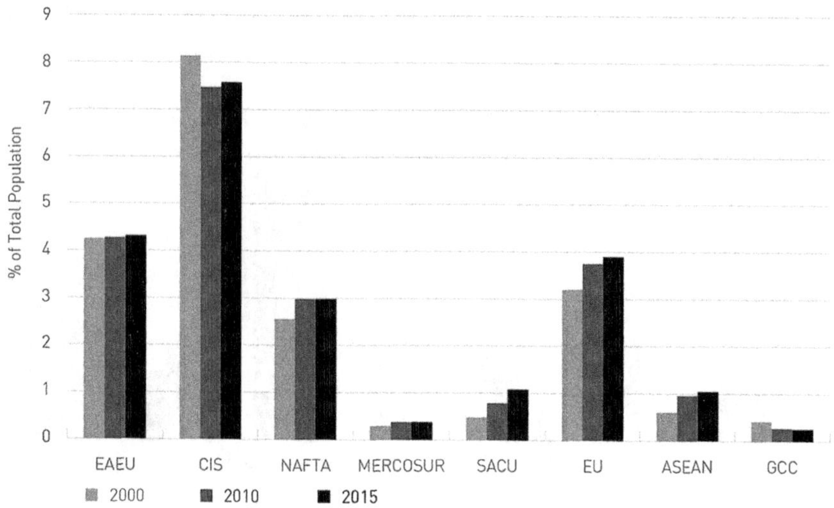

Fig. 6.5 Share of migrants from within the RO in total population. Source: EDB Regional Integration Database, based on UN data (international migration trends)

The overall labour market is already operational—a huge and often underappreciated achievement. There is progress in developing common technical regulations.

The EAEU is not an exception to the rules but rather one of the existing active ROs with a substantial agenda. It has its own share of achievements and problems.[14] It is *normal* in the sense of Shleifer and Treisman's hypothesis of Russia as a "normal country" that can be compared and should not become the subject of a special scientific subdiscipline.[15] The hypothesis of these Harvard economists has been an object of critique. Nevertheless, we believe that its application to the EAEU is fully justified. The Eurasian Union is a "normal" regional integration organization. Its structural features are certainly important, but they are not unique—even those that seem so at first sight. Russia's economic dominance in the EAEU? South Africa's weight in the South African Customs Union is even greater, and the United States economically dominates NAFTA. Exports' orientation towards raw materials? The oil's role is even greater for the Cooperation Council for the Arab States of the Gulf, and the exports from MERCOSUR are mainly raw materials. Initial trade and economic conflicts inside the union? The histories of MERCOSUR, ASEAN, NAFTA, and other regional organizations are full of similar conflicts. Both the EAEU's achievements and its failures are "normal".

There are *several lessons that the EAEU may draw from the international experience of regional integration organizations*. Vinokurov and Libman (2017) compiled a database of ROs and studied the experience of more than 60 ROs around the world, mostly with an economic orientation.[16] ROs are highly nuanced in how they evolve and reach (or fail to achieve) their established goals. A well-developed typology reflects this variety. In addition to "Active" ROs, we distinguish other common RO types such as "Alternative Path" (the RO changes its goals), "Discussion Forum" (the RO's usefulness to member states lies in the possibility of contacts and discussions), "Integration Rhetoric" (used by member states to achieve domestic and foreign policy goals that differ from those officially declared), "Zombie" (makes a lot of noise but does nothing), and "Coma" (exists only in name). Econometric analysis allows us to make several conclusions directly related to the development of the EAEU:

1. An organization grows more stable with time. In other words, an organization is more vulnerable at the early stage of its development. The longer the EAEU exists as an "Active RO", the more likely it is that it will continue to do so.
2. The key to an association's success is the success of the national growth policies implemented by the integration participants. Stable long-term economic growth helps build demand for an effective regional organization. Long-term economic development must take precedence over the formation of day-to-day trade and economic relations between countries, which will produce a positive effect only in the short term. The main question is how the EAEU itself can help form such growth policies: by effectively regulating the Single Economic Space, exchanging "best practices", and interacting with extraregional players (building relations with the EU, creating a network of free trade area, connecting with the infrastructure projects of the Belt and Road).
3. In order for the EAEU to remain active as an RO, the accountability and transparency of its structure are crucial. The clearer the EAEU's

tasks, functions, budget, and organization are to the general public and decision-makers, the less likely it is that the organization's future will be determined purely by bureaucratic inertia. For Eurasia, this also means that economic entities will more frequently use EAEU institutions (e.g., the Court of the EAEU) to achieve their goals. This, in turn, will strengthen the Eurasian integration project.
4. An integration organization should not "expand for the sake of expansion". Such a course will ultimately reduce the effectiveness of a regional organization.

Economic integration is a systemic and fundamental process. Not all effects are immediately apparent—most require years. To maximize the EAEU's positive effect, *the agenda for the next five to ten years covers the following major steps*:

- Complete the single market for goods and services, eliminating existing exemptions. The focus is on common markets for electricity, financial services, oil, oil products, and gas. The plans for these markets are spelled out in the EAEU Treaty (see Sects. 4.1 and 4.3).
- As much as possible, eliminate and/or unify non-tariff barriers within the Union. In practice, non-tariff barriers hamper trade more than import duties themselves. Therefore, they must receive constant and close attention from integration institutions, government bodies, and business. Unlike import duties, non-tariff barriers are "eternal": as you abolish or unify some, others will appear. Countries will always practise protectionism to a certain extent, so there is no alternative to continuously working to minimize NTBs (see Sect. 4.4).
- Coordinate macroeconomic policies, including monetary and financial issues, and thus prevent the Economic Union from "tearing apart". Setting up a common market is not enough. An effective macroeconomic environment where it can function without interruption must also be maintained (for more details, see Sect. 4.7). Imagine a situation where a country devalues its national currencies by 50%, while the other states' currencies hold steady. Manufacturers in the first state can produce goods far less expensively and flood the markets of neighbouring countries with these goods. This is fertile ground for a trade war.

This situation is by no means hypothetical. In the Customs Union's brief history, it has already occurred at least twice—in 2011 in Belarus and in late 2014 to early 2015 in Russia. In both cases, the result was conflict.

- Establish a network of free trade areas and agreements on trade and economic cooperation, including with two key trade and investment partners, the EU and China (Sects. 5.3 and 5.4).
- Effectively coordinate the development of transport and electric power network to raise overall efficiency of cross-border flows.

Addressing these tasks and implementing initiatives in more specific areas (industrial policy, cooperation in agriculture, labour market, a single pension space, scientific and educational cooperation, etc.) will maximize the effect of integration.

As the EAEU and its member states pursue this course, they will face a host of problems and stumbling blocks. In particular, Russian countersanctions and the obligations assumed by Kazakhstan upon accession to the WTO in 2015 are obstacles to the elimination of exemptions from the common market. Common markets for oil, oil products, and gas will be established in conditions where hydrocarbons are exceptionally important to national budget revenues and the creation of a common electricity market promises to be challenging. Eliminating/unifying non-tariff barriers and effectively coordinating macroeconomic policies will be complicated by the resistance of national bureaucracies and the difficulties of interstate communication. Finally, the relationship crisis between Russia and the collective West remains a serious obstacle to the creation of many necessary free trade areas and, above all, a deep and comprehensive agreement with the European Union.

Let us summarize several ideas running through the entire book:

- The EAEU's establishment is a major achievement for its member states after the several "integration false starts" of the 1990s–2000s. The EAEU is the new institutional reality in which businesses, states, and people live and work.
- A combination of political considerations (which vary depending on the member state) and rather weighty economic factors form the foun-

dation of the Eurasian integration's ideology. It is the pragmatic approach to goal-setting and building institutions that has ensured the EAEU's successful establishment after 20 bleak years of "rhetorical integration".

- A comprehensive and generally adequate system of integration institutions has been set up—the Supreme Eurasian Economic Council, Eurasian Intergovernmental Council, Eurasian Economic Commission, Court of the EAEU, Eurasian Development Bank, and Eurasian Fund for Stabilization and Development.
- After a series of rapid initial successes, Eurasian integration faced a number of problems and challenges in 2015–2016. Amid the deteriorating external situation, solving these problems will be much more difficult than before. We can predict much slower progress in the coming years and an increase in the number and intensity of trade and economic conflicts. In these conditions, the next few years will be critical for the organization's long-term future. Member countries would be wise to protect the EAEU in every possible way in the coming years, not sparing their political leaders' time, personnel, and financial resources.

Notes

1. Teng (2013). P. 6.
2. Laruelle (2008). The compelling merits of this analysis include understanding the limited influence of "neo-Eurasians" (such as A. Dugin and A. Panarin) on the real political process, a critical but thoughtful approach to the analysis of L. Gumilev's ideas, as well as a detailed account of the specifics of Eurasianism outside of Russia, especially in Kazakhstan and Turkey.
3. Florovsky (1993). P. 237.
4. Nysanbaev and Kurmanbaev (1999).
5. Laruelle (2008). P. 171.
6. The following books and papers are devoted to the subject of "continental" Eurasian integration: Vinokurov and Libman (2012a, b, 2013).
7. EDB Centre for Integration Studies (2016).

8. A monograph (Libman and Vinokurov 2012) develops this theory and its application to the post-Soviet space (a detailed description of the theory can be found on pages 11–37).
9. Vinokurov (2010).
10. Vinokurov and Libman (2014).
11. Sterzhneva (1999) and Vinokurov (2014).
12. Eurasian Monitor (2007).
13. Vinokurov (2017).
14. Vinokurov (2016).
15. Shleifer and Treisman (2004).
16. Vinokurov and Libman (2017).

References

EDB Centre for Integration Studies (2016). Monitoring of Mutual Investments in CIS Countries 2016. Report No. 39. Saint Petersburg: Eurasian Development Bank. Available at: https://eabr.org/en/analytics/integration-research/cii-reports/monitoring-of-mutual-investments-in-cis-countries-2016/.

Eurasian Monitor (2007). The Russian Language in the Newly Independent States: Status and Prospects. Analytical Report. Available at: http://www.eurasiamonitor.org/rus/research/event-150.html.

Florovsky, G. (1993). The Eurasian Temptation. In: Novikova, L. and Sizemskaya, I. (1993) Russia between Europe and Asia: The Eurasian Temptation. Anthology. Moscow: Nauka, pp. 237–266.

Laruelle, M. (2008). Russian Eurasianism: An Ideology of Empire. Washington, DC: Woodrow Wilson Centre Press.

Libman, A. and Vinokurov, E. (2012). Holding-Together Regionalism: Twenty Years of Post-Soviet Integration. Basingstoke: Palgrave Macmillan.

Nysanbaev, A. and Kurmanbaev, E. (1999). The Eurasian Idea of Chokan Valikhanov. Eurasian Community, 2, pp. 26–31.

Shleifer, A. and Treisman, D. (2004). A Normal Country. Foreign Affairs, 2 (83), March–April, pp. 20–38.

Sterzhneva, M. (1999). The European Union and the CIS: Comparative Analysis of Institutions. Moscow: Moscow Public Science Fund.

Teng, E. J. (2013). Eurasian: Mixed Identities in the United States, China, and Hong Kong, 1842–1943. Berkeley, CA: University of California Press.

Vinokurov, E. (2010). The Evolution of Kazakhstan's Position on Relations with Russia in 1991–2010, MPRA Paper, No. 22187. Available at: https://mpra.ub.uni-muenchen.de/22187/.

Vinokurov, E. (ed.) (2014). System of Indicators of Eurasian Integration II. Report No. 22. Saint Petersburg: Eurasian Development Bank. Available at: https://eabr.org/en/analytics/integration-research/cii-reports/edb-system-of-indicators-of-eurasian-integration/

Vinokurov, E. (2016). Eurasian Economic Union: A Sober Look. Voprosy Ekonomiki, 12, pp. 43–60.

Vinokurov, E. (2017). Eurasian Economic Union: Current State and Preliminary Results. Russian Journal of Economics, (3) 1, pp. 54–70.

Vinokurov, E. and Libman, A. (2012a) Eurasian Continental Integration. Saint Petersburg: EDB Centre for Integration Studies. Available at: https://eabr.org/en/analytics/integration-research/cii-reports/evraziyskaya-kontinentalnaya-integraciya-eurasian-continental-integration/.

Vinokurov, E. and Libman, A. (2012b). Eurasian Integration: Challenges of Transcontinental Regionalism. Basingstoke: Palgrave Macmillan.

Vinokurov, E. and Libman, A. (2013). Two Eurasian Integrations. Voprosy Ekonomiki, 2, pp. 47–72.

Vinokurov, E. and Libman, A. (2014). Do Economic Crises Impede or Advance Regional Economic Integration in the Post-Soviet Space? Post-Communist Economies, 3 (26), pp. 341–358.

Vinokurov, E. and Libman, A. (2017). Re-Evaluating Regional Organizations: Behind the Smokescreen of Official Mandates. Basingstoke: Palgrave Macmillan.

Appendix 1: Chronology of Eurasian Integration, 1991–2017

The following chronology covers 27 years after the breakup of the Soviet Union. It contains events that, in our estimation, had a significant impact on the Eurasian integration and disintegration processes. We consider the economic, political, institutional, and military aspects of this period, paying special attention to economic processes. For each year, we identify two categories of events: those related to economic and institutional transformations and those pertaining to security and military-political issues. Due to the EAEU's exclusively economic orientation, I focus on the economic agenda, while the security agenda has been added sparsely for the sake of the "larger picture".

The initial versions of this chronology appeared in the System of Indicators of Eurasian Integration[1] and in a monograph by Libman and Vinokurov.[2] For the *Introduction to the EAEU*, we have revised the previous versions and added the period from 2011 to 2017, which saw the establishment of the Customs Union and later the Eurasian Economic Union.

E. Vinokurov, *Introduction to the Eurasian Economic Union*,
https://doi.org/10.1007/978-3-319-92825-8

1991: Collapse of the Soviet Union and Emergence of the Commonwealth of Independent States

December 1991	Agreement Establishing the Commonwealth of Independent States, dated 8 December 1991.
	Protocol of 21 December 1991 to the Agreement Establishing the Commonwealth of Independent States, signed on 8 December 1991 in Minsk by representatives of Belarus, Russia, and Ukraine.
	Alma-Ata Protocol, dated 21 December 1991.
1991	Creation of a plan to integrate the gas infrastructure of Russia, Ukraine, and Belarus. State Gas Concern Gazprom seeks to maintain control over its most important assets in the former Soviet Union, above all, over the gas transportation systems in border republics. These attempts are not successful, and Gazprom becomes an exclusively Russian company.

December 1991	Agreement on the Preservation of Joint Command of Strategic Nuclear Forces and Joint Control over Weapons of Mass Destruction in the Arsenal of the Former Soviet Union. As for conventional weapons, CIS member states recognized the principle of creating national armies that are subordinate to the CIS supreme command.
1991	Beginning of the Nagorno-Karabakh conflict (1991–1994).

1992: Cooperation Through the CIS Makes It Possible to Mitigate the Aftermath of the Collapse of the USSR amid the Most Severe Economic Crisis

February 1992	Agreement on Relationships in Trade and Economic Cooperation, dated 14 February 1992.
	Agreement on Principles of Customs Policy, dated 13 March 1992.
May 1992	Agreement on Measures to Ensure Improvement of Settlements Between Economic Entities of the Member States of the CIS, dated 15 May 1992.
July 1992	Agreement on the Status of the Economic Court of the CIS.

(*continued*)

(continued)

October 1992	Agreement on the Single Monetary System and Coordinated Monetary and Currency Policy of States that Retained the Ruble as Legal Tender, dated 9 October 1992.
1992	Industry councils of the CIS, including for transportation and electricity, address the urgent tasks of preserving the unified industrial systems inherited from the Soviet Union.

February 1992	On 14 February 1992 in Minsk, the heads of CIS member states adopt a declaration on the non-use of force, declaration on compliance with the principles of cooperation (which provides for the preservation of unified command of the armed forces for two years), and the Agreement on the Status of the Strategic Forces.
March 1992	Conflict between Moldova and the unrecognized Transnistrian Republic.
	On 20 March 1992 in Kiev, agreements on collective peacekeeping forces in the CIS, on the principles of manning the United Armed Forces of the CIS, and on the status of the CIS Border Forces, as well as a declaration on the non-use of force, are signed.
April 1992	Ukrainian authorities adopt several decisions subordinating the Black Sea Fleet to Ukraine. Russia responds by adopting a decree transferring the Black Sea Fleet to the jurisdiction of the Russian Federation "with its subordination to the Commander-in-Chief of the Joint Armed Forces of the CIS".
May 1992	Between December 1991 and May 1992, in order to minimize the international consequences of the Soviet Union's collapse, the political concept of Russia as the legal successor to the Soviet Union is developed and introduced into international practice. This concept clearly defines Russia's status with respect to four issues: nuclear weapons, membership in the UN Security Council, foreign property, and the Soviet Union's external debt.
	The Collective Security Treaty is signed on 15 May 1992 in Tashkent. Moldova, Turkmenistan, and Ukraine refuse to accede to the Treaty.
July 1992	Peacekeeping forces are deployed in the area of the Georgian-South Ossetian conflict (1991–1992) to monitor the ceasefire and the withdrawal of troops and to maintain order.
August 1992	On 3 August 1992, the presidents of Russia and Ukraine agree to postpone settling the question of the division of the Black Sea Fleet until 1995. The fleet is withdrawn from the CIS Joint Armed Forces and transferred directly to the heads of both states.
1992	Civil war begins in Tajikistan (ends in 1997). Russia sends peacekeeping forces to Tajikistan (October).

1993: Unsuccessful Initiatives Inspired by EU Experience

January 1993	Charter of the Commonwealth of Independent States, dated 22 January 1993. Agreement Establishing the Interstate Bank, dated 22 January 1993, and the Charter of the Bank. Protocol on Coordination of the Operating Conditions of the Interstate Bank in CIS Member States, dated 18 October 1996.
February 1993	Gazprom threatens to suspend gas supplies to Ukraine for non-payment. Gas conflicts become an integral part of Russian-Ukrainian relations.
July–August 1993	The ruble zone collapses. Between 26 July and 7 August 1993, Russia pursues a confiscation-based monetary reform to remove treasury notes of the USSR State Bank from circulation. The reform also sought to separate the monetary systems of Russia and other CIS countries, which used the ruble as legal tender. In 1992–1995, the former Soviet republics introduced their own currencies (most in 1993).
September 1993	Nine CIS countries sign the Treaty Establishing the Economic Union of 24 September 1993; Turkmenistan and Georgia join the Treaty later. Ukraine declares that it will cooperate with the Economic Union's member states as an associate member in certain areas corresponding to its national interests. Inspired by the European Union's experience, on 24 September 1993, the CIS countries sign an Agreement Establishing an Interstate Euro-Asian Coal and Metal Association to ensure mutually beneficial and equitable cooperation in the metals and coal industry, rational development of high-tech production, mutually beneficial product sales, and improvement of the well-being of the CIS. The agreement did not ensure the achievement of its stated objectives, and it was officially terminated on 19 September 2003.

May 1993	The 201st military base is formed in Dushanbe, Kulyab, and Kurgan-Tyube from the 201st mechanized infantry division. The division is stationed in Tajikistan based on an agreement on friendship, cooperation, and mutual assistance signed in May 1993. A special agreement on the status and conditions of the Russian military presence in Tajikistan is signed in April 1999. On 16 October 2004, two countries sign an interstate agreement on the composition and organizational structure of the base.

(*continued*)

(continued)

June 1993	Disintegration of the United Armed Forces. The post of commander-in-chief of the CIS Armed Forces is abolished, and a Joint Staff is created to coordinate military cooperation. During a meeting held on 17 June 1993, the presidents of Russia and Ukraine agree to accelerate the division of the Black Sea Fleet on equal terms. However, the countries never ratified this agreement.

1994: Idea of the Eurasian Union

1994	The Eurasian idea. President of Kazakhstan Nursultan Nazarbayev puts forward the idea of a new integration organization—the Eurasian Union—which contemplates the creation of supranational bodies and a single defence space, the introduction of a single currency, decision-making by a qualified majority, and that decisions so made would be binding on all member states. These proposals met resistance from the majority of CIS countries. The idea of establishing the Eurasian Union was not realized at that time, but it was later embodied in the Eurasian Economic Community, Customs Union, SES, and EAEU.
April 1994	The presidents of Azerbaijan, Armenia, Belarus, Georgia, Kazakhstan, Kyrgyzstan, Moldova, Russia, Tajikistan, Uzbekistan, and Ukraine sign the Agreement Establishing a Free Trade Area of 15 April 1994. The free trade regime extends to trade relations between Russia and all CIS countries, pursuant to relevant bilateral agreements concluded in 1992–1993. Some other CIS member states also conclude bilateral free trade agreements.
October 1994	On 21 October 1994, the Agreement on Formation of the CIS Payment Union is signed by all member states (Ukraine signs it with some reservations). The agreement enters into force for Armenia, Belarus, Kazakhstan, Kyrgyzstan, Moldova, Russia, and Uzbekistan. Agreement on Establishing the Interstate Economic Committee of the Economic Union, dated 21 October 1994. The Committee is a standing coordinating and executive body of the Economic Union and, in fact, the first supranational body of the CIS.

April 1994	On 15 April 1994 in Moscow, the presidents of Russia and Ukraine sign an agreement on a phased settlement of the dispute over the Black Sea Fleet.

(continued)

(continued)

June 1994	Peacekeeping forces are deployed in the area of the Abkhaz-Georgian conflict (1992–1993) to contain military operations, monitor troop withdrawals and disarmament, and ensure the protection of military facilities.
December 1994	On 10 December 1994, Russia and Kazakhstan sign a lease agreement for the Baikonur Cosmodrome for a period of 20 years. In 2004, the term of the lease is extended until 2050.
1994	*Partnership for Peace* programmes. All CIS member states (except Tajikistan, which joins in 2002) are more or less involved in implementing the programme.

1995: The Customs Union's First False Start

January 1995	On 20 January 1995, Belarus and Russia conclude the Agreement Establishing the Customs Union. Kazakhstan and Kyrgyzstan accede to the agreement in mid-1996, Tajikistan—in 1998. The agreement does not work in practice.
May 1995	Agreement Establishing the Interstate Currency Committee, dated 26 May 1995. Ukraine signs the agreement, with the proviso that it enters into force after its introduction of a national currency. Turkmenistan refuses to join the agreement.

January 1995	On 6 January, an agreement on the Russian radar bases in Belarus is signed.
February 1995	On 10 February 1995, an agreement is signed in Almaty on the creation of a unified air defence system.
March 1995	Russian military bases in CIS countries: Armenia.
	On 16 March 1995, an agreement was signed on the placement of a Russian military base in Gyumri for a period of 25 years. No rent is charged, and Armenia commits to provide the base with all necessary utilities. The tasks of Russian troops in Armenia include covering the Russian Federation's southern flank and defending Armenia as a party to the Collective Security Treaty.
May 1995	The mandate of the peacekeeping forces in Tajikistan and Abkhazia is extended. Azerbaijan, Moldova, Turkmenistan, Uzbekistan, and Ukraine refuse to join the agreement on joint protection of external borders.
July 1995	Russian military bases in CIS countries: Moldova.
	On 1 July 1995 in Transnistria, a Russian task force is created out of the disbanded 14th Army.

(*continued*)

(continued)

September 1995	Russian military bases in CIS countries: Georgia. The 12th military base in Batumi, together with three Russian divisions stationed in Georgia, received the status of a Russian military base in accordance with the Collective Security Treaty.

1996: Multivector Foreign Policy

1996	Russia signs bilateral agreements on measures to ensure mutual convertibility and stabilization of national currency rates with Belarus, Kazakhstan, Turkmenistan, Uzbekistan, and Kyrgyzstan.
October 1996	Plenipotentiary representatives of governments and central banks of the CIS countries sign a protocol on the operating conditions of the Interstate Bank, pursuant to which the interested central banks of CIS countries have the right to conclude bilateral agreements with the Interstate Bank on the procedure and rules for settlements under payments and credits.

January 1996	Framework for Conflict Prevention and Resolution, dated 19 January 1996. The mandate of the peacekeeping forces in Tajikistan is extended.

1997: Creation of the Union State of Russia and Belarus and GU(U)AM

March 1997	Framework for the Economic Integration Development of the CIS, dated 28 March 1997.
April 1997	Union State of Russia and Belarus. A corresponding agreement is signed in 1997, building on the Commonwealth of Belarus and Russia, formed in April 1996 with the goal of creating a single humanitarian, economic, and military space. Since January 2000, the union has been officially called the Union State.
1997	Creation of GU(U)AM, an organization that includes Azerbaijan, Georgia, Moldova, and Ukraine (Uzbekistan was a member from 1999 to 2005). GU(U)AM's objectives: development of multilateral cooperation between member states in the areas of democratization and economic development and integration with European countries.

(continued)

(continued)

October 1997	Agreement on Unified Measures of Non-Tariff Regulation in the Customs Union, dated 22 October 1997.

May 1997	The Euro-Atlantic Partnership Council (EAPC), which includes all CIS countries, is created. At present, cooperation between CIS countries and NATO is realized through the EAPC and the *Partnership for Peace*. Additionally, virtually all CIS countries have bilateral agreements and programmes for cooperation with NATO. The agreement on the division of the Black Sea Fleet of 28 May 1997 puts an end to (or rather, as history has shown, temporarily suspends) the dispute between Russia and Ukraine.
1997	Charter on a special partnership between NATO and Ukraine.

1998: Creation of CAEC and Deepening of Russian-Kazakh Relations: The Future Engine of Post-Soviet Integration

1998	Tajikistan joins the 1994 Treaty establishing the Single Economic Space of Kazakhstan, Kyrgyzstan, and Uzbekistan, after which the organization is renamed the Central Asian Economic Community (CAEC). CIS countries adopt several documents on pensions, a visa-free regime, migration, and equal rights for admission to educational institutions. A significant number of these agreements have remained valid and effective to this day.
July, October 1998	Important milestones in relations between Russia and Kazakhstan. In July 1998, the parties sign the *Declaration on Eternal Friendship and Alliance, Oriented Toward the 21st Century* (neither Russia nor Kazakhstan has similar agreements with any other country) and *Agreement on Delimitation of the Bottom of the Northern Part of the Caspian Sea in Order to Exercise Sovereign Rights to Subsoil Use*. Additionally, the parties sign a protocol settling financial issues related to the use of the Baikonur Cosmodrome. In October 1998, the parties sign the Treaty and Programme on the Deepening of Economic Cooperation between Russia and Kazakhstan for 1998–2007 and a package of documents on mutual cooperation.

1999: Another Attempt to Create the Customs Union and Single Economic Space

February 1999	Treaty on the Customs Union and Single Economic Space, dated 26 February 1999.
April 1999	The Protocol of Intentions and Amendments to the Agreement Establishing the Free Trade Area of 2 April 1999 is a framework document that must be adapted to the current laws of each member state. The protocol is signed by the presidents of Azerbaijan, Armenia, Belarus, Georgia, Kazakhstan, Kyrgyzstan, Moldova, Russia, Tajikistan, Uzbekistan, and Ukraine. It introduces a multilateral visa-free regime in the CIS, replacing the former bilateral regime, and abolishes all customs duties and other similar taxes and fees, as well as import and export quotas in mutual trade between members of the free trade area.

April 1999	Azerbaijan, Georgia, and Uzbekistan decide not to extend the Collective Security Treaty of 15 May 1992.

2000: Dissatisfaction with the Level of Cooperation Leads to the Creation of the Eurasian Economic Community

February 2000	Agreement on the Common Customs Tariff, dated 17 February 2000.
October 2000	The Customs Union, established in 1995 and ineffective in practice, is transformed into the Eurasian Economic Community (EurAsEC). The agreement establishing the EurAsEC is signed on 10 October 2000 in Astana by the presidents of Belarus, Kazakhstan, Kyrgyzstan, Russia, and Tajikistan. EurAsEC activities cover a wide range of problems, mainly in economic cooperation and integration. Its ultimate goals are the formation of a Single Economic Space and common market mechanisms and the coordination of member states' approaches to integration into the world economy and trade. Priority areas for EurAsEC activities: transportation, energy, agriculture, and labour migration.

(continued)

(continued)

December 2000	Full-scale simultaneous operation of the energy systems of Russia, the CIS, and the Baltic States is restored for the first time since the collapse of the Soviet Union. By the end of 2000, the energy systems of 14 former Soviet republics operate in parallel—even more than in the Soviet period.

January 2000	The decision to create a single anti-terrorist centre for CIS countries is adopted on 25 January 2000. Peacekeeping forces are withdrawn from Tajikistan.

2001: Shanghai Cooperation Organization

2001	Kazakhstan, China, Kyrgyzstan, Russia, Tajikistan, and Uzbekistan establish the Shanghai Cooperation Organization, building on the Shanghai Five.

2001	For the first time, large-scale *Cooperative Partner* exercises are held in Georgia involving NATO troops.

2002: Collective Security Treaty

January 2002	Russian military bases in CIS countries: Azerbaijan. On 25 January 2002, an agreement is signed on the terms of use of the Daryal-Type Gabala Radar Station.
2002	Agreement Establishing the Collective Security Treaty Organization (Armenia, Belarus, Kazakhstan, Kyrgyzstan, Russia, and Tajikistan). Organization of Central Asian Cooperation. The corresponding agreement is signed in 2002. The new organization replaces the Central Asian Economic Union, which was established in 1998. Its task is to promote regional cooperation and ensure stability in Central Asia. The organization exists until 2005, at which time it joins the Eurasian Economic Community.

2003: Attempt to Create a Single Economic Space (SES) with Ukraine's Participation, Beginning of Large-Scale Expansion of Capital in the CIS

September 2003	The Council of Heads of State of the CIS member states decides to complete the formation of a free trade area and expand economic cooperation. On 19 September 2003, the presidents of Ukraine, Russia, Belarus, and Kazakhstan sign the Declaration, Framework, and Agreement on the Formation of the Single Economic Space.
2003	RAO UES of Russia acquires energy assets in Georgia from AES (USA): AES Telasi (a power distribution company operating low- and medium-voltage networks in Tbilisi and adjacent areas), AES Mtkvari (owner of Block 9 of the Tbilisi state regional electric power plant), and Khramesi JSC (a hydroelectric power plant consisting of two facilities: Khramesi-1 and Khramesi-2). Even during the Russo-Georgian armed conflict of 2008, these assets do not stop working for a minute. During the 2000s, Russia's leading infrastructure companies, primarily Gazprom and Inter RAO, create a network of assets in CIS countries. Gazprom is primarily interested in gas transportation networks and gas distribution. Inter RAO acquires both power generation and distribution networks. Russian and Kazakh capital begins active expansion in CIS countries and continues until the 2008 crisis. The most active investors are Russian companies (oil and gas, ferrous metals, mobile communications, and electric power), as well as Kazakhstan's banking sector.

September 2003	On 18 September 2003, the Collective Security Treaty Organization (CSTO) is established on 15 May 1992 based on the Collective Security Treaty. Russian military bases in CIS countries: Kyrgyzstan. In the summer of 2002, Russia begins to show interest in the deployment of an air group in Kant. Shortly after this, the United States and its anti-terrorist coalition allies build an airbase at Manas Airport near Bishkek. An interstate agreement on the status and conditions of the Russian airbase in Kyrgyzstan is signed on 22 September 2003; the next day the 999th Russian airbase officially opens.

2004: The Initiative to Create a Single Economic Space Involving Ukraine Ends in Failure

February 2004	On 18 February 2004, Russia shuts off all gas supplies to Belarus after Minsk refuses to sign an agreement establishing a joint venture involving Gazprom and Beltransgaz until an agreement is reached regarding gas price for 2004. Minsk offers to pay \$40 per 1000 m^3 gas; Moscow insists on the price of \$50. On 19 February, Russia lifts the gas blockade, which lasted 18 hours and 47 minutes. Belarus starts buying gas at \$46.68, and Gazprom does not receive a stake in the Belarusian gas transportation system.
November 2004–January 2005	The Orange Revolution in Kiev puts an end to the SES.

2004	Georgian-South Ossetian conflict.
Since 2004	"Border" series CSTO joint military exercises.

2005: Conflicts Over Gas

February 2005	On 16 February, RAO UES of Russia and the government of Tajikistan sign an agreement to complete construction of the Sangtuda Hydropower Plant 1. To achieve these purposes, a joint venture between ZAO Inter RAO UES (75%) and the Ministry of Energy of Tajikistan (25%) is created.

(*continued*)

(continued)

March–December 2005	Prices for Russian gas rise sharply. March 1997: A gas price hike is announced for Belarus, but on 4 April, Vladimir Putin promises to keep the price at its current level. On 19 December, the parties finally agree that in 2006 Belarus will receive 21 billion m^3 gas at \$46.68 per 1000 m^3 (in other words, the price does not change). September: The gas price for Georgia for 2006 rises from \$62.5 to \$110. For 2006, Gazprom raises the price even higher—to \$235. November: An upcoming gas price hike to \$110 is announced for Armenia (the 2005 contract stipulates a supply of 1.7 billion m^3 at \$54). The Armenian government expresses doubt that the country can afford to buy gas at such a high price. Russia offers Armenia an interest-free loan as compensation for the price increase. Alternatively, Russia is willing to accept the transfer of ownership rights to one of the power units of the Hrazdan Thermal Power Plant and the entire Armenian gas transportation system. November: The price of gas for Moldova has been raised to \$160. In 2005, Gazprom supplies gas to the country for \$80. For 2007, the price of \$170 is agreed to. November: Gazprom and Azerbaijan agree on payment for gas supplies and gas transit services at market prices. In 2006, Azerbaijan receives gas from Gazprom for \$100 (compared to \$60 in 2005). In 2007, Gazprom intends to raise the price to \$235.

2005	Ukrainian leadership calls for a revision of the agreement on the Black Sea Fleet. Ukraine also demands that various hydrographic items be transferred to it. Russia's lease of a naval base in Sevastopol is paid in part with gas supplies.

2006: Large Joint Projects, Revitalization of Mutual Investments, Establishment of Eurasian Development Bank

January 2006	On 1 January 2006, Gazprom suspends gas supplies to Ukraine. The pipeline system only pumps gas intended for transit to European customers. According to Gazprom, in the period from 1 January to 3 January, Ukraine takes 223.5 million m^3 in Russian gas. On 4 January, a Ukrainian delegation arrives in Moscow. By the evening, an agreement is concluded on gas supplies to Ukraine for $230 for the next five years. However, Ukraine receives gas at $95, since RosUkrEnergo mixes expensive Russian gas with cheap gas from Central Asia.
March 2006	On 27 March, Rospotrebnadzor bans the sale of wine and wine materials from Georgia and Moldova. On 26 April 2006, the Federal Customs Service receives an order to stop importing Georgian Borjomi and Nabeglavi mineral water to the Russian Federation due to non-compliance with Russian quality standards.
	(Since the summer of 2007, more than 40 Moldovan wine-making enterprises undergo a follow-up sanitary and epidemiological examination and receive permission to resume selling their products in Russia.)
June 2006	On 12 January 2006, the presidents of Russia and Kazakhstan sign the Agreement Establishing Eurasian Development Bank (with authorized capital of $1.5 billion). The agreement is ratified in June of the same year. The Bank's head office is located in Almaty. Armenia and Tajikistan become members of the EDB in 2009, Belarus in June 2010, and Kyrgyzstan in August 2011.
December 2006	The new gas conflict between Russia and Belarus ends with a difficult compromise. Gazprom and Beltransgaz later agree on terms for supplying and transporting gas for 2007–2011. The price for 2007 is set at $100 per 1000 m^3. A formula for calculating the price for the period beginning 1 January 2008 is accepted: it is identical to the formula applied to Russian supplies to Europe. The Belarusians agree to prepay 55% of supplies for the first half of 2007 and pay off the rest of the debt no later than 23 July; beginning 1 July, gas will be supplied based on a 100% advance payment.

2006	Abkhaz-Georgian conflict.

2007: Decision of the Presidents on the Preparatory Stage of the EurAsEC Customs Union; Rapid Economic Growth Stimulates Mutual Investment

May 2007	Russia, Kyrgyzstan, Kazakhstan, Belarus, Tajikistan, and Armenia sign an agreement to create a common energy market.
May–August 2007	New gas conflict with Belarus. A joint venture is set up to transport Russian gas through the territory of Belarus. Gazprom and the State Property Committee of Belarus sign an agreement under which Gazprom acquires a 50% stake in Beltransgaz for $2.5 billion.
September 2007	Tajikistan terminates the contract with the Russian company Rusal on the completion of the construction of the Rogun Hydropower Plant. The company is accused of acting in Uzbekistan's interests, since it refused to build a dam 325 m high, which would have allowed Tajikistan to control the water resources of the region. Russia later expresses its desire to resume the project but finds Dushanbe's proposed conditions unacceptable.
October 2007	Framework for Further Development of the CIS and Action Plan for the Implementation of the Framework. Agreement on Customs Union Commission, dated 6 October 2007. Agreement on the Creation of a Single Customs Territory and the Formation of the Customs Union, dated 6 October 2007.

October 2007	An agreement on peacekeeping activity is signed by the heads of state of the CSTO on 6 October 2007 (the agreement enters into force on 15 January 2009).

2008: Russo-Georgian War, Georgia's Withdrawal from the CIS, and Uzbekistan's Actual Withdrawal from the Eurasian Economic Community

January 2008	Agreement on Common Customs Tariff Regulation, dated 25 January 2008.
May 2008	Another former Soviet republic, Ukraine, officially joins the WTO on 19 May 2008. Kyrgyzstan joined the WTO in 1998 and Georgia in 2000.

(continued)

(continued)

August 2008	On 14 August 2008, the Georgian Parliament annuls the documents on the country's membership in the CIS.
October 2008	On 20 October 2008, Uzbekistan suspends its membership in the Eurasian Economic Community.
November 2008	Strategy for Economic Development of the CIS until 2020.
December 2008	Agreement on the Procedure for Calculating and Paying Customs Duties in the Customs Union's Member States, dated 12 December 2008.

May 2008	On 23 May 2008, the National Security and Defence Council of Ukraine decides to begin the procedure for the country's accession to NATO.
	On 20 May 2008, Ukrainian President V. Yushchenko signs a decree on the government's preparation of a bill to terminate Russian-Ukrainian agreements on the Black Sea Fleet's stay in Ukrainian territory in 2017.
2008	Armed conflict between Russia and Georgia in South Ossetia.

2009: The Global Economic Crisis Pushes Former Soviet Republics to Deepen Economic Cooperation; Establishment of the EurAsEC Anti-Crisis Fund

January 2009	In early 2009, Russian-Ukrainian disagreements over gas supplies lead to a gas crisis. The absence of a formal agreement between Russia and Ukraine and the unauthorized taking of gas transported to European consumers through Ukrainian territory push Russia to shut off all gas supplies on 7 January 2009.
	Russia resumes supplies to Ukraine and gas transit to Europe on 20 January 2009.
	On 1 January 2009, Uzbekistan stops transmission of electric power to and from Tajikistan and Turkmenistan.
February 2009	The Commission of the Customs Union—a supranational body created by Belarus, Kazakhstan, and Russia within the framework of the Eurasian Economic Community—holds its first meeting.

(*continued*)

(continued)

February, June 2009	On 4 February 2009, the EurAsEC Interstate Council decides to establish the EurAsEC Anti-Crisis Fund (ACF) in the amount of $8.5 billion and to establish the Centre for High Technologies—an organization for implementing scientific and technical programmes and innovative projects. A package of documents on the Anti-Crisis Fund is signed on 9 June. In 2015, the ACF is renamed the Eurasian Fund for Stabilization and Development (EFSD).
March 2009	Russia presents to experts from CIS countries a draft multilateral agreement on a free trade area. There are about 110 agreements on mutual trade between various CIS countries already in place.
June 2009	On 6 June 2009, the "milk war" between Russia and Belarus begins. Rospotrebnadzor bans imports of dairy products from Belarus on the grounds that the producers did go through the repermitting process in accordance with new Russian technical regulations for milk and dairy products. On 18 June 2009, during a new round of negotiations, the parties agree that Belarusian producers will apply to have export documentation reissued on a phased basis.
June, August 2009	On 10 June 2009, Georgian President Saakashvili announces Georgia's withdrawal from the CIS. On 12 June 2009, the Georgian Parliament unanimously adopts two resolutions on the CIS Interparliamentary Assembly. The official procedure for Georgia's withdrawal is completed on 18 August 2009. CIS international treaties with a limited number of participants and the decisions of CIS bodies then cease to be binding on the country. However, Georgia remains a party to a number of important multilateral economic agreements regulating trade, transportation, and protection of intellectual property in the CIS.
July 2009	The fourth and final 670 MW power unit is launched at the Russian-Tajik Sangtuda Hydroelectric Power Plant.
October 2009	Russia, Belarus, and Kazakhstan approve all the constituent documents of the Customs Union. The procedure for working on the outer perimeter of the Russian-Kazakh and Russian-Belarusian borders is revised. The Customs Union should be fully operational by 1 July 2011. The parties approve a Common Customs Tariff and submit it for confirmation.
November 2009	At the end of the EurAsEC Interstate Council's session, the presidents of the participating countries sign a package of documents on the launch of the Customs Union on 1 January 2010. Agreement on the Customs Code, dated 27 November 2009.

(continued)

(continued)

December 2009	On 1 December 2009, Uzbekistan withdraws from the United Energy System of Central Asia (UESCA). Since Uzbekistan is a central country in UESCA's configuration, the system ceases to function. On 14 December 2009, Turkmen President Berdymukhamedov, Kazakh President Nazarbayev, Uzbek President Karimov, and Chinese President Hu Jintao open the Turkmenistan-China gas pipeline, depriving Gazprom of a monopoly in transporting Turkmen gas. Russia offers Belarus duty-free oil supplies for domestic consumption (6 million tons per year). All other oil supplied to the country is subject to export duties. Beginning in 2010, the reducing coefficient, previously applied to supplies of oil and oil products to Belarus, ceases to have effect (in 2009, the factor was 0.356). The Belarusians insist on continuing to apply the coefficient, but Moscow refuses to compromise. The presidents of Russia, Belarus, and Kazakhstan announce the creation of the Single Economic Space by 1 January 2012. The decision provides for a two-year period to prepare a package of various agreements.

February 2009	On 4 February 2009, the presidents of the CSTO member states decide to establish a Collective Rapid Reaction Force, and on 14 June 2009, the required package of documents is signed.
June 2009	On 14 June 2009 at a CSTO summit, Armenia, Kazakhstan, Kyrgyzstan, Russia, and Tajikistan sign the Agreement Establishing the Collective Rapid Reaction Force. Belarus joins later.
July 2009	On 2 July 2009, the Ministry of Foreign Affairs of Ukraine calls on Russia to return navigational and hydrographic items used by the Russian Black Sea Fleet. Ukrainian courts had previously decided that these items must be transferred to Ukraine, but the fleet command refused to comply.
2009	Planned CSTO exercises "West 2009" and "Interaction 2009" in Belarus and Kazakhstan (coordinated combat practice by the Collective Rapid Reaction Forces).

2010: Start of the Customs Union's Work and Preparation of Agreements on the SES

January 2010	The Customs Union's Common Customs Tariff comes into effect. Beginning in early 2010, Russia and Belarus discuss the volume of duty-free oil supplies to Belarus. On 17 March, the parties agree that all customs duties will be lifted when the common customs area begin functioning in 2012. Until that time, Russia will deliver 6.3 million tons of oil duty-free for Belarus' domestic needs. However, on 25 March, Belarus files suit with the Economic Court of the Commonwealth of Independent States, demanding that Russia abolish the customs duties imposed since January.
February 2010	On 25 February 2010, Gazprom receives a 50% stake in Beltransgaz.
April 2010	On 21 April 2010, gas supply agreements are signed between Gazprom and Naftogaz of Ukraine. In 2010, Ukraine is to receive 36.5 billion m^3 of gas at a discount of $100, but not more than 30% of the gas price. The discount applies to supplies of 30 billion m^3 in 2010 and 40 billion m^3 in subsequent years.
May 2010	On 28 May 2010, the prime minister of Belarus fails to come to tripartite talks in St Petersburg. Russia and Kazakhstan conclude a number of bilateral agreements on the Customs Union. The parties sign documents to enact the Customs Code beginning 1 July 2010 and approve some amendments to the Customs Code. Belarus signs these documents a few days later. The "integration nucleus" of Eurasian economic integration is thus formalized.
June 2010	On 11 June 2010, the leaders of SCO member states sign the regulation *On the Procedure for Admitting SCO New Members*. Considering the organization's requirements, the most likely candidates for membership are India, Pakistan, and Mongolia, which already have observer status. On 18 June 2010, the Council of the EurAsEC Anti-Crisis Fund fulfils the first request for assistance. At a meeting in St Petersburg attended by the finance ministers of participating states (Belarus, Kazakhstan, Kyrgyzstan, Russia, Tajikistan, and Armenia), a decision is made to grant a loan of $70 million to Tajikistan with a fixed interest rate of 1% per annum for a period of 20 years. Gas conflict between Russia and Belarus.
July 2010	The Customs Code comes into force (effective 1 July 2010 for Russia and Kazakhstan and 6 July for Belarus).
December 2010	On 9 December, the heads of the three states sign a package of documents laying the foundation of the Single Economic Space, which is to begin functioning on 1 January 2012.

(*continued*)

(continued)

March 2010	On 4 March 2010, the term of the lease for the Baikonur Cosmodrome is extended until 2050.
April 2010	On 21 April 2010, following talks between the presidents of Russia and Ukraine, an agreement is signed to extend the Russian Black Sea Fleet's stay in the Crimea for 25 years after 2017. The agreement is ratified by the parliaments of the two countries on 27 April. On 21 April, in Kharkiv, a supplementary agreement to the gas supply agreement of 19 January 2009 is signed; the agreement stipulates a 30% discount on gas supplied to Ukraine in exchange for the extension of the Russian fleet's stay in Sevastopol until 2024 (the original contract expires in 2017).
June 2010	The CSTO rules out the use of force to settle the armed conflict in southern Kyrgyzstan. On 14 June, the secretaries of CSTO member states' national security councils decide to provide Kyrgyzstan with assistance by supplying aircraft, equipment, military transport, and so on—but not weapons.

2011: The Customs Union Is Fully Functional; Negotiations on Agreements Pertaining to the Single Economic Space

January 2011	Beginning 1 January, Russian oil companies stop supplying oil to Belarusian refineries due to the absence of new contracts. Negotiations to resume supplies last about a month.
April 2011	Beginning 1 April, transport control ceases at the Belarusian-Russian border within the framework of the Union State of Russia and Belarus.
June 2011	On 4 June 2011, the Council of the Anti-Crisis Fund approves the allocation of a credit facility to Belarus in the amount of $3 billion. The credit is split into six tranches over the course of 2011–2013 pursuant to the stages of implementation of the stabilization programme of the Government of Belarus, which is aimed at stabilizing the balance of payments and increasing the competitiveness of the economy.
	Inter RAO halves electricity exports to Belarus—Belenergo never did find the currency to pay 1.5 billion rubles in debt.
	Amid the crisis, Belarus introduces regulations for exports of food products and bans the exports of several other goods. The government's decision to change foreign trade conditions is due to the need to protect its consumer market.

(continued)

(continued)

July 2011	Gas remains a sore spot in relations between Ukraine and Russia.
August 2011	Products manufactured and imported into the territory of the countries of the Customs Union (Kazakhstan, Russia, Belarus) will be labelled with a special new symbol of quality.
	The Kyrgyz Republic becomes a full-fledged member of Eurasian Development Bank.
October 2011	Decision to start negotiations on Kyrgyzstan's accession to the Customs Union.
November 2011	The heads of the states of the Customs Union sign the Declaration on Eurasian Economic Integration, in which they announce the transition to the next stage of integration building—the Single Economic Space. The presidents also sign the Treaty on the Eurasian Economic Commission.
December 2011	The presidents adopt a decision "On the entry into force of international treaties forming the Single Economic Space of Belarus, Kazakhstan and the Russian Federation", which stipulates that agreements forming the SES take effect from 1 January 2012.
	Russia is officially admitted to the World Trade Organization.
2011	Aggravation of bilateral relations between Russia and Ukraine with respect to gas supplies and gas transit amid intensified preparations of an agreement on Ukraine's political association with the EU.

March 2011	Delegations of the CSTO and the Security Council of the Russian Federation are sent to southern Kyrgyzstan, and the Osh and Batken Regions, to assess conditions and analyse the situation on the border with Afghanistan and to ensure regional security.
December 2011	Moscow hosts summits of the two largest integration structures in the post-Soviet space—the CSTO and the CIS. The outcome of the CSTO summit is measures to limit Western influence in the expanses of the former USSR.

2012: Launch of the SES, Start of the Eurasian Economic Commission's Work, Agreement on a Free Trade Area in the CIS, and Uzbekistan's Withdrawal from the CSTO

January 2012	The international treaties that form the legal basis of the Single Economic Space of Belarus, Kazakhstan, and the Russian Federation come into force, creating the basis for the free movement of not only goods but also services, capital, and labour. To fully implement the "four freedoms", 17 agreements are signed and ratified. They cover a wide range of issues—from general principles of macroeconomic policy coordination to a national labour migration regime.
February 2012	The Eurasian Economic Commission (EEC), with headquarters in Moscow, begins its work. From 2012 to 2015, it employs 9 ministers—3 from each country—and about 800 personnel. The EEC's first chairman is V.R. Khristenko. By 2016, the staff grows to 1200 people and the number of ministers to 10 (2 from each country), considering the accession of Armenia and Kyrgyzstan.
	Rospotrebnadzor bans cheese imports from some Ukrainian producers to Russia. Gazprom continues talks with Kiev regarding gas issues.
September 2012	The agreement on the free trade area in the CIS enters into force.
December 2012	Tajikistan joins the WTO.
	Russian holding company Gazprom completes the acquisition of a 100% stake in Beltransgaz (two 50% stakes for $2.5 billion each).

February 2012	President of Belarus A. Lukashenko approves an agreement between Belarus and Russia on joint protection of the airspace at the Union State's external border and creation of a unified regional air defence system.
April 2012	A meeting of the Council of Foreign Ministers of CSTO countries is held in Astana. One of its main results is the adoption of a statement entitled "On the establishment of cooperation between the CSTO and NATO".
June 2012	The Collective Security Treaty Organization receives a note from the Ministry of Foreign Affairs of Uzbekistan about the suspension of the country's participation in the organization's work.

(*continued*)

(continued)

July 2012	Following Kyrgyzstan, Tajikistan demands that Russia increase payment for locating Russian military bases in its territory. In the Ala-Buka District of the Jalal-Abad Region of Kyrgyzstan, a gunfight breaks out between Kyrgyz and Uzbek border guards on the evening of 17 July.
September 2012	At the conclusion of talks between the presidents of Russia and Kyrgyzstan, documents are signed in Bishkek about the presence of the joint Russian military base in Kyrgyzstan, securing Russia's long-term military presence in Central Asia.
November 2012	The draft of a programme for military-economic cooperation among CSTO member states for the period until 2015 is approved.
December 2012	Moscow and Baku fail to agree on new terms for the lease of the Gabala Radar Station.

2013: Gas and Potash "Wars", Work on the Text of the EAEU Treaty

February 2013	Russia simplifies the migration regime for Tajik citizens. Ukraine attempts to further reduce supplies and reduce gas prices. Gazprom demands \$7 billion from the Ukrainian company Naftogaz for gas not consumed by the end of 2012.
July 2013	Ukraine reduces gas purchases in Russia by 35%.
August 2013	Beginning 14 August, the Federal Customs Service of Russia introduces enhanced control measures on cargo from Ukraine. A "potash war" between Russia and Belarus begins. Minsk accuses Uralkali of inflicting \$100 million in damages. The Board of Directors of Uralkali decides to stop export sales through the Belarusian Potash Company (BPC), having designated Uralkali Trading as the only channel for export product sales.
September 2013	Ukraine begins internal state procedures to prepare an association agreement with the European Union. On 18 September, the text of the document is approved by the government. Ukraine awaits a revision of the gas contract with Russia.

(*continued*)

(continued)

December 2013	Presidents V. Putin and V. Yanukovych hold a meeting of the Russian-Ukrainian Interstate Commission in the Kremlin. At the end of 2013, Russia buys Ukrainian two-year Eurobonds for $3 billion with a 5% coupon rate on the Irish Stock Exchange as a form of financial aid. On 27 December 2013, the Council of the Anti-Crisis Fund of the Eurasian Economic Community decides to grant a $20 million investment loan to Kyrgyzstan to implement the "Financing deliveries of agricultural machinery to Kyrgyzstan" project.

January 2013	Russia and Kazakhstan sign an agreement on the creation of a unified air defence system.
June 2013	Bishkek denounces the agreement with the United States regarding the military base in Manas.
October 2013	Political tension in Ukraine grows.

2014: Signing of the EAEU Treaty, Imposition of Sanctions Against Russia, Change of Power in Ukraine

January 2014	The Government of Ukraine approves a long-term programme for cooperation with the Customs Union until 2020.
February 2014	Devaluation of exchange rates for the currencies of the Customs Union's member states. The Russian government freezes payment of the second $2 billion tranche to Ukraine due to gas debts of $2.7 billion.
March 2014	Dispute between Moscow and Kiev regarding the gas discount. On 20 March 2014, EDB, as the fund manager for the ACF, and Kyrgyzstan sign an agreement on the financing of the "Reconstruction of the Bishkek-Osh section of road, phase IV" project in the amount of $60 million.
April 2014	The EU and United States begin to introduce economic sanctions against Russia amid events in Ukraine and Crimea's reunification with Russia.

(continued)

(continued)

May 2014	Trilateral talks on gas are held between Russia, the EU, and Ukraine. On 29 May 2014, the presidents of the member states of the CU and the SES sign the Treaty on the Eurasian Economic Union (EAEU) at a meeting of the Supreme Eurasian Economic Council. The agreement marks the Eurasian economic project's transition to a new, deeper level of integration.
June 2014	For the first time since 2009, Gazprom halts gas exports to Ukraine.
July 2014	Ukraine actually introduces prohibitive duties on imports of Belarusian beer, milk, and sweets in response to similar restrictive measures by Belarus. Russia tightens bans on Ukrainian products.
October 2014	On 10 October 2014 in Minsk, the Treaty on the Accession of Armenia to the EAEU is signed during a meeting of the Supreme Eurasian Economic Council.
November 2014	The crisis in Russia escalates. Fall in oil prices negatively impacts the economies of Russia and Kazakhstan. Devaluation of the Russian ruble. Representatives of the ministries of finance of Russia and Kyrgyzstan sign an interstate agreement establishing the Kyrgyz-Russian Development Fund in the amount of $ 1 billion.
December 2014	On 23 December 2014 in Moscow, the presidents of Belarus, Kazakhstan, and the Russian Federation on one side and the president of the Kyrgyz Republic on the other side sign the Agreement on the Accession of the Kyrgyz Republic to the EAEU.

February 2014	Change of power in Ukraine, removal of President V. Yanukovych.
March 2014	In Crimea and Sevastopol, a referendum is held on Crimea's reunification with Russia as a constituent entity of the Russian Federation. Laws are signed regarding the adoption of the Republic of Crimea and the city of Sevastopol into the Russian Federation. The Crimean Federal District is established. Civil war begins in the southeastern regions of Ukraine (Donetsk and Lugansk Regions). On 27 March 2014, the "East-Anti-Terror-2014" joint Kyrgyz-Uzbek anti-terrorist command post exercise is held in Uzbekistan.
June 2014	Ukraine adopts documents banning shipments of arms, military equipment, and components for enterprises in the Russian defence industry.
August 2014	In Kazakhstan, the live phase of the "Interaction-2014" comprehensive exercise of the CSTO's Collective Rapid Reaction Force is held at the Spassk training ground (Karaganda Region).
October 2014	Verification of the combat readiness of the CIS countries' joint air defence system is successfully completed.

2015: The EAEU Treaty Enters into Force; Armenia and Kyrgyzstan Accede to the EAEU; FTA with Vietnam

January 2015	Entry into force of the Treaty on the Eurasian Economic Union (EAEU). Armenia's accession to the EAEU. Among other elements of the EAEU, the common labour market begins to function: citizens of the member states have the right to work under national regimes (no quotas or licensing mechanisms; access to health insurance, schools, and kindergartens).
May 2015	Accession of the Kyrgyz Republic to the EAEU. An agreement is signed between the EAEU and Vietnam to create a free trade area—the first FTA of the Eurasian Union.
June 2015	Beginning 15 June 2015, the Anti-Crisis Fund of the Eurasian Economic Community is renamed the Eurasian Fund for Stabilization and Development (EFSD). In addition to financial and investment lending, its funds can now be used to provide grants to the Fund's member states.
July 2015	The Council of the EFSD decides to provide two investment loans to finance the Irrigation System Modernization project in Armenia in the amount of $40 million and the Rehabilitation of the Toktogul Hydropower Plant (Phase 2) project in Kyrgyzstan in the amount of $100 million.
November 2015	Kazakhstan becomes a member of the WTO. Of EAEU's five member states, four are members of the WTO (Belarus is the exception).

March 2015	Beginning 11 March, Russia suspends its participation in meetings of the Joint Advisory Group on the Treaty on Conventional Armed Forces in Europe (CFE), because NATO countries circumvented the provisions of the Treaty "by expanding the alliance", while simultaneously preventing the entry into force of the Agreement on Adaptation, which the Russians insisted on.
September 2015	During the CSTO summit in Dushanbe, member states unanimously express support for an increase in the organization's force component in order to combat terrorism. This support is confirmed in the joint statement "Measures to eliminate international terrorism" adopted by CSTO member states at the 70th session of the UN General Assembly in New York.

2016: Harmonization of the Customs Code and the Common Market for Pharmaceuticals, Beginning of Negotiations with the PRC, Beginning of the Second Four-Year Term of the EEC

February 2016	Change in the membership of the Board of the Commission: at the end of the four-year term of the ministers on the Board of the Commission, they are replaced by a new set of ten ministers, two from each of the five countries. The member states appoint Tigran Sargsyan as chairman of the Board.
May 2016	The EEC receives a mandate to negotiate a non-preferential agreement (i.e., an agreement that does not stipulate the reduction or elimination of customs duties) in the PRC. The regular negotiating track begins in October.
November 2016	The Eurasian Intergovernmental Council, at the level of prime ministers, approves the EAEU Customs Code and a package of documents on the creation of a common market for pharmaceuticals and medical equipment (the Customs Code will enter into force on 1 January 2018).
December 2016	On 19 December, at the meeting of the Board of the Commission, a draft treaty on pension provision for workers of EAEU member states is approved. The essence of the Treaty is a partial introduction of a pension mobility regime.

2017: Work on Non-tariff Barriers, Common Market of Pharmaceuticals, Progress in Deals with China and Iran

April 2017	First White Book on the removal of non-tariff barriers published by the Eurasian Economic Commission. The Commission, first, identifies 185 non-tariff barriers and, second, reports on the consensus among the member states as regards the removal of 61 of them.

(*continued*)

(continued)

May 2017	A common market of pharmaceuticals and medical equipment enters into force.
October 2017	The "General Directions of the EAEU Digital Agenda until 2025" is signed.
December 2017	A "limited FTA" with Iran and a non-preferential deal with China: negotiations on the substance of the agreements have been completed.
December 2017	Six new technical regulations (chemical products, bottled water, etc.) are signed throughout the year.

Notes

1. Vinokurov et al. (2009).
2. Libman and Vinokurov (2012).

References

Aliev, S. (2016). Labour Migration and Social Security for Workers in the Eurasian Economic Union. Moscow: Eurasian Economic Commission. Available at: http://www.eurasiancommission.org/ru/Documents/spreads.pdf.

Alpysbaeva, S., Kenzhebulat, M., Kamzin, A., Kaskeev, S. (2015). Structural Changes in the Mutual Trade of Kazakhstan and Russia in Conditions of External Shocks and Differences in Monetary Policy. Eurasian Economic Integration, 2 (27), pp. 41–51. Available at: https://eabr.org/upload/iblock/c1e/eei_2_2015_alpysbayeva_etc.pdf.

Bertelsmann Stiftung (2016). Free Trade from Lisbon to Vladivostok. A Tool for Peace and Prosperity: The Effects of a Free Trade Area between the EU and the Eurasian Region. Focus Paper. Available at: https://www.bertelsmann-stiftung.de/en/publications/publication/did/focus-paper-free-trade-from-lisbon-to-vladivostok/.

Central Bank of the Russian Federation (CBR) (2017). Cross-Border Transfers of Individuals (Residents and Nonresidents). Available at: http://www.cbr.ru/eng/statistics/Default.aspx?Prtid=tg.

Chayka, K. (2016). Pressing Issues of the Integration Association Law and the Constitutional Law of Member States. Journal of Foreign Law and Comparative Law, 1, pp. 129–133.

E. Vinokurov, *Introduction to the Eurasian Economic Union*,
https://doi.org/10.1007/978-3-319-92825-8

CIS Statistical Committee (2016a). Basic Socioeconomic Indicators of Poverty in CIS Countries. Database "Statistics of the CIS". Available at: http://www.cisstat.com/2base/frame00.htm.

CIS Statistical Committee (2016b). The Labour Market in the Commonwealth Countries in 2015. Database "Statistics of the CIS". Available at: http://www.cisstat.com/2base/frame00.htm.

CIS Statistical Committee (2016c). The Socioeconomic Situation of the Countries of the Commonwealth of Independent States in 2016. Database "Statistics of the CIS". Available at: http://www.cisstat.com/2base/frame00.htm.

Demidenko, M., Korshunov, D., Karachun, O., Miksyuk, A., Pelipas, I., Tochitskaya, I., Shimanovich, G. (2017). Monetary Policy of EAEU Member States: Current Status and Coordination Prospects. Joint Report of the Eurasian Economic Commission and Eurasian Development Bank. Moscow: EEC; Saint Petersburg: Eurasian Development Bank. Available at: https://eabr.org/en/analytics/integration-research/cii-reports/monetary-policy-of-eaeu-member-states-current-status-and-coordination-prospects/.

Denisenko, M. and Chernina, E. (2017). Labour Migration and Earnings of Migrants in Russia. Voprosy Ekonomiki, 3, pp. 40–57.

Dragneva, R. and Wolczuk, K. (eds.) (2013). Eurasian Economic Integration: Law, Policy and Politics. Cheltenham: Edwar Elgar.

Dutkiewicz, P. and Sakwa, R. (eds.) (2015). Eurasian Integration: The View from Within. Abingdon: Routledge.

EDB Centre for Integration Studies (2012). Comprehensive Assessment of the Macroeconomic Effects of Various Forms of the Deep Economic Integration of Ukraine with Member States of the Customs Union and the Common Economic Space. Report No. 1. Saint Petersburg: Eurasian Development Bank. Available at: https://eabr.org/en/analytics/integration-research/cii-reports/a-comprehensive-assessment-of-the-macroeconomic-effects-of-various-forms-of-the-deep-economic-integr/.

EDB Centre for Integration Studies (2013a). Customs Union and Ukraine: Economic and technological cooperation in sectors and industries. Report No. 18. Saint Petersburg: Eurasian Development Bank. Available at: https://eabr.org/en/analytics/integration-research/cii-reports/customs-union-and-ukraine-economic-and-technological-cooperation-in-sectors-and-industries/.

EDB Centre for Integration Studies (2013b). Economic Impact of Tajikistan's Accession to the Customs Union and Single Economic Space. Report No.

14. Saint Petersburg: Eurasian Development Bank. Available at: https://eabr.org/en/analytics/integration-research/cii-reports/economic-impact-of-tajikistan-s-accession-to-the-customs-union-and-single-economic-space/.

EDB Centre for Integration Studies (2013c). Labour Migration and Human Capital of Kyrgyzstan: Impact of the Customs Union. Report No. 13. Saint Petersburg: Eurasian Development Bank. Available at: https://eabr.org/en/analytics/integration-research/cii-reports/labour-migration-and-human-capital-of-kyrgyzstan-impact-of-the-customs-union/.

EDB Centre for Integration Studies (2013d). The Customs Union and Neighboring Countries: Models and Instruments for Mutually Beneficial Partnership. Report No. 11. Saint Petersburg: Eurasian Development Bank. Available at: https://eabr.org/en/analytics/integration-research/cii-reports/the-customs-union-and-neighboring-countries-models-and-instruments-for-mutually-beneficial-partnersh/.

EDB Centre for Integration Studies (2015a). Assessing the Impact of Non-Tariff Barriers in the EEU: Results of Enterprise Surveys. Report No. 30. Saint Petersburg: Eurasian Development Bank. Available at: https://eabr.org/en/analytics/integration-research/cii-reports/assessing-the-impact-of-non-tariff-barriers-in-the-eeu-results-of-enterprise-surveys/.

EDB Centre for Integration Studies (2015b). EDB Integration Barometer – 2015. Report No. 33. Saint Petersburg: Eurasian Development Bank. Available at: https://eabr.org/en/analytics/integration-research/cii-reports/integratsionnyy-barometr-eabr-2014/.

EDB Centre for Integration Studies (2015c). Estimating the Economic Effects of Reducing Non-Tariff Barriers in the EEU. Report No. 29. Saint Petersburg: Eurasian Development Bank. Available at: https://eabr.org/en/analytics/integration-research/cii-reports/estimating-the-economic-effects-of-reducing-non-tariff-barriers-in-the-eeu/.

EDB Centre for Integration Studies (2015d). Labour Migration and Labour-Intensive Industries in Kyrgyzstan and Tajikistan: Possibilities for Human Development in Central Asia. Report No. 31. Saint Petersburg: Eurasian Development Bank. Available at: https://eabr.org/en/analytics/integration-research/cii-reports/labour-migration-and-labour-intensive-industries-in-kyrgyzstan-and-tajikistan-possibilities-for-huma/.

EDB Centre for Integration Studies (2015e). Monitoring of Mutual Investments in CIS Countries — 2015. Report No. 32. Saint Petersburg: Eurasian Development Bank. Available at: https://eabr.org/en/analytics/integration-research/cii-reports/monitoring-of-mutual-investments-in-cis-countries-2015/.

EDB Centre for Integration Studies (2016a). EAEU and Eurasia: Monitoring and Analysis of Direct Investments 2016. Report No. 41. Saint Petersburg: Eurasian Development Bank. Available at: https://eabr.org/en/analytics/integration-research/cii-reports/eaeu-and-eurasia-monitoring-and-analysis-of-direct-investments-2016/.

EDB Centre for Integration Studies (2016b). EDB Integration Barometer – 2016 (Fifth Wave of the Survey). Report No. 40. Saint Petersburg: Eurasian Development Bank. Available at: https://eabr.org/en/analytics/integration-research/cii-reports/integratsionnyy-barometr-eabr-2016/.

EDB Centre for Integration Studies (2016c). European Union and Eurasian Economic Union: Long-Term Dialogue and Perspectives of Agreement. Report No. 38. Saint Petersburg: Eurasian Development Bank. Available at: https://eabr.org/en/analytics/integration-research/cii-reports/european-union-and-eurasian-economic-union-long-term-dialogue-and-perspectives-of-agreement/.

EDB Centre for Integration Studies (2016d). Monitoring of Mutual Investments in CIS Countries 2016. Report No. 39. Saint Petersburg: Eurasian Development Bank. Available at: https://eabr.org/en/analytics/integration-research/cii-reports/monitoring-of-mutual-investments-in-cis-countries-2016/.

EDB Centre for Integration Studies (2016e). Regional Organizations: Typology and Development Paths. Report No. 37. Saint Petersburg: Eurasian Development Bank. Available at: https://eabr.org/en/analytics/integration-research/cii-reports/regional-organizations-typology-and-development-paths/.

EDB Centre for Integration Studies (2017a). Eurasian Economic Integration – 2017. Report No. 43. Saint Petersburg: Eurasian Development Bank. Available at: https://eabr.org/en/analytics/integration-research/cii-reports/eurasian-economic-integration-2017/.

EDB Centre for Integration Studies (2017b). Monitoring of Mutual Investments in CIS Countries 2017. Report No. 45. Saint Petersburg: Eurasian Development Bank. Available at: https://eabr.org/en/analytics/integration-research/cii-reports/monitoring-of-mutual-investments-in-cis-countries-2017/.

Edovina, T. (2017). We must pay for the opening of partner countries' markets by lowering duties. EEC Minister in charge of Trade Veronika Nikishina on plans to expand free trade. Kommersant, February 10. Available at: http://www.kommersant.ru/doc/3214431.

Eurasian Development Bank (EDB) (2006). Charter of the Eurasian Development Bank. Annex to the Agreement Establishing the Eurasian Development Bank dated 12 January 2006. Available at: https://eabr.org/upload/iblock/c91/foundation-documents.pdf.

Eurasian Economic Commission (EEC) (2013). Annotation to the Results of Research on "Determination of Prospective Partners of Customs Union's Member States for Concluding Free Trade Agreements". Moscow: EEC. Available at: http://www.eurasiancommission.org/ru/NIR/Lists/List/Attachments/35/18_12_2013_annot.pdf.

Eurasian Economic Commission (EEC) (2014). Eurasian Economic Union. Questions and Answers. Figures and Facts. Moscow: EEC. Available at: http://www.eurasiancommission.org/ru/Documents/eaes_voprosy_otvety.pdf.

Eurasian Economic Commission (EEC) (2015a). Memorandum on Trade and Economic Cooperation between the Eurasian Economic Commission and the Government of Mongolia is Signed. June 17. Available at: http://www.eurasiancommission.org/en/nae/news/Pages/17-06-2015-2.aspx .

Eurasian Economic Commission (EEC) (2015b). On status of elimination of the barriers for mutual access which prevent functioning of the Eurasian Economic Union domestic market, as well as exemptions and restrictions with respect to the circulation of goods, services, capital and workforce. Analytical Report of the Eurasian Economic Commission. Moscow: EEC. Available at: http://www.eurasiancommission.org/en/nae/news/Pages/25-06-2015-3.aspx.

Eurasian Economic Commission (EEC) (2015c). The EAEU and South Korea Have Signed a Memorandum of Cooperation. November 30. Available at: http://www.eurasiancommission.org/en/nae/news/Pages/30-11-2015-5.aspx.

Eurasian Economic Commission (EEC) (2016a). A further 18 sectors will be included in the single services market of the EAEU. July 5. Available at: http://www.eurasiancommission.org/en/nae/news/Pages/2016-07-06-2.aspx.

Eurasian Economic Commission (EEC) (2016b) A package of documents on the launch of the EAEU's common pharmaceutical market was signed. November 16. Available at: http://www.eurasiancommission.org/en/nae/news/Pages/16-11-2016-5.aspx.

Eurasian Economic Commission (EEC) (2016c). On the Labour Market in the Eurasian Economic Union. 2015. Analytical review October 31. Available at: http://www.eurasiancommission.org/ru/act/integr_i_makroec/dep_stat/econstat/Documents/labourmarket_2015.pdf.

Eurasian Economic Commission (EEC) (2016d). Questions and Answers on the Free Trade Agreement between the Eurasian Economic Union and the Socialist Republic of Vietnam. Available at: http://www.eurasiancommission.org/en/act/trade/dotp/Pages/default.aspx.

Eurasian Economic Commission (EEC) (2016e). The Board of the Commission approves a draft of the Agreement on Pension Provision for Workers of EAEU Member States. December 20. Available at: http://www.eurasiancommission.org/ru/nae/news/Pages/20-12-2016-4.aspx.

Eurasian Economic Commission (EEC) (2016f). The Council of the Commission Recognizes the Wisdom of Negotiations on an FTA with Singapore. December 23. Available at: http://www.eurasiancommission.org/ru/nae/news/Pages/23-12-2016-5.aspx.

Eurasian Economic Commission (EEC) (2017a). Congratulations on the third anniversary of signing the Treat y on the Eurasian Economic Union. May 29. Available at: http://www.eurasiancommission.org/en/nae/news/Pages/29-05-2017.aspx.

Eurasian Economic Commission (EEC) (2017b). EAEU and India began formal negotiations on a free trade agreement. June 3. Available at: http://www.eurasiancommission.org/en/nae/news/Pages/3-06-2017.aspx.

Eurasian Economic Commission (EEC) (2017c). Mongolia is Ready to Conclude an Agreement on a Free Trade Area with the EAEU. June 2. Available at: http://www.eurasiancommission.org/ru/nae/news/Pages/2-05-2017-3.aspx.

Eurasian Economic Commission (EEC) (2017d). Outcomes of the EEC Council: the EAEU new Customs Code will enter into force on January 1, 2018. April 28. Available at: http://www.eurasiancommission.org/en/nae/news/Pages/28-04-2017-3.aspx.

Eurasian Economic Commission (EEC) (2017e). The Eurasian Economic Union in Figures: Brief Statistical Compilation. Moscow: EEC. Available at: http://www.eurasiancommission.org/ru/act/integr_i_makroec/dep_stat/econstat/Documents/Brief_Statistics_Yearbook_2017.pdf.

Eurasian Economic Commission (EEC) (2017f). The Interim Agreement on the Free Trade Area between the EAEU and Iran Will Be Operational by the End of the Year. June 1. Available at: http://www.eurasiancommission.org/ru/nae/news/Pages/1-06-2017-3.aspx.

Eurasian Economic Commission (EEC) (2017g). Veronika Nikishina: Successful Eurasian integration requires having mutually beneficial trade relations with the EU on the one side of the continent, and with China - on the other. April 7. Available at: http://www.eurasiancommission.org/en/nae/news/Pages/7-04-2017-2.aspx.

Eurasian Monitor (2007). The Russian Language in the Newly Independent States: Status and Prospects. Analytical Report. Available at: http://www.eurasiamonitor.org/rus/research/event-150.html.

Florovsky, G. (1993). The Eurasian Temptation. In: Novikova, L. and Sizemskaya, I. (1993) Russia between Europe and Asia: The Eurasian Temptation. Anthology. Moscow: Nauka, pp. 237–266.

Glazyev, S. (2016). Russia Should Play First Fiddle in the Large Eurasian Association (Interview Part 2). Business Online, September 30.

Gleason, G. (2004). The Reintegration of Eurasia: Functional Theory and Inter-state Policy Coordination. In: Khudoley, K. (ed.) Post-Communist Countries in the Globalizing World. Saint Petersburg: Saint Petersburg State University Press.

Golovnin, M. (2010). Interaction of Financial Systems of the CIS Countries. Saint Petersburg: Aletheia.

Gómez-Mera, L. (2013). Power and Regionalism in Latin America: The Politics of MERCOSUR. Notre Dame, IN: University of Notre Dame Press.

Hancock, K. J. and Libman, A. (2016). Eurasia. In: Börzel, T. A. and Risse, T. (eds.) The Oxford Handbook of Comparative Regionalism. Oxford: Oxford University Press, pp. 202–224.

Heifetz, B. (2011). Russian Business in EurAsEC Countries: The Modernization Factor. Moscow: Ekonomika.

Interfax (2017). EEC Minister in charge of Trade: Negotiations with Iran Should Pursue a Win-Win Solution. June 9. Available at: http://www.interfax.ru/interview/566008.

Karaganov, S. (ed.) (2015). To the Great Ocean – 3. The Creation of Central Eurasia: The "Silk Road" Economic Belt and the Priorities for Joint Development of the Eurasian States. Analytical Report of the Valdai International Discussion Club, June. Moscow. Available at: http://ru.valdaiclub.com/files/11300/.

Kaveshnikov, N. (2011). Development of the Institutional Structure of the Eurasian Economic Community. Eurasian Economic Integration, 2 (11), pp. 19–35. Available at: https://eabr.org/upload/iblock/366/n2_2011_3.pdf.

Korostikov, M. (2015). Israel Plans to Establish a Free Trade Area with the EAEU. Kommersant, October 28. Available at: https://www.kommersant.ru/doc/2842046.

Kuznetsov, A. (2014). Russian Direct Investment as a Factor of Eurasian Integration. Voprosy Ekonomiki, 8, pp. 58–69.

Lane, D. (ed.) (2017). The Eurasian Project in Global Perspective. London: Routledge.

Laruelle, M. (2008). Russian Eurasianism: An Ideology of Empire. Washington, DC: Woodrow Wilson Centre Press.

Libman, A. (2014). Commonwealth of Independent States (CIS) and Eurasian Economic Community (EurAsEC). In: Levi, L., Finizio, G. and Vallinoto, N. (eds.) The Democratization of International Institutions. First International Democracy Report. London: Routledge.

Libman, A. and Vinokurov, E. (2012). Holding-Together Regionalism: Twenty Years of Post-Soviet Integration. Basingstoke: Palgrave Macmillan.

Libman, A. and Vinokurov E. (2016). Regional Organizations: Types and Development Logic. EDB Centre for Integration Studies Report. Saint-Petersburg: EDB Centre for Integration Studies.

Libman, A. and Vinokurov, E. (2018, forthcoming). Autocracies and Regional Integration: The Eurasian Case. Post-Communist Economies.

Ministry of Internal Affairs of the Russian Federation (Ministry of Internal Affairs of Russia) (2017). Statistical Information on the Migration Situation in the Russian Federation for 12 months of 2016 with a Breakdown by Countries and Regions. January 30. Available at: https://xn--b1aew.xn--p1ai/Deljatelnost/statistics/migracionnaya/item/9359228/.

Mishina, V. and Khomyakova, L. (2014). The Integrated Currency Market of the Eurasian Economic Area and Calculations in National Currencies: Myths or Reality? Vorposy Ekonomiki, 8, pp. 41–57.

National legal Internet portal of the Republic of Belarus (2016). Decree No. 499 of the President of the Republic of Belarus of 28 December 2016 "On the Draft of the International Treaty". December 31, 1/16815. Available at: http://www.pravo.by/document/?guid=12551&p0=P31600499&p1=1.

Nazarbayev, N. (2012). "Our peoples have lived together for centuries, and the strengthening of neighbourly relations is consistent with the vital interests of millions of people". Speech by the President of the Republic of Kazakhstan at Moscow State University. Moscow, 29 March 1994. In: N. Nazarbayev. When a Thought Becomes Reality. Moscow: Khudozhestvennaya Literatura, pp. 28–33.

Neshataeva, T. (2016). The Court of the Eurasian Economic Union in Action. Eurasian Law Journal, 9 (100), pp. 11–14. Available at: https://www.eurasialaw.ru/index.php?option=com_content&view=article&id=8484:2016-11-15-10-10-35&cati.

News Agency Sputnik (2017). Aramian: Privileges with regard to Goods from EAEU Countries can be Revoked. February 6. Available at: https://ru.armeniasputnik.am/armenia/20170206/6305003/aramyan-privilegii-v-otnoshenii-tovarov-iz-eaes-mogut-bit-otmeneni.html.

Nurymbetova, G. and Kudaibergenov, R. (2010). Foreign Policy Initiatives of the President of Kazakhstan N.A. Nazarbayev. Historical and Documentary Research. Almaty: Kazakh Encyclopaedia.

Nysanbaev, A. and Kurmanbaev, E. (1999). The Eurasian Idea of Chokan Valikhanov. Eurasian Community, 2, pp. 26–31.

President of Russia (2016). Approved draft documents of the Supreme Eurasian Economic Council. December 26. Available at: http://kremlin.ru/supplement/5153 (official website of the President of Russia).

RIA Novosti (2016a). EEC: EAEU Countries Begin Negotiations with Serbia on the Free Trade Area. May 31. Available at: https://ria.ru/world/20160531/1441164875.html.

RIA Novosti (2016b). Shuvalov: The Greater Eurasian Partnership will not be a Counterposition to the TPP. September 5. Available at: https://ria.ru/economy/20160905/1476106027.html.

Shleifer, A. and Treisman, D. (2004). A Normal Country. Foreign Affairs, 2 (83), March–April, pp. 20–38.

Sterzhneva, M. (1999). The European Union and the CIS: Comparative Analysis of Institutions. Moscow: Moscow Public Science Fund.

TASS (2016). Putin Calls for the Creation of a Greater Eurasian Partnership. June 17. Available at: http://tass.ru/pmef-2016/article/3376295.

Teng, E. J. (2013). Eurasian: Mixed Identities in the United States, China, and Hong Kong, 1842–1943. Berkeley, CA: University of California Press.

Treaty on the Eurasian Economic Union (EAEU Treaty) (2014). Moscow: Legal Department of the EEC.

Vinokurov, E. (2010). The Evolution of Kazakhstan's Position on Relations with Russia in 1991–2010, MPRA Paper, No. 22187. Available at: https://mpra.ub.uni-muenchen.de/22187/.

Vinokurov, E. (2013a). Pragmatic Eurasianism: Prospects for Eurasian Integration. Russia in Global Affairs, 2, June 30. Available at: http://eng.globalaffairs.ru/number/Pragmatic-Eurasianism--16050.

Vinokurov, E. (2013b). Pragmatic Eurasianism. Eurasian Economic Integration, 4 (21), pp. 7–20. Available at: https://eabr.org/upload/iblock/a96/eei_4_2013_vinokurov.pdf.

Vinokurov, E. (2014a). A Mega Deal Amid a Relationship Crisis: Why a European-Eurasian Integration Agreement Should Be Discussed Now. Russia in Global Affairs, 5, December 18. Available at: http://eng.globalaffairs.ru/number/A-Mega-Deal-Amid-a-Relationship-Crisis-17221.

Vinokurov, E. (ed.) (2014b). System of Indicators of Eurasian Integration II. Report No. 22. Saint Petersburg: Eurasian Development Bank. Available at: https://eabr.org/en/analytics/integration-research/cii-reports/edb-system-of-indicators-of-eurasian-integration/

Vinokurov, E. (2014c). The Birth of Eurasiaskepticism: Are There Reasons for Panic? Russia in Global Affairs, 1, March 21. Available at: http://eng.globalaffairs.ru/number/The-Birth-of-Eurasiaskepticism-16498.

Vinokurov, E. (2016a). Dushanbe is on the Waiting List. Economist Evgeny Vinokurov on the Effects of Tajikistan's Possible Entry into the EAEU. Vedomosti, August 2. Available at: https://www.vedomosti.ru/opinion/articles/2016/08/03/651491-dushanbe-ocheredi.

Vinokurov, E. (2016b). Eurasian Economic Union: A Sober Look. Voprosy Ekonomiki, 12, pp. 43–60.

Vinokurov, E. and Libman, A. (2012a) Eurasian Continental Integration. Saint Petersburg: EDB Centre for Integration Studies. Available at: https://eabr.org/en/analytics/integration-research/cii-reports/evraziyskaya-kontinentalnaya-integraciya-eurasian-continental-integration/.

Vinokurov, E. and Libman, A. (2012b). Eurasian Integration: Challenges of Transcontinental Regionalism. Basingstoke: Palgrave Macmillan.

Vinokurov, E. and Libman, A. (2013). Two Eurasian Integrations. Voprosy Ekonomiki, 2, pp. 47–72.

Vinokurov, E. and Libman, A. (2014). Do Economic Crises Impede or Advance Regional Economic Integration in the Post-Soviet Space? Post-Communist Economies, 3 (26), pp. 341–358.

Vinokurov, E. and Libman, A. (2017). Re-Evaluating Regional Organizations: Behind the Smokescreen of Official Mandates. Basingstoke: Palgrave Macmillan.

Vinokurov, E. and Tsukarev, T. (2018). The Belt and Road Initiative and the Transit Countries: An Economic Assessment of Land Transport Corridors. Area Development and Policy, (3)1: 93–113.

Vinokurov, E., Demidenko, M., Korshunov, D. (2017). Potential Costs and Benefits of Monetary Integration in the Eurasian Economic Union. Voprosy Ekonomiki, 2, pp. 75–96.

Vinokurov, E., Libman, A., De Lombaerde, Ph., Maqsimchook, N., Moldabekov, Ye. (2009). The System of Indicators of Eurasian Integration 2009. Almaty: Eurasian Development Bank. Available at: https://eabr.org/en/analytics/integration-research/cii-reports/edb-system-of-indicators-of-eurasian-integration/.

Vymyatnina, Y. and Antonova, D. (2014). Creating a Eurasian Union: Economic Integration of the Former Soviet Republics. Basingstoke: Palgrave Macmillan.

World Bank Group (2016). Migration and Remittances: Recent Developments and Outlook. Migration and Development Brief 26, April. Available at: http://pubdocs.worldbank.org/en/661301460400427908/MigrationandDevelopmentBrief26.pdf.

Index[1]

[1] Note: Page numbers followed by 'n' refer to notes.

E. Vinokurov, *Introduction to the Eurasian Economic Union*,
https://doi.org/10.1007/978-3-319-92825-8

MIX
Papier aus verantwortungsvollen Quellen
Paper from responsible sources
FSC® C105338

Printed by Books on Demand, Germany